THE COMMUNITY
OF RELIGIONS

*

The Community of Religions

VOICES AND IMAGES OF
THE PARLIAMENT OF THE
WORLD'S RELIGIONS

*

EDITED BY
Wayne Teasdale
AND
George F. Cairns

Continuum • New York

1996
The Continuum Publishing Company
370 Lexington Avenue
New York, NY 10017

Printed in the United States of America

Library of Congress Cataloging-in-Publication Data

The community of religions : voices and images of the Parliament of
  the World's Religions / edited by Wayne Teasdale and George F.
  Cairns.
      p.   cm.
  Includes bibliographical references.
  ISBN 0-8264-0899-0
  1. Parliament of the World's Religions (1993 : Chicago).
  2. Religions—Relations—Congresses. 3. Religion—Congresses.
  I. Teasdale, Wayne. II. Cairns, George F.   III. Parliament of the
  World's Religions (1993 : Chicago)
  BL21.C646   1996
  291—dc20   96-1036
                                                                CIP

The editors dedicate this volume to all those generous souls engaged in the seminal work of building the Community of Religions. We particularly wish to dedicate it to the noble Tibetan people whose nonviolent, moral struggle is a valuable teaching for humankind. We call upon the Community of Religions to speak with one voice on behalf of the Tibetans, and to focus support for them all around the world. Tibet may seem to be a thorn in the side for those who fear the challenge, but in actuality it is a rare opportunity for the religions and for the consciousness of the planet to be transformed more totally into the Earth Community. What is required in order to realize this vision of transformation is that quality of leadership manifested so luminously in Mahatma Gandhi. This kind of leadership has the attributes of spiritual integrity, moral clarity, political courage, and practical wisdom. We must be willing to take a risk, while seizing the initiative in history, and sparking an awakening in humanity to the larger reality of the Sacred Community to which we all belong. We believe that honestly confronting the issue of Tibet is the first test for the dawning Community of Religions, and its successful resolution will greatly advance the world. With this in mind, we further dedicate this book to risk takers.

Contents

Introduction: Harmony in the Midst of Great Diversity

GEORGE CAIRNS AND WAYNE TEASDALE

The Parliament of the World's Religions (August 28—September 5, 1993) was a historical event of major proportions. It was a breakthrough and a turning point in how humankind can understand itself and in how all of us, coming from so many traditions or no tradition at all, relate to one another in a spirit of genuine acceptance. A new consciousness emerged at the Parliament that is characterized by an evolving sense of community among the religions, the importance of practical spirituality in everyday life, and a profound concern for the planet as a whole expressed in an attitude of universal responsibility.

The Parliament was a miracle of dialogue! It had moments of controversy and strain, but these were part of its genius and authenticity. When one of these situations occurred, Indians reacting to accusations by Sikhs and Kashmiris, in the Plenary for the Dispossessed, it was the Native Americans, under the Crow spiritual leader, Burton Pretty on Top, who brought peace and goodwill to the gathering of several thousand by forming a sacred Hoop Dance. The media never noticed this powerful healing action but simply focused on the disputes. The Parliament was criticized for these disturbances, but Jim Kenney, the chair of the program, remarked: "The Parliament is not tarnished when the real world shows up!" And the real world did show up!

The Parliament, as a profound and broad dialogue, has inspired a continuing process. From beginning to end and beyond, something has guided and *is* guiding this entirely miraculous phenomenon. What this dialogical process reveals is that interreligious dialogue/encounter forms a continuum: from mutual tolerance, to genuine acceptance, to openness, listening, mutual trust, learning and respect, to collaboration on the critical issues the planet faces, to the fostering of deep bonds of community, and then to the evolution of real communion founded on love. The miracle of dialogue is first that it happens but then that it leads to major changes in interactions among persons, societies, cultures, and religions. This significant process holds the promise of lasting peace for the earth.

A word about the compilation of these essays: One of the concerns for editors of collections such as this one is that the collection will be considered uneven in quality and length if a normative level of discourse is not imposed. We have explicitly chosen not to impose such constraints. Instead, we have chosen, as best we can, to honor the voice of each contributor. Since the Parliament itself was an extraordinarily pluralistic conversation, rather than reducing it to a uniform standard that is arbitrary, we have tried to respect this pluralism here. Tens of thousands of articles have been written about the Parliament in the past few years, and most have commented on the diversity, or pluralism of the event. The Parliament was unquestionably the most diverse celebration in history. It is this quality of difference embracing the harmony of community that we want to capture in this work.

Every contributor to this volume, with the exception of Robert Fastiggi, attended and participated in this historic happening. Robert Fastiggi's brief piece was included because he had wanted to come but couldn't and, more importantly, because his view wonderfully expresses the spirit of the Parliament and, indeed, of the whole interfaith movement. He represents all those who didn't attend and the contributions they would have made.

Most of the writers in this book played major roles before, during and after the event. Some are members of the Parliament's Assembly of Religious and Spiritual Leaders. Others are both members of the Assembly and trustees of the Council for a Parliament of the World's Religions (CPWR). The former group consists of the Dalai Lama (one of the twenty-four presidents of the Assembly), the Vatican's Archbishop Gioia, Maha Ghosananda, Burton Pretty on Top, Jim Kenney, Thomas Berry, and David Steindl-Rast, while the latter includes, Paulos Mar Gregorios, Daniel Gómez-Ibáñez, Thomas Baima, Gerald Barney, Ma Jaya Sati Bhagavati, Irfan Khan, and Wayne Teasdale.

Barbara Fields Bernstein was the Program Director, and Jim Kenney was the Program chairperson. Working with a program committee, they masterminded the vast schedule of events in those breathtaking days in Chicago. Barbara Fields Bernstein was also one of the facilitators in the Assembly. Dirk Ficca is the director of the Metropolitan Initiative of the Parliament, organizing a local grassroots organization and a fascinating series of forums, workshops, and other events. Daniel Gómez-Ibáñez was the executive director of the CPWR, while Jim Kenney, formerly a trustee, is now director of the International Initiative of the CPWR. Jackie Rivet-River was the major documentarian of the Parliament, producing the highly acclaimed *Peace Like a River: The 1993 Parliament of the World's Religions,* which has appeared several times on PBS. Joel Beversluis's role as the editor of *A SourceBook for Earth's Community of Religions* (Grand Rapids: CoNexus Press, 1995) is unique. He is a historian of the interfaith movement.

The pieces represented here are of unequal length. There is a reason for this anomaly. The longer articles are reflections developed later. The reader will notice differences of style and expression, e.g., Ma Jaya's heartrending descriptions of her children and students who suffer from AIDS and Burton Pretty on Top's honest portrayal of himself, his Native American viewpoint and particular way of communicating. Ma Jaya's concern is especially relevant to the social dimension. We also included Russill Paul D'Silva's essay and Magdalena Gómez's poem because both gave major performances at the Parliament, and their contribution represents in this volume the spiritual role of art, music, and drama in the interfaith arena.

It is the passionate wish of the editors that this book will not only inform, have historical value, and inspire others, especially those laboring to build bridges between and among cultures, religions and nations, but that it will also prove beneficial to the continuing process of birthing the Community of Religions. We have entered the *Interspiritual Age,* the *Second Axial Age. Interspiritual Community* is an essential, defining reality of this age. The unfolding and expanding of this community will gradually dissipate the fears collected over the millennia, and it will reveal the precious gift of *interspiritual wisdom.*

In this Interspiritual Age, we will gain access to the treasures hidden in the depths of our own and others' traditions of spirituality. These resources have the power to transform our attitudes and behavior toward one another, other species, and the earth itself. They will lead us into awareness of our larger communion with this sacred reality that is home for all of us. The challenge for humankind is to participate actively in this creative process of transformation, while the task of the religions is to inspire in humanity the *will* to change with the energy and courage to sustain it. There is no other work in our time that is more crucial than this work, and few activities are as meaningful. Upon it rests the survival and destiny of our planet.

Part I
. . . .

HISTORICAL
CONSIDERATIONS

*

1

The Importance of Religious Harmony

HIS HOLINESS THE DALAI LAMA, XIV

Nowadays the world is becoming increasingly materialistic, driven by an insatiable desire for power and possessions. Yet in this vain striving, we wander ever further from inward peace and mental happiness. Despite our pleasant material surroundings many of us today experience mental dissatisfaction, fear, anxiety, and a sense of insecurity. There is some kind of vacuum within the human mind. What I think we lack is a proper sense of spirituality.

The reason is simple. We human beings are not produced by machines and our requirements cannot be fulfilled by material means alone. We need material facilities for physical comfort. But these alone cannot provide mental comfort. Under such circumstances religious traditions are very relevant these days. If religion were not of much value in our day-to-day life, I believe we would have a right to abandon it. But I feel that religion actually provides us with tremendous benefit.

Each religion has its own philosophy and there are similarities as well as differences among the various traditions. What is important is what is suitable for a particular person. We should look at the underlying purpose of religion and not merely at the abstract details of theology or metaphysics. All religions make the betterment of humanity their primary concern. When we view the different religions as essentially instruments to develop a good heart—love and respect for others, a true sense of community—we can appreciate what they have in common.

A variety of religions is a natural need. Even our body needs a variety of food. If a restaurant were to sell only one kind of meal, eventually it would have no customers. But because the restaurant offers a variety of food, more people come and enjoy it. Everyone feels that his or her form of religious practice is the best. I myself feel that Buddhism is best for me. But this does not mean that Buddhism is best for everyone else. We all have a right to make our own choice.

Those of us involved with religion should also understand that it is impossible for all human beings to become religious-minded. It is out of the question that everyone become Buddhist or Christian or Muslim, or anything else. Buddhists will remain Buddhists; Christians and Muslims will maintain their own faiths, and nonbelievers will remain nonbelievers. Whether we like it or not, this is a fact and it is very important that we respect other people's views. Whether we like if or not, we have all been born on this earth as part of one great human family. This is not to say that all human beings are the same or that because everyone wishes for happiness that the same things will make each of them happy. Brothers and sisters resemble each other without being identical.

While I do not believe that everybody should become religious-minded, I am convinced each of the various religions can contribute to the welfare of humankind. All the great teachers of the past gave their religious teachings for the benefit of humanity. They did not desire to gain anything for themselves nor to create more trouble or unrest in the world. Through their own examples they advocated contentment, tolerance, and unselfish service to others. They lived saintly lives, not luxuriously like kings, but as simple human beings. While their inner strength was tremendous, the outer impression they gave was of contentment with a simple way of life.

Because all the world's religions have a similar intent, harmony between them is very important. Nothing can be achieved through feelings of discrimination and prejudice. Although I am a Buddhist Bhikshu (monk), I firmly believe that all religions have the same potential to help humankind despite differences in philosophy.

How can religious harmony be achieved? Religious scholars can meet together and discuss the similarities, differences, and values of their traditions. Followers of different religious traditions who have real inner experience should also meet to share these experiences. Occasionally, religious leaders can come together as we did when we prayed together in Assisi, in October 1986.

The Parliament of the World's Religions provides a marvelous forum for just such meetings. The very use of the word *Parliament* is indicative of spiritual pluralism. Delegates from our many religious traditions have the opportunity of meeting together on an equal basis. Just as it is extremely important that political leaders should get to know each other, religious leaders and practitioners must take such opportunities to get personally acquainted. Sometimes religion has been a source of conflict. If such problems arise, religious leaders will be much better disposed to deal with them if they already have friendly relations with each other.

At a time when peaceful coexistence has become a byword for political relations, the need for peaceful coexistence among religious practitioners should be obvious. In the past, unfortunate things have happened when people attempted to propagate their own religion through conflicts with other faiths. Today, it is quite clear that a religious system cannot be disseminated through force. It is impossible to make everyone accept the same religion; nor would it be desirable, and there would be no purpose in doing so.

When we have opportunities to explain our traditions in public, leaders and delegates of different religious traditions have a special responsibility. Of course it is natural to talk about the special qualities of our own tradition. But sometimes while praising our own tradition we tend to belittle those of others. Where is a danger that this will become a source of feelings of uneasiness and misunderstandings.

If we are each to contribute to religious harmony and a more peaceful world, followers of different religions must be true to what they believe. Sometimes we are satisfied simply to say "I am Buddhist," or "I am Christian," without much feeling. If you sincerely practice what you believe, then not only will you get some benefit from it, but other people will benefit as well. It is certainly true that one person can create the positive atmosphere that leads to a happy family and a peaceful community. When you discover the deeper value of your own tradition through actual practice, you will come to recognize the value of other traditions as well. This is how mutual respect and understanding develop. Therefore the first rule of religious practice is to examine ourselves before we judge others.

We have lately seen how new found freedoms, widely celebrated though they are, have given rise to fresh economic difficulties and unleashed long-buried ethnic and religious tensions that contain the seeds for a new cycle of conflicts. In the context of our newly emerging global community, all forms of violence have become totally unacceptable as a means of settling disputes. Let me express my view in the language and spirit of the Universal Declaration on Nonviolence:

Religious groups throughout the world have a responsibility to promote peace in our own age and in the future. It is true that in the history of the human family people of various religions, sometimes even acting officially in the name of their different traditions, have initiated or collaborated in systemic violence or war. At times such actions have been directed at people of other faiths or communities, as well as within a particular religious denomination. This kind of behavior is totally inappropriate for spiritual persons or communities.

It is therefore time for those of us who belong to religious traditions to declare that religion can no longer be an accomplice to war, to terrorism, or to any other forms of violence, organized or spontaneous, against any member of our human family. Because this family is one, our actions must be consistent with this identity of oneness. We have an obligation to promote a new vision of society, one in which war has no place in resolving disputes among states, communities or religions, but in which nonviolence is the preeminent value in all human relations.[1]

If people have faith, accept some ideal and feel they have found the most beneficial way of improving themselves, well and good. They are exercising their right to follow their own choice. If others have no faith, and even consider that religion is wrong, they have a right to their opinion as well.

The purpose of religion is not merely to build beautiful places of worship, but to cultivate positive human qualities such as tolerance, generosity, and love. Therefore, it is quite contradictory that religion should ever become an excuse for war. Since the goals and objectives of religion are genuinely peaceful, the method for accomplishing them should be nonviolent.

Nevertheless, in the present circumstances, no one can afford to assume that someone else will solve our problems. Every individual has a responsibility to help guide our global family in the right direction. Good wishes are not sufficient; we must each assume responsibility. Ideas must be transformed into action. Expressing different ideas in nice-sounding words is easy, but implementing them is much more difficult. The essential point to remember is that however others may behave, the benefits that religion can bring and the contribution it can make to humankind depends on ourselves as individuals and whether we really put our faith into practice. As a Buddhist monk, I try to develop compassion myself, not just from a religious point of view, but from a humanitarian one as well. For me, the propagation of compassion, and through it peace, is part of my daily practice.

Human beings are intelligent, but when strong emotions arise their intelligence becomes ineffective. Therefore it is extremely important to take preemptive measures to avoid conditions or situations that lead to

---

1. *The Universal Declaration on Nonviolence* is a statement I developed with the members of Monastic Interreligious Dialogue, a Roman Catholic group. We signed it on April 2, 1991, in Santa Fe, New Mexico. For the text of the declaration, see *A SourceBook for Earth's Community of Religions,* ed. Joel Beversluis (Grand Rapids: CoNexus Press, 1995), p. 171.

mental disturbance. Whenever we pursue noble goals, obstacles and difficulties are bound to occur. As human beings, we may lose hope. But there is nothing to be gained from discouragement; our determination must be very firm. According to my own meager experience, we can change. We *can* transform ourselves. Therefore, if we all were to spend a few minutes every day, thinking about these things and trying to develop compassion, eventually compassion will become part of our lives.

Generally speaking, religion in the real sense has to do with a positive mind. A positive mind is what ultimately brings us benefit or happiness. The essence of religion is therefore the methods by which these things are generated. The Parliament of the World's Religions encourages us to meet in an atmosphere of mutual respect to exchange our experiences and learn from each other. It is my prayer that by doing so we shall all contribute to a genuinely more peaceful and amicable world. If genuine peace comes and a new global society emerges then we will also contribute to the lasting happiness of all sentient beings.

2

The Two Parliaments, the 1893 Original and the Centennial of 1993: A Historian's View

RICHARD HUGHES SEAGER

The original World's Parliament of Religions of 1893 and its centennial, the Parliament of the World's Religions of 1993, present a historian with an opportunity to reflect upon the significance of two events linked by aspiration, but separated by a century. The organizers of the two Parliaments aspired to convene assemblies that would display to the world the richness of contemporary religious life. Both events were designed to increase understanding and encourage cooperation among different religious traditions and faiths, and both seized the imagination of thousands of observers and participants. At both gatherings, grand theological visions of world religious unity were shared, contemporary social issues were addressed, and deeply divisive religious conflicts were aired.

Yet at the same time the great differences between the two Parliaments are noteworthy because they may point to important shifts that have occurred in the religious world over the course of one hundred years. As displays of contemporary religious life, the two assemblies reflected the spiritual preoccupations of two different eras in American and world history. Each Parliament had a unique institutional history and took on a different organizational form, as a result of different intentions in the minds of their organizers and leaders. The two events, moreover, were marked by strikingly different patterns of dominance and inclusivity.

The similarities and differences between the two Parliaments make them fascinating subjects for historical reflections in a comparative vein.

The century-long gap between them provides the occasion to contemplate what in the world of religious discourse has persisted and what has changed. The continuities and discontinuities between them also provide an opportunity to ponder, in a necessarily speculative way, where we might all be heading as we face together the future and its religious challenges and opportunities, which we can only intuit from our limited perspective today.

The Spirits of Two Ages

The two Parliaments were convened in distinctly different eras in American and world history. On the domestic scene in 1893, Anglo-Protestants remained the undisputed custodians of American culture, but Roman Catholics and Jews were beginning to move into place as important partners in an expanding national mainstream. The nation's optimistic mood, conspicuous in public rhetoric but by no means universal, was informed by progressive postmillennialism—the idea that history was moving forward with increasing rapidity toward the dawn of a glorious new era, propelled by Christianity, democratic institutions, science, and technology.

1893 marked the heyday of the European, Christian empires on the international scene, but the United States was only to enter fully onto the imperial stage five years after the original Parliament, when it went to war with Spain and seized the Philippines. The phenomena we now call globalization was then an exciting, emerge possibility, a result of both the steady rise of global commerce and the development of new technologies. Many people sensed an intimate connection between religion, technology, and the dominance of the West, which resulted in the steamship, electricity, and telegraph being hailed in many circles as products of Christian inventiveness. Ideas about East and West and European and Asian civilization tended to be cast in terms of mutually exclusive dichotomies informed by theories derived from the evolutionary sciences. These theories provided a pseudoscientific basis for widely held opinions about the inferiority of the races, religions, and civilizations of the East and superiority of the Christian West.

In 1993, the world had radically changed both on the domestic and international scenes. In the United States, Anglo-Protestantism was deeply divided along a number of theological, political, and cultural lines, a development foreseen by a few worried observers of the Parliament in 1893. The national mood, while informed by perennial currents of American optimism and idealism, was both jaded and chastened when compared to that in 1893, the result of decades of global leadership during hot and cold wars, periods of unparalleled prosperity that alternated with insecurity, and intermittent dis-ease about some of the far-reaching consequences of science and technology.

By American standards for reckoning the passage of time, the frontier seemed to be ancient history in 1993 and Turner's frontier thesis had been eclipsed as an interpretive national metaphor by globalization theses. Native American cultures were undergoing a multifaceted renaissance fostered by the success of a number of legislative and economic initiatives and by the rise of the politics of identity. The Civil Rights movement had significantly altered the nation, although it had fallen short of achieving the integration envisioned by Martin Luther King, Jr. Beginning in the late 1970s, moreover, many black activists dropped integration as a desired goal and shifted to a pluralistic or multicultural interpretation of the place of African-Americans in the nation's history. At about the same time, Latino and Asian minorities, which grew rapidly after the reform of immigration law in 1965, helped to foster the gradual emergence of a broadly pluralistic understanding of the American dream. Second-wave feminism, while thwarted in its efforts to achieve equal rights initiatives and differentiated to an often confusing degree, had successfully forced a wide range of gender-related issues into the consciousness of the American mainstream.

On the international scene, the idea of a postimperial age seemed to be confirmed by the end of the Cold War and the collapse of the Soviet bloc, even as economic arrangements and political attitudes related to the old empires continued to structure the world in important ways. Globalization had become an omnipresent concern that informed many different fields of endeavor with both positive and negative evaluations, a result of an acute awareness of the degree to which technology, science, industry, and commerce had become dislodged from Western power bases. The world was being transformed by an electronic revolution, but it was a sign of the time that few people hailed the invention of the microprocessor and computer chip as indicative of the genius of Christianity. Ideas about East and West had for fifty years been dominated by the rhetoric of the Cold War. But European and Asian civilizations interacted on a far more even playing field than in 1893, a result of the national liberation movements and the dismantling of political empires that had been conspicuous parts of the first half of the twentieth century.

In a kind of historical shorthand, it might be useful to conceive of the first Parliament as having been held in the heyday of modernity, when the confident dominance of the Christian, Euro-American West encouraged the widespread adoption of overly optimistic assumptions about the consequences of technological development and scientific knowledge. In 1893, challenges to this dominance, be these related to religion, race, or nation, had not come fully into play. The second Parliament was convened in an era sometimes characterized as postmodern. By 1993, many people sensed the highly ambiguous consequences of progress. The authority of the traditions of the West, moreover, which had defined the modern center in 1893, was increasingly challenged by parties that a century before had been consigned to the periphery.

Institutional Setting, Form, and Intention

The first Parliament was institutionally and financially embedded in a web of American commercial and governmental institutions created to construct Chicago's World's Columbian Exposition of 1892–93. This world's fair was a tribute to Christopher Columbus, a triumphalistic celebration of the conquest of the continent, and an announcement of America's economic and political ambitions overseas. The Parliament was conceived in the spirit of the Exposition, and it was organized and managed by representatives of the American religious mainstream. Its steering committee was composed of one Roman Catholic bishop, one Reform Jewish rabbi, and fourteen Anglo-Protestant ministers from as many denominations. The selection of delegates to the Parliament remains somewhat of a mystery (most of the organizational records having been lost), but it seems that, with notable exceptions, individuals received invitations from the leadership in Chicago after consultation with a large advisory committee.

The 1893 Parliament was also meant to be a tightly controlled event. It took on the form of a lecture hall or lyceum and, according to its mission statement, no criticism of any religious tradition was to be allowed. Although controversy disturbed its decorum on a number of occasions, the Parliament was essentially a formal, linear sequence of single speakers, who spoke at a podium before a seated audience during three daily sessions, a format that was maintained throughout the assembly's seventeen days. A good deal of activity took place around the Parliament—denominational congresses, informal conversations, and soirees—but the assembly itself was highly focused. In a fundamental way, if one was not among the speakers or the 3,000 observers in the Hall of Columbus in the Chicago Art Institute (or in the Hall of Washington in the case of overflowing crowds), one was not at the World's Parliament of Religions.

The Parliament's setting and its tightly structured form reflected its organizers' intentions, which was to demonstrate the essential unity of the religions of the world. But, reflecting contemporary understandings of the unequal relation between East and West, most delegates approached religious and theological questions about unity on fundamentally Christian or Western grounds. The theological tenor of the event was informed by the "fulfillment thesis," an assumption influential in liberal religious circles, which saw varying degrees of value in every great religion, but assumed that all were completed or fulfilled in Christianity. Experiential religion was applauded at the Parliament, but the opportunity to experience religions other than Christianity was limited. Voluntary worship assemblies held each morning consisted of the Lord's Prayer or Our Father, called on these occasions "the Universal Prayer." Social concerns such as education, crime, a fair wage, and women's rights received substantial attention from many delegates, both East and West, but this reforming spirit was closely linked to progressive postmillennialism, which tended to bolster the liberal idealism that more or less dominated the assembly.

The Parliament of 1993 had no institutional links to the centennial observances of Columbus's voyage, even though it self-consciously evoked as its precedent the Parliament of 1893. The 1993 Parliament, moreover, followed quickly upon the heels of a Columbiad that might be characterized as having marked the nadir of Columbian triumphalism, with a great deal of public debate over what was to be considered progress and what conquest and pillage in New World history. In the 1980s, Chicago had decided not to host another Exposition. The 1993 Parliament was also conceived and launched by leaders of non-mainsteam religious groups, who then worked to gain the support of Chicago's Jewish, Catholic, and Protestant communities. In large part, delegates and speakers at the centennial were selected by committees representing different religious and ethnic constituencies. These Host Committees played an important role in structuring the 1993 Parliament; they were designed to maximize self-determination by groups that chose to participate in the assembly.

The 1993 Parliament was also highly diffuse in form, more resembling a large convention than a lyceum. Plenary assemblies were held throughout it, which displayed the universality of transcendental aspirations and addressed the social concerns of a wide range of constituencies. These also served to unite in a loosely jointed way an extraordinary range of workshops, panels, seminars, and performances that ran concurrently throughout the Parliament's nine days. For much of the 1993 Parliament, moreover, a convocation of religious leaders met separately to discuss a position paper on a global ethic that could be shared by different religious traditions, an ongoing process that seemed somewhat removed from the rest of the assembly. From an organizational point of view, it is fair to characterize the 1993 Parliament as having been a decentered event; it seemed at times that there were as many different Parliaments as there were participants.

This decentered quality buttressed the organizers' goal of fostering cooperation and respect for the spiritual aspirations to be found in all religious expressions, while avoiding caveats about ultimate reality or a single, authoritative ground for religious unity. A highly general theological consensus did seem to emerge at the assembly but somewhat inadvertently, with universalistic God-talk emanating from the Bahai, Hindu, Jewish, Muslim, and Christian communities. But, the overall tenor of the assembly was such that Jains, Buddhists and Western non-theists were not at a serious disadvantage, a fact underscored in concluding remarks made by the Dalai Lama concerning the need to respect the substantive differences among the religions represented at the assembly. The format for worship at the Parliament, moreover, underscored the decentered quality of the assembly, with a wide range of services in the mornings and evenings sponsored by various Host Committees. A concern for social issues such as the plight of disenfranchised peoples, the consequences of mass migrations, and the threat to the environment posed by industrialism, consumerism, and deforestation played an important role at the assembly. Despite an upbeat air at the 1993 centennial, an urgent and at times dire note was often sounded in addressing these concerns, which was in sharp contrast to the optimistic reformism that dominated the 1893 assembly.

The two Parliaments differed considerably in their institutional settings, forms, and intentions. By late nineteenth-century standards, the first Parliament was a liberal assembly, infused with a progressive post-millennial spirit, while partaking of the Euro-American triumphalism of the age. Its controlled structure buttressed its organizers' intention to present to the world both the essential unity of all religions and the supremacy of Christianity. The second Parliament was marked by a more egalitarian spirit. At the same time, it displayed a more critical concern for the impact of modernity on different peoples, traditions, and the planet. Its decentered structure seemed to mirror the intention of its organizers to affirm the complexity of the religious world of the late twentieth century.

Patterns of Dominance and Inclusivity

The two events were also marked by strikingly different patterns of dominance and inclusivity. Christians dominated the 1893 Parliament with Protestants comprising by far the largest single delegation. As importantly, American Protestant ideas and ideals—be these progressive millennialism or hopes for the universal brotherhood of man—set the tone and agenda for the assembly. The normative God-talk at the original Parliament, whether it was based on traditional creeds, evolutionary ideas, theological fulfillment theses, or ideals of inclusivity, tended to emanate from Anglo-Protestant sources, be those Episcopalian, Presbyterian, Baptist, Methodist, Congregationalist, or Unitarian. Judaism and Roman Catholicism, two religious traditions tied to the mass migrations of the nineteenth century, made important contributions to this Protestant-based theological consensus. But they also made comprehensive and systematic presentations of their own traditions, which had the effect of announcing the arrival of two ancient and distinct traditions in an expanding American mainstream.

The foundations for this new, emergent mainstream were only loosely theological, but the religious limits to this consensus becomes more apparent when considering patterns of exclusion that can be discerned at the 1893 assembly. There were no official representatives of Mormonism, spiritualism, or Theosophy at the 1893 Parliament, all of which were new religious movements with mainstream origins, but considered controversial, of questionable taste, and offbeat. African-Americans were seriously underrepresented and there were no Native American delegates. There was, moreover, no discussion of ethnic tensions within and among Protestants, Catholics, and Jews, even though these were increasingly conspicuous in America's cities. Women's issues were represented by delegates who hailed, by and large, from the more liberal wing of Protestantism. Although women voiced a wide variety of concerns, their comments tended to support the dominant consensus of an emergent, white, Judeo-Christian mainstream.

A similarly formal and essentially conservative approach to forging consensus was apparent on the international front. The organizers of the original Parliament conceived of the religions of the world in terms of "great traditions." As a result, there were no representatives of tribal religions and few delegates from important sectarian and regional variations of a tradition such as Saivite Hinduism or Tibetan Buddhism. Only ten traditions were represented in 1893, these often by only one or two representatives. Hinduism and Buddhism, whose delegations were reasonably large and somewhat diverse, were the exceptions. As importantly, Hindus and Buddhists acted as the catalytic agents for the entire assembly. The excitement they generated on the floor of the assembly is a matter of both legend and historical record and, after the Parliament, they contributed to religious revivals at home and to the importation of Asian religions into America. The 1893 Parliament marked the start of the long march of Hinduism and Buddhism toward the American mainstream from the far periphery.

The question of what group, if any, dominated the 1993 Parliament is difficult to assess, but the shifting roles played by those important in 1893 provide some revealing contrasts. This is particularly so in the case of Anglo-Protestantism. Individual Protestants played important roles in organizing the 1993 Parliament and many were to be found among those speaking on pluralism, religious dialogue, and social issues. There were, moreover, numerous Protestants in attendance. But, formal presentations by representatives of the old mainstream Protestant churches seemed conspicuously absent from the program.

In contrast, a significant number of varied presentations were planned by representatives of Roman Catholicism and Judaism, but neither group seemed concerned to present themselves in a systematic way before the assembly as they had in 1893. Catholics and Jews seem taken for granted as a part of the American mainstream in 1993, even though the presence of Louis Farrakahn and the Nation of Islam precipitated a controversy among Jews regarding their continued participation in the assembly. The numerous Hindus and Buddhists from many different sects and regions, including seekers, Euro-American converts, immigrants, and delegates from overseas, suggested the significant advances toward mainstream status had been made by these "old-line" Asian traditions over the course of a century.

Another striking contrast is in the broad inclusivity that typified the 1993 assembly. Many and varied spiritualist and New Age groups were conspicuous. African-Americans played a powerful role, contributing delegates from the black churches, Islam and the Nation of Islam, and a range of Caribbean traditions. Native American delegates were highly regarded as spiritual teachers, but also as tribal rights advocates and cultural critics. Delegates from Asian immigrant communities relatively new to America—Sikhs, Jains, Zoroastrians, Muslims, and others—were concerned to introduce their systems of belief and practice to the public, much like Jews and Catholics a century earlier. The concerns of women seemed ubiquitous; gender issues were addressed in numerous "little" and "great" traditions and in a wide range of feminine-based religiosities. Overall, there was a pluralistic approach to questions about women and religion with critical feminist perspectives competing with ecofeminism, Goddess worship, and traditional forms of women's spirituality found in the world's major traditions.

Given the diversity of traditions represented in 1993, it is difficult to point to a single group that acted as a catalytic agent. However, earth-based spiritualities, foremost among them neopagans, formed a significant part of the total assembly. A theological controversy, moreover, erupted on the first day of the centennial, which raised questions as to whether these groups deserved consideration as partners in interfaith dialogue and as legitimate parts of the assembly. As a result, the question of inclusivity and its limits was raised at the outset, and the consensus that emerged that favored broad inclusion set the tone for much of the rest of the assembly.

A comparative sketch of the original Parliament and its centennial in terms of shifting patterns of dominance and inclusivity underscores the substantial and important differences between the two events. However, the more speculative question remains: what might the two Parliaments suggest in terms of long-term trends in modern and American religious history?

Continuities and Discontinuities

Continuities and discontinuities between the two Parliaments suggest a few long-term trends that are likely to continue well into the next century. For all their substantial differences, both Parliaments were organized in and infused by an idealistic and essentially liberal religious spirit that has long been seen as characteristically American. At different times, this spirit has found expression in national moods that have been both world-embracing and irritatingly naive and in national missions that have been alternately generous, coercive, and ill-conceived. But, in its better moments, this spirit has made events like the Parliaments become realities. The contrast between 1893 and 1993 suggests that the national, racial, and religious triumphalism that was part and parcel of the liberalism of the first Parliament has been chastened, at least in many different quarters, over the course of the century. It may well be that a healthy, rigorous, and realistic form of American religious liberalism will serve as the platform for a third Parliament in 2093.

The two Parliaments also suggest a long-term trend in which religious affiliation, race, and ethnicity are of decreasing importance as criteria for inclusion in an American mainstream. Boundaries clearly drawn at the 1893 Parliament had fallen at the centennial, replaced by multicultural and pluralistic sensibilities. A few observers dismissed the centennial's eclectic flare as mere novelty, but it managed to bring together— not without controversy to be sure—many Anglo-Protestants, Jews, Roman Catholics, African-Americans, Asians and Asian-Americans, Native Americans, and representatives of a wide range of new spiritualities. This should not be dismissed as trendiness. It was more an indication that a wide range of people were ready to see something like a religious rainbow coalition become a new, increasingly broad, and pluralistic American mainstream.

But given that mainstream Protestant churches dominated the Parliament in 1893, their absence as a programmatic presence at the centennial remains a serious development, one that became a source of considerable speculation and some hand-wringing. This development was attributed to a variety of factors—a lack of institutional savvy on the part of the centennial's organizers and/or theological skittishness, an overly cautious mood, renewed conservativism, and general world-weariness on the part of the mainstream Protestant churches.

Whatever the immediate causal factors, this contrast between 1893 and 1993 seems to mirror another long-term trend in American religious history. The old Protestant mainstream was as much an ethnic as a religious identity. The liberal/fundamentalist schism around 1920 undermined its traditional role as America's chief custodian and religious leader. Its more recent fragmentation into a number of major camps, each competing for the traditional place of honor, has served to diminish further its public authority. In the meantime, the shift from the Anglo-conformist assumptions of the last century to the multicultural ideals that increasingly prevail today has significantly altered the way we describe America, which has provoked in turn a kind of ethnic identity crisis in the old Protestant mainstream. The outcome of the Protestant search for a new identity as both a people and a religion is likely to continue and will be an important factor in determining the shape of American religiosity in the twenty-first century.

A comparison of the two Parliaments may also shed some light on the protean questions frequently posed about modernity and the postmodern. As a period and style, modernity is often characterized as optimistic, future-oriented, and this-worldly. In retrospect, modernity's confident brio may be attributed to the ameliorative capacity of science and technology, the rising prosperity brought about by industrial society, and the broadening of the democratic ethos and franchise. Part of this confidence, however, may be attributable to forms of geopolitical theologizing conspicuous at the Parliament in 1893—the assumption that the world can be neatly divided between superior and inferior religions and civilizations, between a defining, authoritative center and a passive, dismissable, and malleable periphery.

Postmodernity is often linked to ideas about pluralization and globalization, and it connotes for many a commitment to freedom of expression and action for those excluded or marginalized by historically authoritative centers. The 1993 Parliament was a postmodern event insofar as it pointed to multiple centers, many of them emerging from peripheral status, a situation participants and observers alike seemed to find both religiously profound and spiritually exhilarating. The 1993 Parliament's exuberant, at times chaotic, spirit was a testimony to the capacity of all people to strive for transcendence through a wide range of different and highly particular traditions, beliefs, and actions. But this spirit demanded no appeals to fulfillment theses. The centennial was a multireligious event, well suited to an age when genuinely plural civilizations both at home and overseas are struggling to come of age.

It is hopefully a long-term trend that ideas about racial and religious superiors and inferiors are losing their capacity to convince. But, while postmodern pluralism is experienced as liberation by many people, the absence of a defining center is for others an occasion for anxiety, an emotional reaction compounded by unsettling advances in the sciences, ongoing revolutions in technology, and uncertainties in the national and global economy. As an orientation to the world, postmodernism makes few claims that an increase in freedom is going to allay contemporary anxieties. Nor does it provide much solace in terms of authoritative, traditional theologies. The Parliament of 1993 seemed a witness to the fact that people from many different religions and traditions are attempting to move ahead together into an uncertain future in good faith, whether they ultimately place that faith in God, the Goddess, the dharma, or serendipity.

A Chain of Parliaments

One hopes that Chicago will rise to the occasion and convene another centennial of the World's Parliament of Religions in 2093. One also hopes that a sequence of three Parliaments will reveal the confident optimism associated with modernity to have been combined with the pluralistic commitments of postmodern sensibilities. It is, moreover, wonderful to think that the world might have a Parliament in Chicago every hundred years. They are extraordinary occasions that allow calls to be sent out, visions to be formulated, and unpredictable throngs of people to be gathered in. As many observers pointed out in 1893, they are living oracles from which one can glean insights into the preoccupations of an age. They are of inestimable significance to their participants and, as evidenced by the 1893 Parliament, they help the world to change.

One centennial Parliament now stands in concrete relationship to the original. With these two, there is a kind of point/counterpoint statement. Like a pair of bookends, they have the religious history of the twentieth-century—its aspirations, revolutions,and anxieties—stored between them. A third would yield a trinity, the fourth a quaternity, the fifth, the start of an indefinite sequence, and so on into the future, each centennial epitomizing an era in its own right, while creating a historical continuity.

Future historians of religions would be delighted to analyze the linking together of such a chain of Parliaments. Each one will elicit from their participants deep spirituality and great sincerity, cast against a landscape of concerns that change with each century. Each will prompt commitment and self-sacrifice on the part of those who organize them, inspire visionary leaps of faith among those who speak at them, and call forth extraordinary responses from those who attend them. By nature, these future Parliaments will be both grand and grandiose events, much like the two in the past, and will continue to lure historians, who are necessarily blind to the actual frame of things, into interpretative excess and speculative flights of fancy.

Part II
. . . .

THE 1993
PARLIAMENT OF
THE WORLD'S
RELIGIONS

*

3

Dancing Honeybees and Sacred Snakes

KEITH CUNNINGHAM

The symbols in our lives grow out of the intersection of our personal experience with the eternal tropisms of our human being. Symbols are mythic images. A symbolic dimension suffuses every instant of our consciousness, but there are heightened moments where a great symbol seems to take conscious form before our eyes. At such moments we could be said to be living a myth in the truest sense. My personal experience at the Parliament of the World's Religions contained such moments, and other people I met, from different faiths and different parts of the world, voiced to me many of the same impressions. I could say that collectively we had some awareness of having become part of a *living process* that can only be very dimly conveyed to those who were not there. Of course when you are living such an intense collective experience you are immersed in the flow of it. The broader perspective revealing the essential *living form* of the experience may only emerge later. So it was only with the distance of some months that I could begin to see the Parliament as a symbol *in the act of forming itself,* as a mythic image. Symbols implicitly have to do with boundaries: crossing boundaries, the dissolution of some boundaries, and the obstinate presence of others. The birth of any new idea requires boundaries, like the placenta or the eggshell, which separate the inside from the outside and concentrate the incubating energy within. At heightened, mythic moments we experience the living symbol crossing the boundary from the unconscious into consciousness.

The creative process leading to the formation of a living *symbol* is different from that leading to the development of an effective *sign*. All of us arriving at the Parliament were greeted by the *insignia* of the Parliament on banners, on buttons, on literature and communiqués, on our personal identity badges. The insignia of a core hub with nine concentric "flames" radiating outward became familiar to us, but it had no part in our inner lives. It had been *invented* by someone—or by a committee—as an effective sign to represent the Parliament. It was conventional: created by convention. One could call it generically mandalalike. But could it become a living symbol? Did it come to life for some, or for many?

The insignia is an instance of a sign, created by the conscious mind, which may take on the power of a symbol *only* if it penetrates, and resonates back from, the depth of the soul. More commonly the symbol rises from the welter of our inner experience, and, like the dream, is a crystallization and transformation of it. The Diamond Body or Truth Body of Buddhism, as a symbol of our spiritual potential bears a relation to our physical body like the relation of a quartz crystal to the endless chain of an organic molecule. It makes us *see* the imperishable and eternal within ourselves. But this would be no more than a poetic metaphor were it not that the diamond expresses the *experience* of a sudden clarity and gemlike consciousness that is transcendent of language and logic. Symbols articular the experience of heightened power or consciousness and point beyond the experience itself to its unfathomable source. We are continually experiencing this flux of the sacred in our lives—and not only at those moments, or through the particular avenues, officially sanctioned by the institutions of our society. "Any object, intensely regarded," Joyce reminds us again, "is a doorway opening to the eon of the gods."

Therefore, I would like to focus on three collective experiences from the Parliament, intensely regarded by many, that began to take on the quality of living symbol. There were constant topics of conversation at the Parliament, they were on people's minds, they became channels for energy. They were not specific or unusual events, but classes of universal experience—universal because implicit in the structure of the experience itself, and therefore inevitable—in which almost everyone participated, and which by their very nature spoke to the heart and awakened the mythic core. In contrast to this, no one spoke about the Parliament's insignia. It was simply *there,* a given, like the hotel building itself.

First, then, and in fact the point of entry for everyone arriving at the Parliament, was the chaos of good-natured milling confusion always surrounding the third-floor registration area and the entrance to the Grand Ballroom where the plenary sessions were held. This was the "solar plexus" and nerve center of the entire Parliament, if not the locus of its higher brain function. One could go into one of the seminar rooms and leave feeling lofty and mentally enlightened, but here on the third floor was the intense experience of *life*. The life of the street, the life of the bazaar. One was pressing, bumping, and rubbing against literally dozens of people from every part of the world in making one's way across the lobby, exchanging touches, exchanging scents, exchanging looks, all in a sea of frothing, bubbling languages. This was the immersion experience, and it became a daily ritual. Here one lost much of one's separateness and became part of a larger collective life. It was like being in the melee of chromosomes during the mitosis of a cell. I heard people call this *"the beehive."* The symbolic and mythological associations with bees and beehives draw us into a sacred context both broad and deep, speaking of community, nourishment, eros: the dance of life.

The second living symbol that took its significance from the collective life of the Parliament I shall call the *Circle Dance*. The *dance* that joins us all together took several striking forms. The Native American elders, in their opening sacrifice and blessing for the Parliament, stood and concentrated their energies around an invisible but palpable center. Their movements took the form of a circle addressed directly to the sacred energies of the unconscious—and of the world. By *acting* on behalf of all present and on behalf of all of the Earth's creatures, they established what many felt to be, and perhaps in fact was, the moral center of the Parliament. Two days later, during a stormy plenary session, the "Voices of the Dispossessed," when speakers had been rudely shouted down by impassioned voices from the audience and it appeared that all the Parliament's ideals for itself threatened to become a nightmare, it was again the calming center created by the Native Americans that was crucial. The dance for peace they began on the stage embraced everyone without distinction, all of the contending parties. Soon the dance spilled from the stage in snaking lines that wound through the entire ballroom, hundreds asserting *through their bodies* their experience of unification and solidarity. This was not an act of rhetoric. Nor was it a *performance*. It had absolutely to come from the heart. So, importantly, as a symbol compensating for a destructive trend in the mass consciousness of our time, the spontaneous collective gesture of the dance broke through the division between "actor" and "spectator." By this act the Parliament came to life: with a cry.

The "dance" became another leitmotif of the Parliament, a source of continued affirmation. I believe it expressed better that any other single gesture what reconciliation *means* to the whole integrity of the mind-body system. In many of Jesus' parables, like that of the "Prodigal Son," reconciliation leads to feasting, dancing, and celebration, or the party is the setting for the miracle event. It is the *dance* of the returning scout that galvanizes the beehive into focused action. The inherently dramatic shape of the plenary crisis and its resolution seemed to touch those deep centers of motivation where the mind-system and the instinct-system meet. This is the mythic dimension. Recalling that extraordinary event throughout the week always brought back the *energy* of the moment. It was already an act of commemoration, already the beginning of a mythology. The presentation by Brother David Stendl-Rast, presciently entitled "The Great Circle Dance: Religion and the Religions," seemed to encompass perfectly and define this new possibility of reconciliation. Finally, the Parliament ended with a dance, which symbolically brought all the "dancers" of the different faiths together and sent the energy of the Parliament out into the larger world.

And so the *portal,* or doorway, where energy is carried across the boundary between the world of the Parliament within the Palmer House and the world outside, presented a third set of universal and inevitable experiences that took on the aspect of a living symbol. Inside, six thousand delegates and participants were working hard to forge a vision of a sustainable, responsible, and sacred future for the Earth and its creatures. Many were asked to sacrifice long-cherished points of view and to review the entire posture of their faith traditions. Outside, life went on as usual. On the sidewalk, representatives of fundamentalist groups sold papers accusing the Parliament of devil worship. Meanwhile, the Chicago daily newspapers paid scant attention to the Parliament, beyond seizing upon a few incidents that intimated scandal or titillation, or upon the presence of proven media "stars" such as the Dalai Lama. Chicago is a pragmatic city, a city of big shoulders. It is a city whose essential mythic identity remains that of "hog-butcher to the world," even if that takes the contemporary form of hog "futures" on the commodities exchange. This is not Rome or Jerusalem, Varanasi or Assisi. The contrast could hardly have been more abrupt, and it was the portal that "mediated" the energies of "inside" and "outside."

I mention this not to emphasize a dualism between sacred and profane, but to recognize that the walls of the hotel presented a natural boundary between two modes of activity, however they may be defined, that constitute one of the fundamental dialectics of human evolution. The perpetually revolving doors (another circle dance) of the Palmer House, leading to the bustling street, symbolized the *threshold crossing* each delegate and participant at the Parliament would face upon returning to their own societies with this new vision of sacred global possibility. This was the return threshold, as the registration area with its ebullient confusions had been the entry threshold.

Such thresholds are universal mythological motifs that always appear in conjunction with *initiation*. What had been initiated at the Parliament would have to cross the return threshold back to the world, there to meet what Joseph Campbell calls "the jury of sober eyes": the challenge of all those who have *not* seen. Thus it was of crucial importance on a symbolical level, which means on a deep energy and motivation level, that the final event and dance of the Parliament was held outside the boundary of the hotel, in Grant Park's concert shell. This was a deliberate threshold crossing that carried the energy of the Parliament into the city, and from there across the globe in a spirit of birth and celebration. It completed a sacred, initiatory cycle and showed great sensitivity to the importance of symbol and ritual on the part of the Parliament's planning committee. Literally the final word, the recessional hymn, so to speak, was given to the electrifying voices of the Chicago Soul Children's Choir. The energy was passed to a new generation and out into the world.

The Life of a Symbol
in the "Forest of Signs"

These symbols of the beehive, the circle dance, and the threshold crossing, grew out of the implicit structuring forces within the direct collective experience that made up the Parliament. They pointed to an initiation, the beginning of something new, and by their resonating presence made initiation possible. That is to say, these symbols that hovered in the background of awareness helped to create an accord between the intellect and the impulse systems of the body. They got everything flowing together in a subtle way. They were "living" symbols to the extent that they were begotten at once by life and by the human imagination, imparted momentum to human action, evolved in interaction, and continued to generate new experience. They were "religious" to the extent that they helped "bind us back" (re-ligio: to bind back) to what it means to form a living human community: not just a bunch of people getting up and talking. Together they could make up parts of a mythology, but what kind of mythology would it be?

Now, if we were a traditional mythopoeic people, we would gather associated symbols and images from our inner and outer worlds around this core as a way of sustaining and concentrating the vital energy of the initiation experience, and of communicating the essence of it to those who were not there. The bee, the snake, and the portal would become theriomorphic and objective representations of the idea. They connect the mythic image to an essential, ritual *enactment* unified with the wisdom of the body and the instincts. We would dance them again, draw them, keep them alive. The circle, the waving line, and the doorway as graphic symbols would have the power to commemorate and rekindle our energies. We would husband our sacred symbols the way the sacred coals of the hearth are always kept glowing. We would midwife them into blossoming aesthetic and cultural forms.

There are two dangers at this point in the life of a symbol, and these two dangers point, I believe, to the exact difficulty of our present situation. The first danger has already been voiced by Joseph Campbell. It is the danger of overinterpreting and concretizing the symbol. If, in our zeal to guard, protect, and nurture the sacred experience we have shared we declare the symbols *themselves* to be sacred—the snake, the bee, the portal, the circle of flames—rather than their referents in our experience, then we have already made the fundamental mistake. Then we become angry when someone, an "outsider," desecrates our insignia, turns the phrases meant to remind us of the sacred into absurd and offensive bumper stickers, or directs a Senate subcommittee to investigate us. The old walls go up. This is such a large subject in itself, that here I would like only to remark that the *first* problem was to obstruct the flow of the psychic energy itself. It's a little like people who fall in love, and then make such a shrine of the moment and the place where they met that the relationship isn't fully living in the present.

The second danger is the other pole: that the symbol will become trivialized, banalized, profaned: that it will cease to be able to evoke any depth-level response from us at all. Its outer forms will become mere decoration, swallowed up in the churning, meaningless flow of images. Its energy will have become dissipated. This is a new, pervasive problem in our spiritual life, because most of us do not live in traditional societies, and those who do will almost certainly see their worlds collapse. Instead we live in a turbulent time where images have a half-life of only flickering seconds. That dazzling sight of the Earth in space, which amazed in 1968 and which many held to be the foundational image of a new era of global peace, has been so overused that it has lost its ability to move us. The evocative images and heart-pounding music of *2001: A Space Odyssey,* were immediately turned to the more profane purpose of selling salad dressing. When we see this happen we feel disappointed, but powerless to halt the seduction of the spirit by the commercial impulse. Beethoven's Ninth Symphony and likewise the temples of Asia become just so much "stimulus" material to accentuate a product. The developed world lives a veritable bulimia of mass-produced images. It is implicitly one of our freedoms. There is another, entirely secular mythology that properly belongs to *this* world, one that I believe is rather desperately seeking roots to ground itself in an experience of the sacred, and one with which we imperatively must engage.

Stories and Memes

Our role in the cosmic story seems forever to be that of the Sorceror's Apprentice. Our creations, like the irrepressible broomstick that Mickey Mouse animates with his puerile magic in *Fantasia,* tend to take on lives of their own beyond the limited intentions of their creators. From languages and tools to aldermanic subcommittees and operas, they evolve, multiply, interact, beget offspring, and behave in other ways like living things. In what I consider to be one of the most insightful approaches to the problems of continued human evolution in an envelope of human artifact, psychologist Mihaly Csikszentmihalyi has developed the concept of the *meme* to explore the nature of human products, including stories and images, as a separate life form. Csikszentmihalyi defines the meme, from the Greek *mimesis,* as "any permanent pattern of matter or information produced by an act of human intentionality. Thus a brick is a meme, and so is Mozart's *Requiem.* Memes come into being when the human nervous system reacts to an experience, and codes it into a form that can be communicated to others."[1]

The central problem, as he points out, is that while at the moment of its creation, the meme is part of a conscious process directed by human intentionality, immediately afterward it begins to react with and transform the consciousness of its creator. "Once free from their creators, do memes continue to serve our purposes?" Csikszentmihalyi compares memes with genetic alleles and sees a useful analogy. Memes also obey the evolutionary rules of competition, diversification of forms and habitats, and apparent drive for survival.

> Information contained in memes is passed on by different mechanisms than those involved in transmitting genetic information. Memes require only our minds to feed on, and they will replicate images of themselves in consciousness. A catchy tune I hear on the radio may colonize my mind for days, surviving there thanks to the psychic energy I devote to it. If the tune is good enough, others may hear me whistle it and take it up, too.[2]

Even if taken merely as a helpful metaphor, Csikszentmihalyi's concept opens the possibility of finally investigating the relationship of Mickey and the broomstick in a scientific context not dominated by the

---

1. Mihaly Csikszentmihalyi, *The Evolving Self* (New York: Harper/Collins, 1993), p. 120.
2. Ibid., p. 122.

rhetorical twists of Madison Avenue or the underlying political agenda of Deconstructionism.

The Image, the Sacred, and the New Paradigm

We are in a time of profound paradigm shift, of transition from one form of civilization to another, where all our social and cultural values will be transformed. The important question about the paradigm shift is whether it will shift fast enough for new, more appropriate systems and institutions to come "on line" before the old ones collapse altogether. Will a new way of being rescue us from our present follies? Our patterns of interaction with our media constitute one of the keys that will determine how quickly and how broadly the new paradigm of global possibility is "seen." This is because we have given over to the media a tremendously influential power to either entrain us in the patterns of the old paradigm or prepare the ground upon which the new becomes visible.

The question of how we interact with the media is more complex than the more localized questions as to whose side the media favors on political issues, or whether minority views are adequately represented, or whether we can demand more sense and less violence from network TV. All of the above are important elements in the context. But one larger learning in the past thirty years of media study is that media are contexts of contexts intricately coconditioned with those vast loops that constitute economics, politics, culture, religious dogma, social mores, etc. The mass media partake of the synergistic momentum of the whole.

What then of the new paradigm? Paradigm shifts occurs when knowledge is reframed in a new context that is more vivid and compelling than the old. The new context, as a mythic image, is more "charming"; it invites libido. As the collective libido flows into the new image rather than follows the worn path we find ourselves in a new "reality." The starting point for the process is reframing the familiar, so that we see therein a "reality" to which we had previously been blind.

I believe that the faith traditions today are in a position to foster a new religious harmony in which the depth-level of each may be mirrored in all of the others. Today's mixing of cultures means increasing interfaith contact and interfaith marriage. A quest for direct spiritual *experience* and an emphasis on personal rather than institutional religion are becoming the actual spiritual movements of our time. Entering the creative dialogue now will mean adopting an essentially mythological viewpoint in relation to all experience whatsoever, whether deemed sacred, secular, or profane by our religious traditions. The mythological viewpoint suggests that the sacred is what is happening right *now,* through the perpetually self-revealing depth and mystery dimension of our direct experience, though necessarily with different inflections and with different emphases in our many cultures. What the faith traditions have to offer in this setting is to relate us to this totality via their living symbols—and via the unshakable connection to the ground of our being provided directly by mystical experience, and indirectly via ritual and sacred art. It is for the faith traditions to provide a grounding that may counterbalance our modern tendency toward acceleration, deracination, and dehumanization. In this effort the faith traditions will hopefully unite, accept that the cultural horizons of their origins are broken, set aside for the sake of our common humanity their exclusionistic demands, and seek together out of their deep and shared wisdom the new symbols to bring the many symbolic languages into a unified force for good.

It is either this or be marginalized as a quaint cultural relic. It is either this or submit to that *other* symbolic language, evocative of human desire but without sacred depth and ultimately destructive of the Earth and her creatures, which cries its siren song from billboards and television commercials. The dehumanized language of a short-sighted economic pragmatism, the language of mass and statistic, the language of the seduction of the spirit by programmed appetites, will otherwise control the debate over our path into the future. What will be the response of the faith traditions? Will they find their point of unity and turn the flaming tongues of their truth outward to the larger dialogue, as the Parliament insignia would urge us to do? I believe it was Benjamin Franklin, at another key moment in history, who said, "We must all hang together, or surely, we will all hang separately."

Somehow it always comes back to the question of relationship. Can we keep our relationship to each other, to our world, and to the mystery of our being alive and in movement? Can our grounding in our religious traditions keep leading us—right *now,* in this eternal moment—to the Ground, the Tao?

I go walking by the lake, Lake Michigan, my lake, which is itself such a mythic presence in my own life, evoking the great sense of mystery as its colors continually shift against the endless horizon. Today is stormy and silvery. Great rafts of sea ducks are migrating about a mile out. Flights of more than a hundred pass, settle, fly on. And out there I also see two small kayaks. I wonder what they're doing on a day like this. For fifteen minutes, they don't seem to move. Maybe they're just watching the ducks, but maybe they're having some trouble. They may have trouble, but they are not lost. They are in the midst of beauty. I have someone call the Coast Guard just in case. But as I walk back home a poem by an Eskimo woman comes back to mind, a true "poem for our climate." It seems to clarify so much:

> And I think over again
> my small adventures
> when with a shore wind I drifted out
> in my kayak
> and I thought I was in danger.
> My fears,
> those small ones
> that I thought so big,
> for all the vital things
> I had to get and to reach.
>
> And yet there is only
> One great thing,
> the only thing:
> to live and see in huts and on journeys
> the great day that dawns,
> and the light that fills the world.[3]

---

3. K. Rasmussen, *Reports of the Fifth Thule Expedition, 1921–24* (Copenhagen: Gyldendalske Bogenhandel/Nordisk Verlag, 1929), cited in: G. Kepes, *Sign, Image, Symbol* (New York: George Braziller, 1966), p. 234.

4

A Parliament of the People

BARBARA FIELDS BERNSTEIN

The human being is a work of art. Though we haunt the world's archives of myth and scripture; scan eternity for clues to the nature of reality and the soul, the program of the 1993 Parliament of the World's Religions revealed that the presence of divine integrity nests in the warm, wise hearts of the people.

From seed to fruit, the Parliament program unfolded in a state of grace. Its story reads like a biography, narrating the experience, talents, and vision of an extraordinary *character* whose life has lent special meaning to our times. In this case, however, the character was not a single individual but a collage of qualities sculptured into a Genius of the Collective Whole. Humility and rare kindness presented themselves there, as did woundedness, confusion, and ego. Love and fear arrived early, attended by full congregations. For eight whirlwind days the Collective Genius spoke, instructed, sang and danced, debated, responded, prayed, meditated, laughed and cried, embraced, argued, learned, worried, stayed up too late, listened and was heard, became leader, disciple, and empowered.

From the perspective of Program Director for the 1993 event, I have since described the experience as a "microcosm of human excellence." Parliament organizers provided a strong and well-defined container— the beautiful Palmer House Hilton for a span of eight days—in which all participants could safely choose to suspend habits and expectations, liberating space within ourselves to become new, more and better than we had ever been before. It seemed as if we had fallen collectively in love—we *cared,* at last, to understand one another. And in caring to understand, we dared to venture outside the prisons of our own needs and fears. In truly honoring "other" we recognized ourselves, and in those graceful moments we were wonderful.

Of course, some of us may have been thinking that if—when it was all over—we did not prefer this thrilling new level of consciousness, we could simply go home and resume being whoever we were before we came, none the worse for having been better!

Overview of Process

Many religious and secular organizations approach the problems of the human community as if both problems and communities are solitary phenomena. Yet the complex matrix of critical global issues, further measured against philosophical and religious orientations, precludes the simple ground for which we soulfully yearn. The Parliament program was born into chaos and renaissance from the outset. By virtue of its stunning religious, cultural, linguistic, and geographical diversity there appeared to be no common thread in the tapestry. Paradoxically (the appropriate adjective for most emerging truths), it was precisely this diversity that turned up clues to an eight-day reunion of the human family.

The making of the Parliament program required the unconditional acceptance of as diverse a collection of interests, topics, ethics, personalities, styles, motives, processes, and outcomes as anyone can imagine. As program planners, we were obliged to volunteer at the front lines of a great struggle for authenticity, lest we fail to model the very responses and expectations we implored of presenters, participants, and the event as a whole. To the best of our ability, we gave up value judgments, attempts at predictable control, and a great deal of ego attachment in order to surrender to the wisdom of the organic *Process,* right up front. We steadied our skills, found our faith, and then got on with the work.

We saw the paradigm begin to shift before our eyes. Over a period of eleven months, the program staff compiled a monstrous database containing over thirteen hundred detailed program proposals. These were submitted by fifteen major faith traditions orchestrated by hierarchies within their associated Host Committees, two hundred official cosponsors representing religious factions and independent spiritual, secular, scholastic, and monastic communities, and hundreds of independent applicants from every quarter. The protocols customarily relied upon in a conference setting to determine who spoke about what, to how many, at what time, in what room—not to mention why—simply broke down. Personally, I was ecstatic about this. The playing field was equalizing itself by reason of its own complexity!

The Program and Plenaries

The program began each morning at 7:00 A.M. with special meditations planned by members of a wide variety of faith traditions, and open to all. Each evening, sometime before midnight, the program concluded with a thematic plenary featuring world-reknowned speakers, and creative performance pieces. Throughout the week, cultural and educational programs were held at institutions and museums throughout the city of Chicago. During the final three days of the event, the Assembly of Religious and Spiritual Leaders met in closed afternoon sessions at the Art Institute of Chicago.

The Opening Plenary was a celebratory pageant in which music from East (The Drepung Loseling Monks) and West (The Music of the Baroque, and Native American Singers) accompanied a stunning interfaith processional through the aisles of the Grand Ballroom. Welcomes, blessings, and invocations from each of the world's major faith traditions greeted the eager assembly of registrants. One week later, the Closing Plenary in Chicago's Grant Park included a profound and charming keynote address by H. H. the Dalai Lama, invocations from the Parliament Presidents, and remarks of thanksgiving and farewell from CPWR board members. The vibrant dance styles of the multi-cultural Call for Peace Drum and Dance Company, and a rousing final concert by the 200-voice Soul Children of Chicago Choir brought an audience of thousands to their feet in exhilaration during the Parliament's final hours.

Preceding the evening Closing Plenary in the park was an afternoon of music. In the sunny, perfect warmth of the late-summer day, Arlo Guthrie, Stephen Halpern, a specially formed band of Rastafarian musicians, The Drepung Loseling Monks, and superstar Kenny Loggins, all graciously contributed their talents to create a musical spirit that could not have been bought at any price.

The week-long series of thematic plenaries, "Interfaith Understanding," "What Shall We Do?", "Visions of Paradise and Possibility," "Voices of the Dispossessed," "Voices of Spirit and Tradition," "From Vision to Action: Celebrating Dialogue," "The Inner Life," "Life in the Community," and "The Next Generation," were nine full-scale productions, weaving together with live multimedia performance the challenging commentary of social activists and youth participants, moving personal stories told by religious and spiritual leaders, Native American prayer ceremonies, and the cultural and political expressions brought by representatives of third-world communities. Stage Manager and Program Assistant Tracy Nicholas was assisted by Elizabeth Stroll in the complex orchestration of these productions.

Evening after evening, the full-to-capacity Grand Ballroom harbored a spectrum of spontaneity from outbursts of heated debate to mass tai chi chuan exercises, punctuated by laughter, tears, and song-and-dance circles engaging the entire audience. Registrants overflowed into other meeting rooms throughout the Palmer House to watch proceedings on huge screens connected by closed circuit television.

Major Presentations, Workshops, and Special Symposia

From Tuesday through Friday of the Parliament week, the lifeblood of the program flowed through an intricate maze of over eight hundred major addresses, seminars, lectures, and workshops. Over forty sessions were available concurrently from morning to evening in carefully scheduled program "slots" throughout the hotel. While the most highly revered religious and spiritual personages and noted leaders in a wide variety of secular fields captivated large audiences, hundreds of smaller groups gathered in breakout rooms on the topmost floors of the hotel. Participants deftly negotiated their way, first through the 152-page descriptive program catalogue, and then through a mindful wonderland of workshop spaces divided among six focus areas: (1) "The Earth, Science, and Technology," (2) "Social Challenge," (3) "Community and Culture," (4) "The Language of the Spirit," (5) "Religions of the World," and (6) "Body and Mind."

A number of thematic areas were considered so important to the global community that special symposia were organized in order to consider their issues as comprehensively as possible. "The Conference on Pluralism" convened for four days of working sessions and presentations on the subjects of "Identity," "Conflict," and "Globality," with regard to religious and cultural diversity in today's world. The conference was coordinated by Professors Jeffrey Carlson of Depaul University and Robert Schreiter of Catholic Theological Union.

The Science Symposium, "Cosmic Beginnings and Human Ends," brought together distinguished members of the international scientific community to discuss areas in which scientific and technological developments are raising issues of concern to the world's religious communities. Professor Clifford Matthews, University of Illinois Department of Chemistry, was assisted by Program Chair Jim Kenney in coordinating these thematically linked programs.

The Symposium on "Religion and Violence," addressed the critical problem of religious-based war, from interpretations regarding its scriptural roots, through consideration of present struggles in various parts of the world, to possible strategies for our peaceful common future. Ronald Kidd of the Institute for World Spirituality coordinated several programs included in this series.

The Business Symposium, "Ethics, Values, and Spirituality in the Workplace," considered questions of changing paradigms in corporate settings and in economics. Brian Bacon and David Johnston assisted in the planning of this symposium.

"The Media Panels" engaged representatives of the American print and broadcast media to debate the responsibilities of communications to growing public consciousness, from the points of view of both mainstream and alternative news press, and publishing. Anne Simpkinson of *Common Boundary* magazine graciously helped Barbara Bernstein to organize these panels.

"The Academy" of the Parliament was a component designed to give focused expression to members of the international academic community. With coordination assistance from Professor Daniel Ross Chandler of Loyola University, more than sixty papers from the world's leading colleges and universities revealed "cutting-edge" thinking on a wide range of themes related to religion, spirituality, and critical issues.

Fine Arts

Authentic cultural performance art was a major experience at the 1993 Parliament. The Palmer House Hilton's famous Empire Room came alive full-time through the week with international performance pieces in music, dance, drama, and poetry presented by talented artists from every faith tradition in attendance. In addition, a five-hour global extravaganza, "The Festival of Sacred Performing Arts," held the rapt attention of its audience in the Grand Ballroom.

A world-class Fine Arts exhibit portraying the visual, conceptual spirituality of painters, designers, and photographers from around the globe drew crowds for seven days in the upper exhibition hall of the hotel. As has been the way of the creative spirit since ancient cultures, a magnificent showing of work called forth the sacred in the language of archetypes and symbols. Salvatore Conti of the Kashi Foundation curated the exhibit with assistance from Ms. Chickie Alter of Alter Associates.

A preview of the feature film *Baraka—A World beyond Words,* produced by Samuel Goldwyn Company attracted almost one thousand viewers to its screening at the Art Institute of Chicago. Mr. John Raatz of The Visioneering Group, California, facilitated the contribution of this stunning gift to the Parliament.

A full-time Video and Film Festival was held in the Palmer House to applaud the work of professional and amateur videographers and directors who have contributed significantly to the vision of bringing spirit into the worlds of creativity and global action.

Communications and Networking

Working without budget or personnel—restraints imposed by an excessively bureaucratic vision of priorities dictated by executive, administrative, and logistic organizers—friends of the Parliament made a nonetheless valiant attempt to create a two-pronged communications network among Parliament participants, on-site and beyond the event.

The Together Foundation, Burlington, Vermont, contributed hardware, software, personnel, a bottomless basket of apples, and an abundance of heart to run the TogetherNet computer network seminar in Hans Keller's sixth-floor booth throughout the entire Parliament week. Several thousand people received free software and user instructions to get "on-line." To date, users around the world are maintaining friendships, sharing advice, and designing projects by means of this interactive telecommunications technology.

Using a brilliant "Participant Interaction Messaging" design prepared by Nadia McClaren, a set of twelve communal newsletters entitled *Your Voice* was produced on-site, an average of two per day. Participants-at-large were able to contribute thoughts, opinions, and responses to proceedings via messages written by hand on "post-it" notes, or given verbally to newsletter managers. Tim Casswell, Nadia, Robert Pollard, Sharon Drew Morgan, and a task force of dedicated volunteers stayed up through the nights in order to enter, organize, and format messages on computer terminals. Private donations solicited by Brian Muldoon at Monday evening's plenary, "From Vision to Action: Celebrating Diversity," funded this eleventh-hour endeavor. The newsletter team paved a well-trod path between the Palmer House and a local copy facility to keep stacks of newsletters supplied to participants, free of charge. To our great frustration, overly zealous CPWR logistics and housekeeping teams systematically removed many newsletters as soon as they appeared on public tables throughout the hotel.

Using this same interactive messaging system on the second day of the Assembly of Religious and Spiritual Leaders (the only time allotted during the Parliament for active conversation among leaders) the twelfth issue of *Your Voice* was dedicated exclusively to the ideas of these respected guests. Ironically, *Your Voice #12* became the only substantive record expressing the views generated freely and spontaneously by the Assembly itself.

The Parliament of the People

Held during the lunch hour, (with a promise by volunteer crews to return 800 chairs to their formal "theater-style" arrangement before the 2 P.M. lecture), the "Parliament of the People" attracted thousands of participants eager to express themselves over the course of four consecutive days. Under the highly conscious leadership of Brian Muldoon and a vision inspired by Barbara Marx Hubbard, a team of professionals in communication techniques variously referred to as "facilitation," "conflict resolution," "community- and consensus-building," "diversity training," and "dialogue process," volunteered their time and energy to ensure that a true attempt to establish a sense of community, as well as meaningful communication among the "little people" of the Parliament, would be made. Facilitation Team members encouraged interactive conversation among participants by organizing enthusiastic crowds into more intimate small-group circles clustered in the Red Lacquer Ballroom of the hotel.

Working with unwieldy numbers, complicated diversity issues, and an obviously low-priority scheduling status, a great deal of planning, expertise, and love was poured by the entire team into the challenge of designing the "Parliament of the People." What emerged was a four-day, four-part journey through which every single person was fully included and given opportunity to articulate her or his: (1) Vision, (2) Obstacles perceived in the face of reaching that vision, (3) Proposals for action, and (4) Personal commitments.

Through a sensitive yet systematic process, the views and feelings of each participant were brought forth among peers. Sometimes represented by a group-elected spokesperson; other times with an open mike in hand while a trailing line awaited its turn; often in front of video camcorders hastily set up in the adjoining foyer, the *individual* voices of the world's religious and spiritual constituents were given forum. For this component of the program, bodies overflowed the large ballroom into the corridors beyond—ever patient, courteous, and profound.

What occurred at the Assembly of Religious and Spiritual Leaders was another matter altogether. Twenty-five additional team members were dispatched to facilitate dialogue at the tables of the (dis-)organized Assembly of Religious Leaders, which met for three afternoons at another location. Surprisingly late and little comprehensive planning had gone into this lofty Parliament component whose main, and perhaps single intentional feature, was the brandishment of the virtually complete *Global Ethic* document for signatures. Executive organizers came across, understandably enough, as overwhelmed by the illustrious gathering of religious talent. It has been suggested by critics since the event that one key notion was overlooked—it is the nature of religious leaders to *lead* or, at the very least, to *participate* in the process preceding their endorsements of significant universal statements, no matter how well-intentioned.

Thoughtful analyses submitted by table facilitators identified any number of design problems that, had a more progressive planning model been undertaken by CPWR Assembly organizers, might have been avoided. Facilitators were not, in fact, invited to participate in the design of, or even to submit feedback regarding the process they were asked to integrate at Assembly tables. This was, they argued, as fundamental a mistake in creating a successful model for actual dialogue as it was for organizers to put the *Global Ethic* literally "on the table" for signatures during the very first hours of the opportunity-rich Assembly. While the great gathering was, as honored guest Dr. Raimon Panikkar concluded, "a really good try!", most professionals in the field of dialogue (not to mention other process analysts, scholars, and religious leaders, themselves) concluded that this perhaps "once in a lifetime" moment for authentic dialogue had been painfully undercultivated.

Commentary

The overall program of the Parliament was unique in two major ways: first, by deliberately addressing the interface between religion, and critical environmental, economic, political, scientific, and social justice issues that traverse all boundaries between sacred and secular, the dialogue leaped to another level. Programs were evaluated and selected for their ability to root issue-oriented presentations in a deeper field of values, ethics, and spirituality. Polarized ideologies and policies regarding environmental stewardship or human rights abuses, for example, sought consensus within broader strategies to sustain our common future, and to fortify a more proactive commitment to compassion and peace. Taking respite from habitual grievances, we could afford to spend time in our common good. Patches of clarity broke over the turbulent horizon and, together, we dared again to hope.

The second unique feature of the Parliament program has less to do with the content, or *products* of its individual presentations, but speaks ever more subtly to its *metaprocess*—the layer of dynamic meaning that enfolds both medium and message within the very *nature* of the communication flow. I refer to the infrastructure of power, itself. Many stories of power were told by the 1993 Parliament of the World's Religions—the politics of organizational bureaucracy, the protocols of inter- and intrareligious hierarchy and celebrity, overt and covert games of intimidation, the exploitation of good grace and goodwill through "politically correct" rhetoric, and the subterfuge of powerful spirits by power struggles, to name a few.

This postmodern era of information exchange is fueled by an evolution from products to services, and from services to technologies as the import/export trade of global culture. If we mobilize to act intelligently, these technologies will be perceived as precocious hardware in respectful serve to the needs of human communication in an era of crisis. Events such as this centennial celebration, the 1993 Parliament of the World's Religions, are in a unique position to provide ongoing coordination and direction for the massive web of individuals and organizations who attend, often at considerable difficulty and expense to themselves. Understanding the individual-to-group dynamics of these gatherings becomes important as a matter of "quality control." The infrastructures that *define power* in the planning of an event as massive as this Parliament bear close scrutiny, as they are none other than archetypes for the way constructed social realities are shaped and shared in the context of a much larger, future arena.

Most conferences and large gatherings are structured in terms of a clear hierarchy. A body of program organizers, guided by the focus or theme of their event, use traditional parameters to determine the selection of speakers. Almost invariably, the most visible and elite collection of individuals as possible is assembled for both the quality of their contribution, and their prestige. Charismatic leaders and figureheads, well-known authors, prizewinners, so-called experts and authorities are featured on the proverbial VIP guest list. The Parliament program was no exception. It boasted as impressive a speaker roster as conference organizers could ever hope to engage, and whose role it was to deliver wisdom via major addresses to large audiences in fine ballrooms.

But, truly and fortunately, there emerged another Parliament—the Parliament of the People—because the brilliance of spirit cannot be veiled by vanities. The Parliament program proved a healthy challenge to the prevailing model of hierarchy. For every religious leader and secular expert who spoke there, forty more "grassroots leaders" shared their more anonymous wisdom with one another.

The integrity and tenacity of the human heart allows much to be created from little. The Parliament of the People stood up to contradictions, demonstrating that one can fully observe and revere the practices and tenets of her religious tradition—a tradition that happens to be engaged in bitter struggle with another—yet, standing side by side in a hotel elevator, still respond with warmth and rapport to the very person whose adherence to his own tradition would deem him the "enemy(?)" This simple observation, multiplied a thousandfold throughout the week, inspired in many of us sufficient humility and innocence to ask: *Whose interests and politics are we, as the religious and spiritual People of the world, supporting?* Conspiring (literally "breathing together") to touch and to be moved, seeds were sown for the future of reverence and governance on this planet.

The mothers, brothers, sisters, fathers, and friends who comprise the human family are interested in the safe growing of children, the alleviation of suffering for whatever cause and by whatever means, and in what service we can provide to the earth upon which our food is cultivated, whose water we drink, and whose air we have no choice but to breathe. We rightfully embrace our philosophies, literature, scriptures, rituals, moral codes, ethics, politics, opinions, and dreams. But we never intended that they be corrupted into weapons of wounding on so personal and universal a scale.

In a revolutionary anthology edited by Susan B. Thistlewaite and George F. Cairns entitled, *Beyond Theological Tourism: Mentoring as a Grassroots Approach to Theological Education* (Orbis Books, 1994), Thistlewaite points out:

> But virtually no one has done a theological anthropology that takes account of the *differences* in concrete social locations for the *transaction* of becoming human in the process of trying to transform the world. That is, how do we describe what it means to become human together when the real, material differences between human beings are made central? Furthermore, how is this relationship in difference constructed when we are engaged together in the act of world transformation? Do concrete differences and acting together constitute the possibility of a new human being?[1]

Here at the turn of the century, the religious conversation has been enhanced by the advent of a new species of international organization

---

1. Susan Thistlethwaite, "Beyond Theological Tourism," in Susan Thistlethwaite and George Cairns, eds., *Beyond Theological Tourism* (Maryknoll, NY: Orbis Books, 1994), p. 10.

devoted to "interfaith dialogue." The latest of these is the institutional-ized Council for a Parliament of the World's Religions. These organizations share at least three characteristics: (1) the search to engage influential religious leaders in their activities, (2) a struggle over inclusion (i.e, which traditions are invited to participate and which are excluded) and representation (to what extent, if any, do delegates carry the official sanction of their tradition), and (3) a general agreement that the religious and spiritual *grassroots* populations of the world should be somehow involved, but no genuine attempt—in the form of a *plan*—to do so.

In his book, *The Matchless Weapon—Satyagraha,* James K. Mathews quotes one of M. K. Gandhi's admirers: "The great secret of the popularity of Gandhi's political creed and methods is that he has given back to the people their own ideas." Or in the words of St. Augustine: "Men go to gape at mountain peaks . . . and yet they leave themselves unnoticed; they do not marvel at themselves." As we continue our work, forming new organizations and planning future gatherings, here is the question that must be asked: What is the meaning behind this tendency of powerkeepers to suppress, ignore, or innocently omit the world's so-called ordinary people from discussions "behind closed doors"? Is it in fact a matter of holding influence and authority a little too "close to the chest?" Is it merely a question of logistical complexity, even as communications technologies reconfigure civilized culture? Or does it have something to do with the rhythm of time, itself, which sustains the spirit's yearning by pulsing back and forth between high and low, the One and the Many?

Andrew Harvey, the Anglo-Indian mystic teaching at the California Institute of Integral Studies, includes this post script in a compilation of interviews with Mark Matousek, *Dialogues with a Modern Mystic*:

> There is one way, and one way only that the planet can be saved in time—and that is through a massive worldwide transformation which is simultaneously spiritual, practical, mystical and political . . . what is needed is a worldwide, highly organized spiritual civil disobedience movement. Millions of ordinary people all over the world must take to the streets if at all possible; and as long as possible non-violently, and simply demand:
>
> No more destruction of the environment.
> No more inner and outer pollution.
> No more mad expenditure on lethal and horrifying weapons
> We have had enough!

Without question, we are riding the waves of Great Change, helpless to do more than look deeply into ourselves for the wisdom to remember the nature of the whole. For now, at least, that vision will carry us through. I, for one, will never receive a greater blessing than to have walked among the Parliament of the People. In a rare window of circumstance we lived up to all our legends, shared heartbeats, re-claimed our faiths and our faith, honored others in the purest sense of that word and, most dazzling of all, celebrated the Mystery.

5

Voices of Vision:
The Parliament and Beyond

JACKIE RIVET-RIVER

Having lived in Chicago all of my adult life, I find that a healthy kind of inner-city paranoia has settled into my bones. But for one week in September 1993, at the Palmer House with 8,700 strangers from more than 150 countries, I felt perfectly safe. That was the feeling the Parliament of the World's Religions emanated.

Recall that emotion when you arrive home and are swept up and into the warmth, freedom, and comfort of it all. Standing in those crowded elevators with scarcely room to move, the air was charged not with distant, blank stares at the ceiling but with laughter and ease. The hallways and lobbies rang with greetings. People embraced one another. The grand lobby, stately and elegant, became a garden of rare and exotic flowers, the diaphanous robes and gowns blossoming upon satin sofas. And yet, no faces were familiar. The robes and gowns were not like mine. The accents, expressions, and speech patterns were foreign. The ideologies, theologies, and spiritual beliefs had little in common. But paradoxically, as the children of a plenary called The Next Generation were to sing, we were one family.

We came to the Parliament as documentarians, sponsored by the Chicago Sunday Evening Club, an organization that had broadcast ecumenical sermons on the local PBS-TV station for thirty-two years. They had struggled financially and theologically to make the commitment to this project. The challenge was to try to capture the spirit of the gathering. Thus, on August 28, 1993, our taping began.

How can one documentary possibly reflect the seven hundred events of this exciting week that had taken the Parliament Council five years of planning? How could one hour possibly do justice to a schedule that read like the Who's Who of Religion and Spirituality? How could one glean the highlights from a directory resembling the yellow pages on interfaith dialogue: Akasha Singers with Sri Chinmoy, H. H. The Dalai Lama, Native American Smoke Ceremony, the meditative advice of Thich Nhat Hanh, the spiritual laughter in Tai-Chi, sagely advice from a former Deputy Secretary General of the United Nations, deep respect for all religions from Zoroastrians, reverence for all life from Jains, dialogue among Buddhists, Muslims, and Mormons, seminars on entropy and ecology, violence and ethnic cleansing, homelessness and hopefulness.

We worked cooperatively with the Bahai Media Service and the Earth Network, and had four cameras rolling from nine in the morning until ten o'clock at night. David Hardin and Robert Black, our Executive Producers, and I, as the Writer/Director, made a commitment early on that our documentary would focus on human rights abuses, the desecration of our planet, capture an overview of the week, seeking out moments of candor, healing, celebration, and similarities.

After years of planning, the opening ceremony of the 1993 Parliament of the World's Religions began. It would mark the first time in a hundred years that the spiritual and religious leaders of the world would set aside their differences, joining together in sisterhood and brotherhood.

The opening procession commenced. It was solemn and wondrous, an elegant tapestry of humanity. Dr. Daniel Ibanez-Gomez, Executive Director of the Council for the Parliament of the World's Religions, chanted prayers of many faiths as the saffron, violet, and turquoise colors flowed into the Grand Ballroom. Those who had been forgotten a hundred years ago were there: women, children, Native Americans, African-American, Indigenous peoples from around the Earth.

The chants of Drepung Loseling Tibetan Buddhist monks melded with Native American drums, Rastafarian flutes, and the voices of the ensembles, Chicago's own Music of the Baroque.

The opening statements went directly to the heart of the subjects we hoped would be raised. These figures challenged, called for courage, action, solutions, reconciliation. It was a time of ownership for much of humankind's anguish and for our planet's agonies. In what follows, we want to give a catalogue of the most powerful voices at the Parliament.

Professor Diana Eck, a Protestant and Director of the Pluralism Project at Harvard University observed: "A hundred years ago at the Parliament of the World's Religions, the Chairman of the Parliament said, 'Henceforth the religions of the world will make war not on each other, but on the great evils that afflict mankind.' But wars continue and our religious traditions continue to provide the fuel for the world's strife."

Rabbi James Rudin, the National Interreligious Affairs Director of the American Jewish Committee remarked: "Over fifty wars are going on now which are based in part on religion. But we live in a time of unprecedented opportunities to build human bridges of understanding, not just between, but among all of us who are peoples of faith."

Professor Hans Küng, a Roman Catholic from the University of Tubingen, Germany pointed out: "There will be no peace among the nations without peace among the religions. Therefore, the religions themselves have to use every possible means to clear up misunderstandings, to do away with stereotype images of the other religions, to break down hatred and to reflect on what they have in common."

The Venerable Thich Nhat Hanh, a Buddhist and Vietnamese Zen Master exhorted us to: "remove the notions and the barriers that have divided us. Why don't we act together as living beings, because our problems are the same: violence, hurt, division, despair. Why don't we get together?"

Ravi Singh, a college student, Sikh, and the Committee Chair of the Next Generation Plenary Session, wisely counselled: "We must see each other as friends rather than enemies, yet learn from the past rather than dwell on it. We must put aside the labels of being a Hindu, a Muslim, a Sikh, a Baha'i, a Christian, a Zoroastrian, a Buddhist, a Jain or a Jew. And if we do this, we will have peace."

Maulana Dr. Farid Esack, a Muslim Professor of Religion at Selly Oak College in England, reflected: "Religion is intertwined in the history of subjugation and resistance in South Africa. It is likely to play an equally ambiguous role in the postapartheid era. If people committed to the enduring struggle for justice neglect the religious terrain, the reactionary forces will have that much more access to an enduring ingredient of the South African life. No nation has ever undergone lasting renewal without an appeal to its innermost values. The religions of South Africa can enable the nation to rediscover these values, often buried under generations of religious and ideological muck. What is needed is a peace not based on silence, a peace not based on acquiescence with injustice, but a peace that is real, a peace that is rooted in human dignity, a peace that is based on a relationship of equality, whether it is between males and females, between black and white, or Hindu and Jew."

Ladjamaya Green, an activist, dramatist, and a Baha'i from Colorado, forcefully asserted: "Racism runs deep. It infects the hearts of both black and white Americans. And neither should assume that the responsibility for the elimination of prejudice and of its effects belongs exclusively to the other. To build a society in which the rights of all its members are respected and guaranteed, both races must be animated with the spirit of optimism and faith in the eventual realization of their highest aspirations. Both must recognize that unity is essential for their common survival."

Molefe Tsele, a Protestant graduate student in theology in South Africa, predicted: "We in South Africa believe that, in as much as religion was used to dehumanize us, in the same way true religion can play a role in healing, humanizing, and liberating us. And so I thank you and say to you that many, many years to come, our grandchildren will ask us in South Africa in the same way as the African-Americans are asking their grandparents, 'How did you survive slavery?' we will be asked, 'How did you survive apartheid?' My answer is simple . . . by faith."

Joseph Montville, the Director of the Conflict Resolution Project in Washington, D.C., said, "There's a very bitter split, an historic split, between Orthodox Christianity and Western Christianity that must be addressed and one of the things the Yugoslav tragedy has pointed out is the necessity of addressing this seriously. I noticed in working in the conflict between Catholics and Protestants in Northern Ireland, that one of the most effective ways of persuading the Protestant minority, which feels really besieged, is when Irish Catholics, either from the north of Ireland or the United States, are actively involved in promoting dialogue, because they are more than promoting dialogue, they are bearing personal witness to a willingness to forgive."

Boldly, Dr. Gerald Barney, Executive Director of the Millennium Institute observed: "We Christians hate and kill people of other faiths as we have been doing most recently in Bosnia. We pay lip service to protecting Earth, but in our heart feel that the Earth is insignificant and irrelevant since our real home is in Heaven, which is not on Earth."

Professor Susannah Heschel from Case Western Reserve University said, "From the time of the disappearance of the dinosaurs until a hundred years ago, the rate of the extinction of living species remained constant, but since the late nineteenth century the number has risen to over 10,000 each year. We are raised as Jews to feel agony over the burning of a book, and we venerate also the marvelous expressions of spirituality in art and architecture. But then where is our agony over the disappearance of an entire living species? . . . We often use language that condemns the rape of the earth and invoke the metaphor of Mother Earth. As a woman this concerns me. The language we use is not an accident. There is a reason we speak of the earth in female metaphors. The problem is that the earth suffers from our sexism as women suffer from our sexism. What is the connection between our treatment of nature and our treatment of women? The misuse of nature follows from seeing nature as something to be ruled, manipulated, guided, controlled, and dominated as inferior matter, separate from us. It is no accident that we speak of Mother Earth. Women have shared similar exploitation."

Then frail yet powerful Thomas Berry, a Geologian eloquently remarked: "We can eliminate the most beautiful forms of birds, the butterflies and all of that, but we fail to realize, spiritually even, that the outer world is necessary to activate the inner world. If we destroy the grandeur of the forest, we lose a wonderful dimension in the inner world of the human. When the world is trivialized, when the planet is trivialized, when the butterflies disappear, when we no longer hear the song of the birds, when children in the cities cannot see the stars, the possibility of being truly religious disappears. If we lose the soaring birds, we lose a dimension of our imagination and of our spirituality. We lose poetry; we lose music; we lose the grandeur of life. If we tear the mountains down, then what is going to evoke from us a sense of wonder and grandeur? What is going to evoke in us a sense of the divine?"

Archbishop Paulos Mar Gregorios, Orthodox Metropolitan of Delhi, India, confessed: "There is a lot that religions have done to each other about which we ought to be sorry and we ought to ask pardon and we ought to ask for reconciliation."

The crowd was shocked into wakefulness by these words that surely must have touched every heart. To own the responsibility that organized religion carries a heavy burden and much of the blame for warfare and human rights abuses around the globe was shocking, indeed, and redeeming. This week held out the promise of redemption and reconciliation. Was it a goal too grand? Would this august gathering have the strength and courage to tear down the barriers and begin a new journey into the future, together?

Proudly, emotionally, Burton Pretty on Top, a Native American Crow, spiritual leader and pipe carrier took the podium: "We're here for a very short, short time. Let's use this short time to be the best Buddhist that we can be, to be the best Moslem that we can be, to be the best Jew that we can be, to be the best Christian that we can be. My brothers and sisters, let's be the best that we can be of what God has given to us and celebrate diversity; confront this bigotry and eliminate it permanently so that into the future our children and their children's children will see the benefits and the reaps of our work today."

H. H. The Dalai Lama was presented with a statement of solidarity by Brother Wayne Teasdale, a Roman Catholic who is a member of Monastic Interreligious Dialogue. Brother Wayne and many Catholic monks and nuns took a stand that held great political as well as religious and spiritual consequences. They pledged solidarity with the Tibetan people, urging the international community, particularly the United Nations, to express collective outrage at the brutal and callous actions of the Peoples' Republic of China. This was a touching and triumphant moment during the busy week. His Holiness sat quietly, his hands held gently by Brother Wayne's, his impish grin now a thin line as he listened with his heart to the words that held such meaning for him and his people.

At a gathering of several hundred one morning in the Grand Ballroom, there was a particularly polemic speech made by a Sikh regarding Hindu oppression in India. Shouting from the audience interrupted him. Tempers flared; voices were raised in anger, ushers hurried in to hush and calm. Council members moved in to mediate. For a few moments there was not just unrest in that great room among those gathered few, but the potential to start a media frenzy that could have devastating repercussions halfway around the world. Violence could erupt, religious riots could resume. Then, spontaneously, people in the audience stood, joined hands and very quietly started singing, "We shall overcome." The song flowed from the back row, building, arching, lifting as it swept up to the stage. There stood Thomas Yellowtail, the Crow Nation Religious Leader with Thomas Banyacya, the Traditional Spiritual Leader and Interpreter of the Hopi prophecies, both well into their ninth decade, along with Burton Pretty on Top. They began to chant. Behind them Native American drummers and singers joined in. The Elders explained that healing could take place if everyone would join in a circle, forming a Sacred Hoop. Brown hands reached out to grasp yellow hands, and white and red and young and old.

The gentle drumming began to build until it became a common heartbeat for everyone in the room. Shoulders swayed, feet began to pound with the pulse of the drums. Then the circle began to move around the room; snaked onto and down from the stage, and streamed to the back of the great hall. Where there had been anger and fear now there was an aura of peacefulness, compassion, acceptance. It was a moment of true grace.

The Creator, called by many names, poured love and healing into that gathering and the presence of the spirit was palpable. Then Dr. Yvonne Delk, a black woman, Protestant and Executive Director of the Community Renewal Society of Chicago took the podium. "We know that the path to hearing is not easy. We know that the wounds between us run deep. And yet we yearn for a day when we together can make affirmations that will affirm all of us . . . that will continue to name the issues and name the pain, but always affirming the hope that, together, ... together, we can find a way to speak and to offer hope and peace in the midst of our world."

What an irony that at the Parliament of 1893, there were few women and no Native Americans. Now, in 1993, those two previously forgotten groups came bearing the gifts of partnership and healing. Religious and spiritual leaders from around the Earth were gathered in that circle. Perhaps some of the Hopi prophecies were coming to pass. It must have been a spiritual mountaintop for the Elders, realizing visions so long held dear, holding this Sacred Hoop so surely. Only days after the Parliament's closing ceremony where he whispered a prayer in Crow, Thomas Yellowtail died.

Each afternoon during that week, leaders held closed council at the Art Institute. There they struggled together to come up with a statement each could sign. Dr. Hans Küng, Professor of Ecumenical Theology at the University of Tubingen, authored a paper entitled Global Responsibility: In Search of a New World Ethic. He had been working on it for several years at the request of the Parliament Council. It was hoped that all would sign it and that it would become the working document of this congress. Many did sign it. Many felt it was a profoundly significant beginning. Others felt it fell short of its mission. Dr. Robert Muller, Former Assistant Secretary General of the United Nations, proclaimed: "If you create an international secretariat or a permanent Parliament or a world spiritual agency everything will change, because then the religious leaders will receive from these people, from their workers, from their representatives working daily together, the advice as to what we should do next. This is, in my opinion, the most important single result that could come out of this Parliament."

Children from more than thirty faiths presented a wonderful evening plenary called The Next Generation. Everyone in our crew was excited about this evening because we had taped the Executive Committee earlier that day. These six young people sat around a table and tried to explain to us just how deeply they had been changed by working together on their presentation for the Parliament. Ravi Singh, the Chairperson, said he had learned that Sikhs, Hindus, Buddhists, Jains, Jews, Muslims, Catholics, and Protestants could join together and see each other as human beings. He saw that color must stop being a barrier. He said they believed that was the only hope for the future of all humankind, for all creatures and for this planet. He maintained that each of them, as leaders of tomorrow, had made a commitment to that belief. There was great strength in their diversity. The spirit of respect and love among them was astounding. When they mounted the stage they had forgotten no one. A teenager in a wheelchair captivated the audience with his poignant storytelling. Children danced and performed dramas. They explained the essence of many religious and spiritual traditions with precise simplicity. As they stood together, singing "This Little Light of Mine," their voices clear as crystal, full of unity and wisdom, we truly believed, there is hope for the flowers.

Each day the Major Presenters roster offered up a smorgasbord of choices. Each day we came away from the taping enriched by the experience. There was a common thread that flowed from speaker to speaker. At least, this seemed to be true of those we chose to videotape for our documentary. Each presenter seemed intent upon solutions that would bring about a better tomorrow. Each seemed dedicated to breaking down walls of ideological and theological barriers; not to deny those differences, but to rise above them and seek a common harmony. Senator Leticia Shahani, a Brahma Kumari from the Philippines, said: "In a better world, people live in ways that preserve nature's ecological balance, in an environment that is beautiful and clean. In a better world, the planet's natural and abundant resources are shared equitably and the basic human needs of all people are provided for."

Ivanka Vana Janic, a Christian and head of the Zones of Peace Transnational Project, warned: "Since all of us are responsible in various degrees for the desecration of life and the planet itself, we now turn for guidance and help to our religious and spiritual leaders so that we may shape our future more wisely and compassionately in a nonviolent way. Their calling is to promote, preserve, and establish peace wherever and whenever possible. However, religious and spiritual leaders need to take a more assertive role in the exercise of their rightful leadership."

Again, Dr. Gerald Barney challenged: "Now, I have a request to you, our spiritual leaders—a request that I make on behalf of not just all humans, but on behalf of the whole community of life. Would you devote the next seven years of your lives to helping six billion people learn from each other and from Earth how to live sustainably, justly, and humanely on the Earth in the next millennium? Would you help us all—would you help the Earth—dream a new dream? Would you put away hatred and work together in ways previously unimagined and unimaginable? Would you develop a community of the Earth's faith traditions that is an example of the kind of open communication, mutual respect, acceptance, cooperation, and goodwill that should characterize the emerging global community of nations and peoples? Would you lead the way to a planet-wide spiritual celebration of Earth's entry into a new era? Would you bring every person, every community, and every country to the celebration with appropriate gifts? And most importantly, would you and your faith tradition come too, bringing a gift that will change the course of Earth? If you will, then the Original Source of Creative Energy will show us all a new future. Then, with hope in our hearts, we can die in peace, all six billion of us . . . die to our old, immature twentieth century ways of being and thinking. We can cross the waters together and we can celebrate Earth's arrival in a new era in a way that will be remembered forever."

Dr. L. M. Singhvi, a Jain and the High Commissioner of India to the U.K., asked: "Are we prepared to conclude a universal covenant on interreligious cooperation for peace, for the relief of those in distress and deprivation and the preservation of planet Earth? Are we prepared to form a coalition of the world's religions for human rights and human obligations, for ecology, for distress relief and peace? Are we prepared at carry forth the message of Rio on the environment and the message of Vienna on human rights through our deliberations in the Parliament at Chicago? Above all, are we prepared to proclaim and abide by a Universal Declaration on Nonviolence? Are we prepared to redeem our pledges to ourselves in the spirit of 1893 and to enlarge them and carry them forward into a holistic, secular and spiritual reality? I say our answer has to be yes, yes, yes!"

And so the 1993 Parliament of the World's Religions in Chicago came to a close beneath the stars of a late summer sky. In the bandshell at Grant Park just across Columbus Drive from the Art Institute where the Global Ethic had been signed that afternoon, many of the leaders took the podium for closing statements and prayers. One of the most poignant was given by Nick Hockings, a Baha'i, Naive American Ojibway Traditional Dancer and Cultural Teacher who brought the crowd of several thousand to their feet with his greeting, "Hello, my relatives!" He went on to observe: "This Parliament attests to the wisdom of our faith keepers, attests to the wisdom of our spiritual leaders, and it's up to each and every one of us at look at each other not as strangers, but to reach our hands out to one another in friendship; not to judge people by the color of their skin, but search their hearts. So this is a beginning time, and I thank you."

With that, brothers and sisters in the audience joined hands again, dancing, crying with joy, and made another Sacred Hoop. The stage filled with men and women and children of every color who began to drum and dance, each in his or her own tradition and the pulse of their music joined the heartbeat of Mother Earth. We closed our documentary with this celebration that was so full of rejoicing, commitment, family, and safety, with these words read by the academy award winning actress, Ellen Burstyn: "No one can be sure just where this great river of peace will flow. Will the promises and pledges flood over this planet like a joyful conjoining of the dance? Will the celebration bring forth a song that will sail the river, its melody soaring to the sky with messages of gentleness, compassion, and caring? These gathered religious and spiritual leaders made a covenant, giving their commitment to making this world a better place and asking each of us to join them, to glide upon this river like a leaf carrying seeds of hope and unity, flowing out and into the oceans, rising up into the heavens, and raining down peace upon the parched places of our earth."

And with the glorious energy of the Soul Children of Chicago praising God in gospel singing that made our bones vibrate and our souls nearly burst open like a fine Fourth of July fireworks display, the Reverend James Forbes, from Riverside Church in New York, exultantly invited us to: "Go forth with a joyful Amen!"

6

Gazing into the Cosmic Soul: A Participant's Reflection on the Parliament

GEORGENE L. WILSON

It was August 28, 1993. As I entered the Palmer House, which hosted the 1993 Parliament of the World's Religions, I was embraced by a lobby filled with abundantly differing folk, dressed in an array of costumes and speaking in a great variety of tongues. I knew then that I was in for eight days of an extraordinary experience. The Program invited participation in some nine hundred choices of major presentations, lectures, seminars, workshops, films, dances, prayers, and performances. Truly, I thought, this event had been planned by folk who worship at the altar of Divine Abundance! The possibilities invited me to open my eyes into the soul of the cosmic Sacred and to gaze into this "too much" so that I might receive enlightenment. I accepted the invitation with eagerness and asked "The different than I am" and "The beyond my consciousness" to be my Parliament companions.

The Opening Ceremonies began with the procession of the world's religious leaders in all of their ritual vestments. My "plain dress" was but another proper attire in this sparkling diamond of faceted beauty. I was home! Besides, Chicago is homeland to me. I was born, raised, educated, and spiritually formed in this city. I have offered most of my ministries in and around this greater metropolitan area. Presently I reside and minister in an anchor hold, a community-based house of solitude, silence and service, in a western suburb of Chicago. These realities, as with all of life's experiences, both enhance my perspectives and limit my insights. But now, in this familiar geography, all was new. This gathering of the Parliament was like a freshly lit hearth in my home space.

As I sat and received the blessings and warmth from the opening ceremonies I remembered the words given to me by a spiritual mentor many years before. "As you journey through life," he said, "go with open eyes and with a heart ready to receive. See how the Holy One lives among the peoples. Receive the blessings of each people as they show you how they temple the Sacred. Then return home. Be a fire for others to gather around and to gaze into as they receive the stories you share from your blessings." These words were spiritually formational in me. Living with them has awakened me to the way or the practice that I am to attend to during this earth walk: Gazing is my practice. In this practice I commune with the twelfth-century Christian saint, Clare of Assisi, who in one of her teachings said that the way to pray is *to gaze*. After gazing, she said, one can consider, contemplate, and imitate. I have also come to know that this Franciscan way of prayer or practice is similar to the Buddhist way of "Benevolent Glancing." The invitation of this practice is to *behold each now*. The *now* is the *all* of the spiritual path.

Each awakening person comes to see, to gaze, with three eyes: the eye of the body, the eye of the mind, and the eye of the soul, or the heart, or the Self. At the Parliament I looked with the eyes of my body and saw anew that we are all in relationship with each other and with the earth. With the eyes of my mind I beheld the differing life situations, joys and sorrows and the abundant variety of expressions of the spirit that we, as the kin of the world, experience and manifest. And with the eyes of my soul I gazed into the eyes of the kin of the world's religions only to receive benevolence from each soul's returning glance. There were no strangers among us. The fire of Divine Reality blazed in each person's hearth. In the mutuality of our exchanging gaze each of us was transformed into the kin of the cosmic soul: we were the Kin-dom of God.

With this wisdom I lived and breathed the blessings of this historic gathering. This exchange of soulful gazing was the one ritual in which all religions could participate as a body. Our differences knew a common practice. For a few brief days we practiced a *global ethic* of beholding and blessing. For me, the event of the Parliament of the World's Religions was like a retreat for the practice of gazing. The practice issued deep radical perceptions and expanded the edges of my limits outrageously. It was as if . . .

A center,
the inner temple

I brought to the Parliament,
had grown larger & smaller;
deeper & lesser;
challenged & refreshed.
The world's family had hung their prayer flags
and kindled fires
in my sanctuary.
As one living being we gazed into the Cosmic Soul.

The experience of the Parliament changed my vision. It was as if the soul of the cosmos met my glance with bold embrace. For a week of creation we coincided as if there were but one homeland where blessing was the law of the land. We exchanged the breath and fire of life in word and ritual, in poetry and dance, in confirmation and challenge, in tears and laughter, in fears and faith, in inspiration and invitation to global awareness as well as to a global ethic. Because of the experience of the Parliament my heart has grown more loving. My spirit breathes more fully. My desire for "unity coinciding in diversity" longs more passionately. I suspect I will forever be changing the filters through which I gaze and receive. Faithfulness to this practice always offers the possibilities of new vision! I now know more deeply the cosmic soul's challenge to remain anchored in the silence and solitude and in service of the Holy One who chants "OM" in unison with all.

Part III

MAJOR
PRESENTATIONS
AT THE SECOND
PARLIAMENT

∗

7

In Darkness Grows the Green

MAGDALENA GÓMEZ

A soul cornered by Death's
unwelcome visit to the mind
cowers in darkness;
illusions gathered as gold
purchase denial.
A friend sold on the auction block;
faithful Wisdom goes with her.

Death sings to the rising sun
reminder to live
dance,
dream,
hope,
extend a hand beyond
a casual, passing reach
through the edge of one more day.

Despised gypsy
rattles bones in fleshy cages
where we do not welcome ourselves
as who we are,
but as what we do
and do, and do and do
forgetting to live,
becoming the stranger.

Magdalena Gómez and Reverend Paul Manship presented a play they authored, called *Sacred Visions,* at the Parliament on September 3, 1993.

An intruder is defined
by a locked door;
welcome,
embrace,
devour what comes,
what will come;
within a dark womb
the first howl awaits.

Be still
Be still
Be still

Seek the eyes of Death
as Lover,
bestowing compassion;
as Prophet,
foretelling the uselessness
of anything less
than love.

8

What Shall We Do?

GERALD O. BARNEY, JANE BLEWETT,

AND KRISTEN BARNEY

There is a sense, Earth is no longer orbiting peacefully about the Sun. Earth is careening toward the spiritual equivalent of a massive stone wall. The brutality of humans to each other; the "ethnic cleansing," the ignoring of hunger and poverty, the acts of terrorism and the environmental destruction and loss of natural beauty are already draining us of the spiritual and emotional energy we need to change course, and the situation is growing worse daily. We are becoming numb, unable to feel and react as we must if we are to put Earth back into a peaceful orbit. Changing course will require an immense amount of energy. Not the energy that comes from coal, gas, oil, or even nuclear fuel, but rather spiritual and emotional energy, enough to change the thinking and lives of six billion people. Can so much energy be generated? Can so many people become empowered to think and live differently? Perhaps.

The Millennial Moment:
Thinking Like *Earth* and Our Gifts

It is our conviction that a unique opportunity to set Earth on a new course is offered by the 1999–2001 period, and we are working steadily to make the most of this opportunity. We invite spiritual leaders, and others too, to join us in this effort. The opportunity relates to the fact that deep in the human psyche is a compulsion to celebrate anniversaries, birthdays, and other recurring dates. The entry into the twenty-first century and the third millennium will be a psychological experience vastly more profound than any anniversary we humans have yet experienced. Already hotel ballrooms are being booked along the Greenwich meridian by people who want to be the first to enter the twenty-first century. Concord supersonic jets are being chartered to fly people across time zones so that they can attend parties and celebrate the entry into the new millennium twice. These are just the beginning signs of the emotional energies that will be released during the 1999–2001 period, which can be called the millennial moment.

This occasion, the entry into the new millennium, has special significance for Christians as the approximate bimillennium (2000th anniversary) of Christianity, and there is danger that it could come to be seen as an exclusively Christian event. The Gregorian calendar, however, never was an exclusively Christian calendar. Beginning the year at 1 January was a pagan Roman custom resisted by the Church, and most scholars now agree that the Nativity of Christ did not occur in C.E. 0 (or 1) but rather before Herod's death in 4 B.C.E. Furthermore the Gregorian calendar has become the calendar of commerce and science throughout the world. The entry into the new millennium must be understood to be an anniversary of Earth to be enjoyed and celebrated by peoples of all faiths. Earth's entry into the next millennium is a planetary "transitional" event, and as a "mega anniversary" it has potential for reinforcing the identity of human beings, first and foremost, as citizens of Earth, as "Earthlings." This potential must be developed and utilized.

In most cultures, the transition from an old state to a new one (birthdays, graduations, marriages, funerals) is marked by celebrations having three elements. The first element is a period of preparation and grieving. During this period, we prepare to give up our past condition or to "die" to our old state. For our entry into the new millennium, we must prepare to give up our old, twentieth century ways of thinking and living.

The second element is a moment of transition, the actual giving up of the old state and the entry into the new. It requires a symbolic act of change, such as the embrace or kiss at a wedding, the movement of the tassels at a graduation, the closing of the casket or the lighting of the pyre at a funeral. For our entry into the twenty-first century, we need a new symbol, perhaps crossing a stream or river to a new place and a new way of being.

The third element is the celebration of the new and its possibilities. Music, dance, singing, and other forms of celebration are appropriate and needed. Gifts are an essential part of the celebration. Gifts are our way of expressing our good wishes and support for the new, and also a means of helping to assure that something good and enduring comes of the new. For our entry into the new millennium, we must celebrate the opportunities and possibilities of the new era not only with music and joy, but also with generous gifts for the poor, for our enemies, and for Earth on this most extraordinary occasion. Earth's entry into the next millennium cannot be just another major event. It cannot even be just the event of a lifetime. Or of a hundred years. Or even of a thousand years. That would not be enough. This must be the event of the whole Earth-time, the whole history of Earth. This must be the moment when humans interchange bad and good, unreal and real, and set themselves and Earth on a new course.

Over the next five years all six billion of us humans must prepare to die to twentieth century ways of thinking and being. We must also prepare to see the possibilities and opportunities in our new condition in our new millennium. To make these preparations, all six billion of us must devote the next five years to learning from each other about Earth and how to live sustainably and peacefully on Earth. Every person must learn to think in a way that leaves room in one's mind for the thoughts of others. Every person must come to understand much better how Earth's natural systems function and how human institutions, governments, political systems, social systems, international organizations, corporations, and spiritual institutions operate and influence the future of Earth. Every person must learn again the immense power and value of life. (Does all the money or wisdom in the whole world have the power to restore a single life?) Every person must learn to *think* like Earth, to *act* like Earth, to *be* Earth.

As a part of this learning process, we must all think through how our part of Earth can contribute to the new. Each person, each family, each corporate institution, each community, each country, each faith needs a plan to contribute to the new. What laws must be changed, what traditions, what beliefs, what institutions? We also need ideas of appropriate gifts for Earth on this anniversary. What gift can a person give? What can a family, a corporate institution, a community, a country, a faith give to Earth on this momentous anniversary?

For this event to do what it must, the spiritual leaders of Earth must help lead the way and help plan the events. We humans, all six billion of us, depend on our spiritual leaders to make this happen. Only the spiritual leaders of Earth, the recognized and the not-yet recognized, command the emotional energies needed to move heads of state, leaders of corporations and other institutions, and ordinary citizens to the acts of generosity and changed thinking and living that must occur.

We need the spiritual leaders to lead us in teaching each other about Earth and how to live sustainably on Earth. We need them to help us all design a once-in-an-Earth-time celebration of Earth's entry into a new era. We need them to bring every person, every community and every country to the celebration with their gifts. And most importantly, we need them to bring to the celebration a gift from their own faith tradition, a gift that will help change the course of Earth. What gift could each faith give Earth?

To do what must be done, Earth's spiritual leaders of all faiths and all traditions must work together in ways previously unimagined and unimaginable. We must count on each of us to develop a community of Earth's faith traditions that is an example of the kind of open communication, mutual respect, acceptance, cooperation, and goodwill that should characterize the emerging global community of nations and peoples. Each tradition has at its core a vision of Divine harmony that it urges its followers to embody in the social sphere. These visions have evolved in distinct historic and geographic contexts. The religions have not successfully been able to transcend their own historical origins so as to express their visions of unity in a fashion appropriate to the needs of the pluralistic global society that is taking form at the beginning of the new millennium. The greatest single scandal in which Earth's faith traditions are now involved is their failure to practice their highest ethical ideals in their relations with one another.

In his recent message acknowledging the Church's error in the conviction of Galileo, Pope John-Paul II introduced some thoughts that might provide a basis not only for increased understanding and respect between science and religion, but also between religions. To paraphrase and abbreviate the Pope's argument: The church must teach the truth, but what are we to do when a new scientific datum seems to contradict the truths of the faith? There are two things we must do. First, it is a duty for theologians to keep themselves regularly informed of scientific advances in order to examine whether there are reasons for introducing changes in their teachings.

Second, it is necessary to recognize the distinction between sacred Scripture and its interpretation. If it happens that the authority of sacred Scripture is set in opposition to clear and certain reasoning, this must mean that the person who interprets scripture does not understand it correctly. Truth cannot contradict truth, and we may be sure that some mistake has been made. From the Galileo affair we can learn a lesson that remains valid in relation to similar situations. In Galileo's time it was inconceivable to depict the world as lacking an absolute physical reference point, which could only be situated in the Earth or in the sun. Today, however, after Einstein and within the perspective of contemporary cosmology, neither of these two points of reference has the importance they once had. The lesson, therefore, is that often beyond two partial and contrasting perceptions there exists a wider perception that includes them and goes beyond both of them. This lesson of Pope John

Paul II might point the way for a new approach to the distrust, hatred, and violence that currently plagues interreligious relations. Might there be beyond the "partial and contrasting perceptions" of the many faith traditions "a wider perception that includes them and goes beyond ... them?"

As soon as we humans learn to think like Earth, we together will see a new future for Earth. Then we can die in peace, all six billion of us, to our old ways of thinking. We can cross the waters together. And we can celebrate Earth's safe arrival in a new era in a way that will be remembered forever.

Optimism, Hope, and Confidence

Many people, especially young people, look at our situation and prospects and ask, can we be optimistic? We have acted too slowly to help tens of millions of people, and if hundreds of millions, even billions are to be spared the same fate, massive changes are needed over just the next few years. Can we be hopeful? There is a difference between being optimistic and being hopeful. An optimistic person has a habitual disposition to expect the best possible outcome as the most likely. A hopeful person has a reasoned commitment to and faith in a good outcome, even though it may be unlikely in the light of past experience.

There is reason for us all to be hopeful but not optimistic. We can be hopeful because Earth is such a fertile, supporting place. We can be hopeful because Earth is showing remarkable resilience in the face of tremendous abuse. We can be hopeful because we now have a much greater understanding of Earth and its limits. We can be hopeful because we humans are recognizing that, as a species, we cannot indefinitely increase our numbers and our demands on Earth. We can be hopeful because we humans are beginning to recover from our erroneous notion that we are separate, above, and independent of all other life. But perhaps something more than hope is justified. At least one person, Father Thomas Berry, thinks so:

> [We] need to realize that the ultimate custody of the earth belongs to the earth. The issues we are considering are fundamentally earth issues that need to be dealt with in some direct manner by the earth itself. As humans we need to recognize the limitations in our capacity to deal with these comprehensive issues of the earth's functioning. So long as we are under the illusion that we know best what is good for the earth and for ourselves, then we will continue our present

course, with its devastating consequences on the entire earth community.

(Berry, T. *The Dream of the Earth,* San Francisco: Sierra Club Books, 1988, p. 137)

Our best procedure might be to consider that we need not a human answer to an earth problem, but an earth answer to an earth problem. The Earth will solve its problems, and possibly our own, if we will let the earth function in its own ways. We need only listen to what the Earth is telling us. Here we might observe that the basic mood of the future might well be one of confidence in the continuing revelation that takes place in and through the Earth. If the dynamics of the universe from the beginning shaped the course of the heavens, lighted the sun, and formed the earth, if this same dynamism brought forth the continents and seas and atmosphere, if it awakened life in the primordial cell and then brought into being the unnumbered variety of living beings, and finally brought us into being and guided us safely through the turbulent centuries, there is reason to believe that this same guiding process is precisely what has awakened in us our present understanding of ourselves and our relation to this stupendous process.

Let us all listen to and allow ourselves to be guided by the creative energy that shaped and lighted the universe from the beginning. Let us all awaken to a new understanding of ourselves and the continuing revelation that takes place in and through Earth. Let us take back our lives from cynicism, optimism, additions, and despair. Let us act with conviction and confidence, but let us act!

The Catholic Church
and Other Religions

ARCHBISHOP FRANCESCO GIOIA, OFM CAP.

It is life that allows us to know and to understand others. Life lived together. The "word" is only a door that introduces us into the profoundly mysterious and deeply fascinating world of the other. I wish to open the "door" of the Catholic Church. Yours will be a friendly visit whose goal is to see, to listen, to reflect. I shall be your discreet and respectful guide. I'll not tire you and will not disturb your heart. I'll serve you, satisfying your desire to know without limiting your freedom. I propose here a simple anthology of Catholic teaching. A "gathering of flowers," which is the etymological meaning of the term "anthology." I have chosen the literary anthological genre to facilitate direct access to the sources of the teachings of the Catholic Church, without interpretation of theologians.

The span of time taken into consideration embraces exactly the last thirty years, from the Second Vatican Council to the present. During this period, both the Catholic Church and other religions entered a new climate of dialogue, a period that witnessed the growth of a climate of friendship characterized by reciprocity, respect, confidence, and intense collaboration. In what follows, I will concentrate on four fundamental themes: (1) aspects of truth and goodness, (2) dialogue, (3) salvation, and (4) peace. Let us set off on our visit to this marvelous "garden"; there are flowers for all.

This presentation was given at the Parliament on September 1, 1993. In the documents quoted here we have chosen to use inclusive language.

1. Aspects of Truth and Goodness
Present in All Religions

The Catholic Church, celebrating the Second Vatican Council (October 11, 1962–December 8, 1965) "looked beyond the limits of the Christian horizon" and considered with fraternal attention those "religions which retain the sense and the concept of God, One and Creator, provident, the high and transcendent, which profess the cult of God with sincere piety and whose creeds and practices found the principle of moral and social life.[1]

The Council faced directly the matter of the relations between the Catholic Church and other religions[2] and instituted a proper organism able to take care of practical aspects[3]—The Pontifical Council for Inter-religious Dialogue in the Vatican.

The position of the Second Vatican Council is extremely clear: every religion has aspects of goodness and truth. The conciliar degree, *Nostra Aetate,* declares: "The Catholic Church rejects nothing of what is true and holy in these religions. She has a high regard for the manner of life and conduct, the precepts and doctrines which, although differing in many ways from her own teaching, nevertheless often reflect a ray of that truth which enlightens all people."

Indeed, she speaks of "seeds of the Word"—the seeds of the Son of God Jesus Christ—seeds that lie hidden among the different religions (*Ad Gentes* 11). The Second Vatican Council underlines some particular positive aspects of the various religions.

"In *Hinduism* [people] explore the divine mystery and express it both in limitless riches of myth and the accurately defined insights of philosophy. They seek release from the trials of the present life by ascetical practices, profound meditation and recourse to God in confidence and love" (NA 2).

"*Buddhism* in its various forms testifies to the essential inadequacy of this changing world. It proposes a way of life by which [persons] can, with confidence and trust, attain a state of perfect liberation and

---

1. Paul VI, "Discourse of Opening of the Second Period of the Council" (29.9.1963), in *Insegnamenti* (Libreria Editrice Vaticana 1963), I, pp. 183–184.
2. The Council confronted directly the problem of the various religions in the Decree *Nostra Aetate* (AE). The Council spoke about this problem in other documents, especially in *Lumen Gentium* (LG), *Ad Gentes* (AG), *Gaudium et Spes* (GS), *Dignitatis Humanae* (DH), *Dei Verbum* (DV), *Apostolicam Actuositatem* (AA). See *The Documents of Vatican II,* ed. Walter Abbot, S.J. (New York: Guild Press, 1966).
3. With the Apostolic Letter "Progrediente Concilio" (11.5.1961), Paul VI founds the Secretariat for non-Christians, whose goals are written in the Apostolic Constitution "Regimini Ecclesiae" (15.8.1967).

reach supreme illumination either through their own efforts or by the aid of divine help" (NA 2).

"So, too, *other religions* which are found throughout the world attempt in their own way to calm . . . hearts . . . by outlining a program of life covering doctrine, moral precepts and sacred rites" (NA 2).

Concerning *Islam,* "the Church has also a high regard for the Muslims. They worship God, who is one, living and subsistent, merciful and almighty, the Creator of heaven and earth, who has also spoken to [humankind]. They strive to submit themselves without reserve to the hidden decrees of God, just as Abraham submitted himself to God's plan, to whose faith Muslims eagerly link their own. Although not acknowledging him as God, they venerate Jesus as a prophet, his virgin Mother they also honor, and even at times devoutly invoke. Further [more], they await the day of judgment and the reward of God following the resurrection of the dead. For this reason they highly esteem an upright Life and worship God, especially by way of prayer, alms-deeds and fasting" (NA 3).

The Church feels herself "spiritually bound to *Judaism*" with which she has a "great spiritual common patrimony." The Jewish people are "most dear for the sake of the fathers" (*Lumen Gentium* 16). In fact, it is from them that Christ was born according to the flesh (cf. Rom. 9:4–5), Child of the Virgin Mary. "The apostles, the pillars on which the Church stands, are of Jewish descent, as are many of those early disciples who proclaimed the Gospel of Christ to the World" (NA 4).

2. Dialogue: Pope Paul VI's Teaching in *Ecclesiam Suam*

The sincere acknowledgment of the aspects of truth and goodness present in all religions constitutes a solid foundation for dialogue. Dialogue is the term that recapitulates the methodology adopted by the Catholic Church for approaching the followers of other religions (NA 2; AG 16, 41) and the entire world (*Gaudium et Spes* 92). Long silences, violence, wars between Christianity and other religions, especially with Judaism and Islam (NA 3–4), must be forgotten by dialogue on a level of mutual comprehension and love (NA 3–4; AG 11, 26).

Pope Paul VI in an official document, his Encyclical Letter "Ecclesiam Suam" (6.8.1964)[4], outlined with astonishing profundity of knowledge and psychological clarity the specific goals of the dialogue that the Church tries to pursue with followers of other religions. This document

---

4. *Insegnamenti, Encicliche* 1971, pp. 33–49.

can be considered the "Magna Carta" of dialogue. Conscious that "the duty consonant with the patrimony received by Christ is spreading, offering, announcing the Gospel (n. 66)," the Church should enter into dialogue with the world in which she lives. The Church becomes word; the Church becomes message; the Church becomes dialogue" (n. 67).

Paul VI goes on: the choice of dialogue is not optional, but it imposes itself because of its "transcendent origin." In fact, "Religion, of its very nature, is a relationship between God and [us]. Prayer expresses such a relationship in dialogue" (n. 72). For the Followers of Christ, the history of salvation narrates exactly this "long and changing" dialogue (n. 72), which "was opened spontaneously on the initiative of God" (n. 74) and is "destined for all without distinction" (n. 78).

Then he says: the Church has a message for every category of humanity: "for children, for youth, for [persons] of science and learning, for the world of labor and for every social class, for artists, for statesmen, and for rulers. Most of all, the Church has words for the poor, the outcasts, the suffering and the dying, for all men and women" (n. 111). But the Church wants particularly to dialogue with "those men and women who adore the One and Almighty God" (n. 111).

Dialogue is to be directed to everybody. It "will take cognizance of the slowness of psychological and historical maturation and of the need to wait for the hour when God may make our dialogue effective.[5] Not for this reason will our dialogue postpone till tomorrow what it can accomplish today; it ought to be eager for the opportune moment; it ought to sense the preciousness of time. Today, i.e., every day, our dialogue should begin again; we, rather than those toward whom it is directed, should take the initiative" (n. 79).

Dialogue is "an example of the art of spiritual communication" (n. 83), interwoven with simplicity and *clarity* (n. 95); *meekness,* which avoids pride and—"it is not bitter, it is not offensive"; "it promotes *trust* and friendship" and "calls for pedagogical *prudence* which strives to learn the sensitivities of the hearer" (nn. 83–84). A sincere dialogue also requires times of loving silence and the ability to accept the other: "Before speaking it is necessary to listen, not only to a person's voice, but to their heart. A person must first be understood; and, where they merit it, agreed with. In the very act of trying to make ourselves pastors, fathers, and teachers of persons, we must make ourselves their brothers and sisters. The spirit of dialogue is friendship and, even more, is serv-

---

5. In *Evangelii Nuntiandi,* among the "signs of love" that have been done by those announcing the Gospel, for Paul VI "The first is respect for the religious and spiritual situation of those being evangelized" (n. 79), *Insegnamenti* 1975, XIII, p. 1487.

ice" (n. 90). "In a dialogue thus articulated one discovers how different are the ways which lead to the light of faith, and how it is possible to make them converge on the same goal" (n. 86). Thus emerges the real goal of dialogue; that is the discovery of "elements of truth also in the opinions of others" (n. 86).

From this point of view, the Church does not want to refuse "the respectful recognition of the spiritual and moral values of the various religion forms." On the contrary, with them she wants "to promote and defend common ideals of religious liberty, human brotherhood, good culture, social welfare, and civil order" (n. 112). But we need to be aware that the Church cannot be allowed to be taken by the passion of her mission; in the diffusion of the message of Christ, which pushes her to dialogue with the world and particularly with the followers of other religions, she must be aware of the danger of syncretism: "an immoderate desire to make peace and sink differences at all costs is, fundamentally, a kind of scepticism with regard to the Gospel" (n. 91).

3. Salvation

The question of salvation has received different answers in various religions. The doctrine of the Church in this regard can be summed up as: (1) "God wants everyone to be saved" (1 Tm 2, 4); (2) "Everyone needs salvation" (LG53); (3) "Christ died and is risen for all" (cf RM 8:32–34); and (4) "the Church is the universal sacrament of salvation" (LG48), that means a "sign and instrument of communion with God and of unity among all" (LG1), "at once manifesting and actualizing the mystery of God's love for all" (GS 45).

A first consequence of these principles is that the plan of salvation is for all peoples. "First of all for that people from which Christ was born according to the flesh," that is, the Jews. After "those who acknowledge the Creator, in the first place amongst whom are the Muslims: these profess to hold the faith of Abraham, and together with us they adore the one, merciful God, mankind's judge on the last day."

Finally, all peoples: "Those who, through no fault of their own, do not know the Gospel of Christ or his Church, but who nevertheless seek God with a sincere heart, and moved by grace, try in their actions to do his will as they know it through the dictates of their conscience— those too may achieve eternal salvation. Nor shall divine providence deny the assistance necessary for salvation to those who, without any fault of their own, have not yet arrived at an explicit knowledge of God, and who, not without grace, strive to lead a good life. Whatever good or truth is found amongst them is considered by the Church to be a preparation for the Gospel and given by him who enlightens everyone that they may at length have life"[6] (LG16).

Another inevitable consequence of the Church's doctrine on salvation is the validity and necessity of her missionary activity: "So, although in ways known to himself God can lead those who, through no fault of their own, are ignorant of the Gospel, to that faith without which it is impossible to please him (Heb. 11:6); the Church, nevertheless, still has the obligation and also the sacred right to evangelize. And so, today as always, missionary activity retains its full force and necessity" (AG7).

The fact that various religions have given different answers to the problem of salvation does not prevent their followers from working together in some stages that are common to every project of salvation, such as the struggle against sin, suffering, poverty, violence, injustice, and against evil in all its manifestations. Salvation also means human development. This is at the heart of all religions. "The primacy is always one of the Spirit[7] but we cannot forget the fundamental needs of the whole human being." The concept that salvation also embraces human development is a recurring idea in the teachings of the Church.

4. Peace

I wish peace for all of you. We cannot reach salvation and, above all, human development without peace. Peace is a universal value accepted by all religions. On her part, the Catholic Church has always been a promoter of peace. But, in the last thirty years, the defense of peace has become a predominant preoccupation of her activity and teaching.

In 1967, Pope Paul VI launched an initiative to celebrate at the beginning of each year a "World Day of Peace," by sending a message to all people of good will. What is proposed is not necessarily a Catholic celebration, but something which embraces "all true friends of peace."[8] Pope Paul VI calls attention to the fact that peace is not a simple, ingenuous, and dangerous utopia. It is the new law of humanity that comes forth and arms peace with a tremendous principle: "All of you

---

6. The Council affirms that the grace invisibly works in the heart of all people of good will (cf. Rom. 8:32 and GS22).

7. Paul VI, "To the faithful in the Solemnity of Pentecost" (Rome 17.5.1964), *Insegnamenti* 1964, II, n. 6, p. 342

8. "We address Ourself to all persons of good will to exhort them to celebrate 'The Day of Peace,' throughout the world, on the first day of the year, January 1st, 1968." *Insegnamenti* 1967, V, pp. 620.

are brothers [and sisters]!" (MT 23:8).[9] This causes Pope Paul VI to say that "the Church, in this world is not an end in itself, she is at the service of all people; she is the bearer of love and promoter of peace[10] and is a Church open to good relations with all other Christian communions, with other religions as well as with all people of good will.

Concern for peace has become a priority in almost every religious denomination. It seems to be evident to all that an essential task of every religious denomination is to contribute positively to the peaceful coexistence of peoples. To this end the Pope "appeals to all believers that they work indefatigably to establish an ambience in which peace, so greatly desired by humanity, can flourish."[11] Furthermore, peace presupposes justice, longanimity, patience, waiting and pardon. Peace is good for all, so all have the obligation to cultivate it, defend it and promote it. Good must supplant every conflict. "Peace is the foundation of every new civilization, it is not just a contingent pause in history, but a stable foundation of human society."[12]

The theme of peace dominates the pastoral activity of Pope John Paul II and marks certain high points of his Pontificate, as in the meetings of Prayer for Peace in Assisi, the city of St. Francis, with the representatives of various religions. These meetings, such as the one in Assisi between the followers of Christ, Confucius, Buddha, Muhammed, and other religions, have left a mark on the mentality and the religious history of humanity, when people of different religions, though using different words, invoked the same God, and with the same intention, which was to foster understanding and love among all human beings.

The prayer, "that they may be one" in Jesus' Last Supper finds an initial realization: "That if you love one another, all will know that you are my disciples" (Jh 13:35), Jesus said, and it was this they attempted to do. It is what they have tried to do in Assissi. My dear friends, there is a "gospel," a "good news" for all: it is that of friendship, of love among all. Friendship will help us to accept with serenity the inevitable pain that all forms of dialogue bring, especially interreligious dialogue. It would be good to recall that a ray of sunlight does not illumine if it has not first "struck" the eye. Thus, a word of friendship does not bear fruit if it has not "disturbed" by unsettling our internal balance.

---

9. Paul VI, "Message for the World Day of Peace" (18.10.1975), *Insegnamenti* 1975, XIII, p. 1135.

10. Paul VI, "Discourse of opening of the IV Session of the II Vatican Council" (14.9.1965), *Insegnamenti* 1965, III, p. 479.

11. Paul VI, "To the representatives of Japanese Buddhism" (Rome 7.11. 1966).

12. Paul VI "To the faithful at the General Audience" (Rome 11.4.1963), *Insegnamenti* 1973, XI, p. 329.

In fact, before God allows himself to be "possessed" by us, he disturbs us in a thousand different ways, at times with an anxious silence, at times with an impetuous word that invites us to conversation, now with his action hidden in the daily events that close the way just begun in order to open a new way. Only by passing through fear and trembling can one come to confident, filial, and blessed adoration. May God accompany our walk and illumine our path!

10

Elements of *Nirvana*

SAMDECH PREAH MAHA GHOSANANDA

- (Translated by Wayne Teasdale)

Nirvana, the "blowing out of desire," blissful omniscience, has a number of levels, dimensions of meaning, for it is a profoundly rich experience and form of consciousness. It is first of all the ultimate state of consciousness, and as such, is beyond all determination, all form, concept, image, feeling, or emotion. Its various levels of meaning and function include: an intrinsic or absolute dimension, and a metaphysical, etymological, psychological, and ethical understanding. There are other meanings as well, because, again, it is a very rich experience, awareness, philosophical perception.

Nirvana in its *intrinsic* sense or meaning is Absolute Peace, Supreme Blessing, Ultimate Bliss. These terms name, refer or suggest pure happiness or beatitude. There is no limit to the peace, blessing and bliss of nirvanic awareness. Nirvana is not the kind of ordinary peace that we know in the course of normal human experience. It is something totally unlimited and fully actual, not in a state of becoming, not affected by the problem of impermanence.

Metaphysically, nirvana is the only real mental health, the only genuine sanity, the comprehensive vision of reality as it is, without the corruptions of time, space, and becoming, without the tragedy of finitude. The metaphysical sense of nirvana means that one has the whole picture, and so is in a state of perfect perspective and so also, of perfect mental health.

In terms of its *etymological* significance, nirvana means or connotes "without passion," free of the egoistic drive, transcending the need to be something or someone, beyond the pull of the desires that bind, enslave, and trap us in samsara, or the cycle of birth, death and rebirth. This particular meaning of nirvana actually suggests the way out of the problem of life—suffering, anxiety or *dukkha*—as the going beyond desire, passion, or the egoistic impulse to be a separate "self."

On the *psychological* level, nirvana is the cessation of the possessive attitude expressed in statements like: "This is mine; this is me; I am this or that, or simply I am, or this is my self, I own this or that," etc. Psychologically, there is a passing away of individuality, but not of consciousness.

Lastly, in its *ethical* meaning, its moral content, nirvana refers to the inner transformation that takes place when a person is free of desire. It is the extinction of the afflictive, negative emotions of anger, hatred, violence, greediness, and delusion. Nirvana is the ultimate destiny of humanity, each one of us, the state of sharing in transcendent Consciousness, absolute being, unending bliss of *sunyata,* or emptiness and fullness simultaneously. Nirvana is the goal, and our original nature, according to the Buddhist tradition. It is only when we are truly established in nirvanic awareness that we can learn and practice compassion toward all beings.

11

Inward Journeys:
Life as Art Form

BYRON L. SHERWIN

"Why did God create human beings with *two* eyes, rather than with one or three or four?" a disciple once asked his master, Rabbi Mendel of Kotzk.

"Because human beings need no more and no less than two eyes," answered the master. "They need one eye for looking outward, at the world. And, they need a second eye for peering inward, into the self."

Of Abraham—the parent of the three great Western faiths—the talmudic rabbis and the hasidic masters said that only once Abraham realized that creation was an invitation to encounter the Creator was he prepared to journey inward to encounter the spiritual potentialities locked up within himself.

In the biblical text, God's first words to Abraham are *"Lekh lekha"* meaning "you go out." This is one of the two parts of the polarity that the spiritual life embraces—going outside the self, transcending the self to encounter the world. The second part of the polarity relates to the inward journey. According to the hasidic master, Judah Aryeih Leib of Ger, this dimension of the spiritual journey is also indicated by the words *"Lekh lekha,"* which can be translated as "go to yourself," i.e., travel inward.

Jewish spirituality revolves around this polarity of the inward and the outward, the journey out to the world and the journey in to the self. One without the other is incomplete.

Abraham began a spiritual journey that each of us can elect to continue today. Abraham is the first of a long line of spiritual pilgrims represented by his physical and spiritual heirs—Jews, Christians, and Moslems. The choice each Jew, Christian, and Moslem must make is whether to join the spiritual pilgrimage initiated by Abraham.

No voyeur on a tour of the world, the spiritual pilgrim—like Abraham—is an exile in search of a spiritual homeland, an ephemeral subject in search of an elusive predicate. The spiritual pilgrim is one who strives for self-transcendence rather than for social approval. For such an individual, life is a continuous adventure in awareness, a perennial pilgrimage in perception. The eyes of the spiritual seeker inhale wonder and exhale awe.

According to rabbinic legends, Abraham's quest began with an encounter with nature. His great innovation was the discovery that nature is not divine, but is instead a visa to encountering the divine. Abraham detected that to worship the world is idolatry, to consider nature as divine is like considering a book as having no author. For Abraham, the universe is a book written by God. Through studying the book, one can move closer to its Author. Encounter with creation is an overture towards the Creator of the oeuvre. Through awareness of the splendor of the universe and its plenitude, we are issued an invitation to meet the majesty of God. Commenting on the verse in Psalms, "I look at the heavens, the work of God's fingers" (Psalm 8:4), Rabbi Nahman of Bratzlav told this parable:

Once a prince lived far away from his father, the king. Each day he longed for his father's presence. One day, he received a letter from his father, and he was overjoyed and treasured the letter. Yet, the joy the letter gave him only increased his longing even more. He would sit and cry, "Oh, if I could see my father and touch his hand. Merciful father, how would I love to touch and kiss your little finger." And while he was crying, feeling the longing for the touch of his father, a thought came into his mind. "Do I not have my father's letter, written on his own hand? And, is not the handwriting of the king comparable to his hand?" And, suddenly, a great joy burst forth in the heart of the prince.

In the encounter with creation, the story of "Eyes" and "No-Eyes" is the story of the spiritually enriched and the spiritually deprived. "Eyes" and "No-Eyes" find themselves on a path in the midst of a dense forest. "No-Eyes" feels obliged to traverse the path with dispatch. The goal is to arrive at the destination as quickly, as efficiently, and as comfortably as possible. Trudging along, "No-Eyes" ignores the mystery and the marvels of the forest. "No-Eyes" remains oblivious to the beams of sunlight that dance upon the leaves, to the gentle caress of the breeze upon his face, to the symphony of the animals that scamper in the brush, and to the manifold panorama of color and hue that envelops the traveler. When "No-Eyes" stops to look at a plant or at an animal, it is only to recall its name, merely to remember to which botanical species or which zoological category it has been assigned. For "No-

Eyes," nature is a potential enemy to be dissected, mastered, and controlled. Calculating what to do upon reaching the clearing of the forest, "No-Eyes" remains oblivious to the pregnant drama of the moment.

"Eyes" walks along the same path. For "Eyes," each step, each instant is replete with wonder. Each tree is an unmasked miracle in disguise. Each moment is a marvel bursting with beauty. "Eyes" hears the birds and sees the sunbeams calling out their salutations. The very journey is a joy. The grandeur of nature is inebriating. For "Eyes," each instance is a destination, each glimpse a revelation, each breath a precious gift, each step opens a door to awe. For "Eyes," each glance testifies to the Artist who created it all. Each murmur betrays the presence of the Composer of the symphony of life.

At the end of the path, "Eyes" and "No-Eyes," meet. "No-Eyes," when told of "Eyes" adventures, refuses to believe they both had traversed the identical path. "No-Eyes" fancies "Eyes" as a hallucinatory dreamer. But "Eyes," who represents the spiritual pilgrim, would rather be perpetually entranced by the ineffable splendor of creation than rush through life like a window-shopping tourist in search of a bargain. No celibate where the world is concerned, the proclivity of the spiritual seeker is toward a romance with creation. For the spiritual seeker, the sensual can be the prelude to the spiritual. Marveling in creation is foreplay for sacred intercourse with the Creator. The natural world is a garment that conceals the supernatural dimension of existence. The spiritual seeker desires to divest the world of its outer garment so as to enter into intimacy with the divine concealed beneath it.

In the midst of gently exchanging a series of shared caresses with creation, the spiritual seeker discovers that just to be is a blessing bestowed by the Source of all blessings. Existence becomes coexistence with the remarkably diverse expressions of divine creativity that comprise the fellowship of creation. In the moment of deepest intimacy with creation, spiritual elation borders on revelation. The spiritual pilgrim becomes aware that he or she is "God's partner in the work of creation." Being created in the image of the Creator entails spiritual development as a created being as well as a creative being. The spiritual life is a life lived in partnership with God.

God is the ultimate creator, the ultimate artist. As a being created in the image of God, as the most superlative artwork of the divine imagination, as the partner of God in the work of creation, the human task is to complete God's unfinished artistic masterpieces—the world, and the self. Like the world, each of us is an unfinished masterpiece of God. Like a master artist, God leaves completion to the apprentice of what had been initiated by the master. Each of us is an artistic apprentice of

God. The spiritual journey is the task of creating our own lives as a work of art. The task of the spiritual life is the creation of our lives as an art form, as a work of art of which both the Creator and the apprentice cocreator can be proud.

In creating life as a work of art, each of us is an novice serving a perpetual novitiate. There are always concealed possibilities encoded in each of our souls waiting to be revealed. During a single life, the soul may transmigrate many times. Only with death is the definitive edition of each life complete. Until then, there always are new melodies to compose, new songs to sing, new pages of the novel that is our life yet to be authored. As the rabbi of Kotzk once said, "In creating life as a work of art, one who thinks he or she *has* finished, *is finished!*"

It is told that once a disciple of Levi Yitzhak of Berdichev asked his master, "Why does each tractate of the Talmud begin with page number two, rather than with page number one?"

"To teach us," replied Levi Yitzhak, "that no matter how much we know, we must always remember that we are still beginning, that we have not yet even gotten to the first page."

The Jewish New Year, Rosh Hashanah, begins in the seventh month of the Hebrew calendar and not—as one might expect—in the first month. One of the commentators observes that the reason is to teach us that one can begin anew at any time, and not only in the beginning. The spiritual quest, the quest to create one's life as an art form, may still begin in midlife, or even toward life's end. As the hasidic masters taught, it is never too late and never too early to remove the rust that corrodes one's soul.

The soul is a seed implanted within each of us. Each person is like a tree that may choose whether and when to bring forth its own fruit. At life's end, one may return a diminished form of what was received, or more than one received, at life's beginning. Each person has the choice to corrode or to create, to pollute or to improve, what one initially has been granted.

For Jewish spirituality, human existence is too precarious, life is too fragile, time is too precious, not to be taken with the utmost seriousness. Commenting on the verse in Ecclesiastes (9:8), "Let your garments always be white; let not oil be lacking on your head," Rabbi Israel of Rhyzen commented, "A person should view himself or herself as being dressed in white silken garments with a pitcher of oil on his or her head, walking a tightrope over an abyss. A single wrong small step and one's garments become stained. A single irretrievable step and one falls into the abyss below."

For Jewish spirituality, performance of sacred deeds are the seeds toward creating one's life as a work of art. The sacred deed is faith in the form of action. The sacred act is not primarily viewed as a way of providing oneself a portion in the World to Come, but as a way of providing God with a presence in *this* world. Performance of the sacred deed is how we as creatures bear witness to our Creator. Commenting on the verse in Isaiah (43:12), "You are my witnesses says God," a talmudic rabbi said: "If you are My witnesses, then I am God. But, when you are not My witnesses, it is as if I am not God."

The spiritual quest is a perpetual adventure of hide-and-seek, rather than a game of "trivial pursuit." The spiritual pilgrim is a person in search of the divine masked by creation.

It is told that the grandson of Rabbi Barukh of Miedzyborz was once playing hide-and-seek with a friend. The boy stayed in his hiding place assuming that his friend would come and look for him. After waiting a long time, it was clear that his friend had decided not to try to find him. The boy ran into the study of his grandfather complaining about how his hiding had been in vain. Upon hearing the story, Rabbi Barukh began to cry. "Why are you crying, grandfather?" asked the boy. "Because," said Rabbi Barukh, "God, too, says 'I hide, will no one come to search for Me?'"

For the spiritually developed individual, there is but one entity that one can be sure is no illusion, no ephemeral fancy, no passing fad, no public relations stunt—and that is God. God is the anchor for each individual's spiritual quest as he or she attempts to navigate through the currents of absurdity, the whirlpools of trauma, the shifting winds of historical change. God is the meaning beyond absurdity, the source of the truth beyond deceptions, ultimacy beyond the transient. As God may be found hiding behind the disguise of creation, God may also be found absconded within the self. In this view, the search for spiritual self-awareness, the inner journey, is simultaneously a quest for encounter with the divine.

Beginning in the sixteenth century, Jewish mystics began to describe the individual soul as "a part of God from above." In this view, each individual is an incarnation of God, each person carries an element of divinity within. From this perspective, the quest for self-knowledge and the quest for encounter with the divine begins not only with a journey into the world, but also with a journey inward, into the self. Without self-encounter, there is no self to seek that which is beyond the self. Self-awareness is a path that, if properly traversed, can lead to the innermost chambers of the palace of God. Self-awareness is a critical step in the creation of life as art form. A person who encounters the world, a person who embarks upon the outward journey but who fails to encounter the self and the divine within the self, who does not also embark on the inward journey, becomes a conclusion without a premise, a contradiction, a spiritual fallacy.

Through the performance of sacred deeds that shape life as an art form, the individual human being can offer the divine a home within the self. Each person may extend an invitation to the divine to become incarnated within his or her own self. In this regard, the Zohar—the central work of the Jewish mystics—states:

> Happy is the person who lets God dwell in every single organ of his or her body, making a place for the divine to dwell there . . . so that no organ is devoid of God.

For Christianity, God became incarnate in one person. But, for the Jewish mystics, the divine may become incarnated in *each* human person. For Christianity, God incarnated the divine in a single human person. For the Jewish mystics, each human being—through the performance of sacred deeds, can incarnate the divine within themselves.

In a similar vein, Rabbi Mendel of Kotzk commented on a verse in Deuteronomy (6:6): "These words shall be upon your heart." "Why," he asked, "does the verse describe the word of God as being *upon* the heart, *on* the heart, rather than *in* the heart? Because," he said, "the word of God lies upon the heart, waiting for the heart to open so that the word of God may enter the human heart. God dwells where the human being lets the divine enter."

Each person is an envelope bearing a divine message, a divine Presence. The spiritual challenge to each person is to convey and to bear witness to this message by the way in which we live. By realizing the presence of God implanted within each person, each individual can bring about not only the realization of our own individual spiritual selves, but also the augmentation of the Source of all selves. The danger, however, is that we may become messengers who either lose or forget the message.

According to Jewish spirituality, there are four converging paths to the creation of life as an art form, four roads to spiritual self-development, four paths that can lead to the divine: the world, the self, the sacred deed, and, the sacred word. The sacred word is a road and a rope with each of us at one end and God at the other end.

Just as one can encounter the Author of the book that is the world through the *work* the Author has composed, so can one encounter the author of the *word*—the author of the Torah—through study of the letters and the words that comprise it. The sacred word is a setting for the rendezvous of the human and the divine. Commenting on the verse in Exodus (25:8): "They shall make Me [i.e., God] a sanctuary so that I can dwell among them," Rabbi Moses Hayyim Ephraim of Sudlykow said, "This verse means that each of us must create a sanctuary within ourselves for God to dwell. But how can we take God so that God dwells within us? The way is through the Torah which is God's Name. Since the Torah is God's Name, it is identical with God."

According to the Gospel of John (1:1), "In the beginning there was the word and the word was with God, and the word was God." However, according to the Jewish mystics, it is the opposite. In the beginning there was God, and God becomes the word. God infused the divine Name, the divine presence, into the letters and the words of the text of the Torah. By entering the word, we encounter the divine. The quest for God, for truth, for self-knowledge, for instruction in creating life as a work of art, begins with the Torah, with the word of God, with meeting God in the word *of* God, the word that *is* God, the word where the divine presence dwells.

In Hebrew, the word for letter is *"teivah."* But, *"teivah"* is also the word for "ark." The Baal Shem Tov interpreted God's command to Noah as a command to each person: "Enter the *'teivah'"*; enter the letter. By entering the holy letter, through study of the sacred text, through praying the sacred word, one enters the word; there one can realize a rendezvous with God.

By encounter with the world, one can become God's partner in the work of creation. By entering the word, one can become God's partner in the work of revelation. One can become a coauthor of the Torah, a cocreator of the sacred text. As Rabbi Moses Hayyim Ephraim of Sudlykow wrote:

> Until the sages interpreted it, the Torah was not considered complete, but only half-finished. It was the rabbinic sages through their interpretations that made the Torah whole.

Just as in the spiritual quest, one is always beginning, so in the understanding of the words of the Torah, no one but God has the final word. The liturgical blessing over the reading of the Torah describes God as the One "who *gives* the Torah," i.e., the Torah is perpetually being given, always being revealed, continuously being understood.

As the quest for self-knowledge is perpetually continuous, the quest for the knowledge of the Torah is always ongoing. The quest for truth is never-ending. Indeed, the truth is that *the* Truth cannot be fully known in our world of falsehoods and illusions. As the Jewish philosopher Franz Rosensweig put it, "Truth is a noun only for God; for human beings truth must remain a tenuous adjective."

For the Jewish mystics, since truth is a spiritual reality, it can only be truly known in a completely spiritual realm, which our world, alas, is not. We only can know partial truths, truths tainted with falsehood, compromised truths, what Martin Buber termed "moment truths."

The spiritually adept person is one who is aware that our most dearly affirmed convictions may only be deceptions traveling incognito, that our supposed intellectual sureties may simply be grand illusions, that what we tend to equate with reality may merely be an illusion in the mind of God, that human history may only be a bad dream from which God will one day awaken. For the spiritual pilgrim, skepticism should not be an invitation to despair, but an antidote against intellectual vulgarity and arrogance. Doubt is not a catalyst for hopelessness, not an invitation to cynicism, but a weapon in the constant battle against self-delusion. In the spiritual quest, hypocrisy is a greater danger than heresy, self-delusion a more urgent fear than failure. When asked, "Who is a *hasid*? Who is pious?" Rabbi Bunam of Przysucha replied, "A *hasid* is one who does more than the law requires. The law demands that one not deceive one's own neighbor. A *hasid* is one who goes above the letter of the law. A *hasid* is one who endeavors not to deceive his or her own self." But, even worse than self-deception is deceiving the self and remaining oblivious to it. As Rabbi Mendel of Kotzk put it, "It is bad enough to be in a state of exile. But, it is even worse to be in a state of exile and not even know it."

At the heart of the spiritual journey is the promise of self-transformation. Various spiritual disciplines offer road maps as to how such self-transformations can be achieved. The Jewish mystics perceived the spiritual quest as an encounter with one's own self-realized spiritually developed self, which they considered as being a limb of God. Once this encounter with the vision of one's self-realized self had been achieved during an intensified mystical experience, the subsequent task became to effect the transformation of the self from who and where one is, to where one can be and to who one can become, to transform the self from potentiality to actuality. The challenge then is to find oneself by losing oneself in God. In this view, once a person succeeds in envisioning his or her spiritually realized self, one can then embark upon the task of revisioning one's spiritual profile, i.e., one can focus on how to make the transformation from who one is to who one can be and should become.

For the Jewish mystics, the performance of sacred deeds and the study of sacred texts are critical components in this process of self-realization. In discussing this process, the Jewish mystics refer to two similar Hebrew words: *"zel"* and *"zelem."* *"Zel"* means "shadow"; *"zelem"* refers to the "image of God," to the individuating principle that defines who each of us can become. In other words, one may choose to remain a *zel,* a shadow of one's potential spiritual self; or one can opt, through spiritual development, to realize one's potential as *"zelem,"* as "the image of God," as one's realized spiritual self.

In the final analysis, the spiritual journey is a challenge to become who each of us can be. For Jewish spirituality, the spiritual journey is not an attempt to escape the world but to transform it, not to obliterate the self but to fulfill it.

There is an old Jewish tradition related to Rosh Hashanah that God records each person's deeds in a book. Upon the death of each individual, he or she is presented with the book of his or her own life. In this view, through his or her deeds, each person composes a novel that represents his or her own life. At life's end, the last words are written. The definitive edition is completed. At that point, the volume becomes the provenance of the critics. The question each person must therefore face as he or she goes through life is: What will the reviewers say about the book, about the story of my life, about the quality of the work of art that is my life?

12

Until the Pain Is Over

MA JAYA SATI BHAGAVATI

The babies were sleeping and tucked into their cribs. Little Nisha had just turned nine months; she was incredibly cute, and we were grateful still to have her with us. Trent was crawling around the floor. He had full-blown AIDS and suffered from muscular dystrophy. Jeremy, our oldest little boy, had been playing with a caregiver's lipstick and had fallen asleep on the couch. With the lipstick smeared all over his face, he looked like a little old lady who had had too much to drink the night before. He was three and proud of the feeding tube that came out of his little belly. If he liked you enough, he'd let you put his food in the tube. Deena was lying on the other couch, pouting because one of my students wasn't rubbing her feet hard enough.

"Little Miss Thing, stop pouting," I said.

She smiled and said in her perfect English, "He's quite slow, isn't he, Ma?" Deena had been raped at seven and now, at nine, she was dying from AIDS.

I was in Connor's Nursery in West Palm Beach, sitting on a blue couch with the yellow flowers and talking with Laverne, little Tran's mommy. Connor's Nursery is a home for babies and children under six who have AIDS. Deena was such a heartbreaking case that they had stretched the rules and taken her in. Laverne had lost her son, Tran, to AIDS a few months before; she also had AIDS. She worked at Connor's to forget her grief and to help Tran's little friends.

I had just received an invitation to speak at the Parliament of the World's Religions, which would be held a few months later in September. They had asked me to submit a description of my work and why I did it.

I couldn't help thinking about all the church and temple doors that are closed to my people with AIDS just when they most need the openness of religion. I looked around the room, my eyes focusing on Laverne's thin form and beautiful ebony face; her eyes were the darkest chocolate brown. Her first little boy had died from AIDS a few years before. Laverne gave and gave and never stopped giving. Her year-old baby girl was quite sick with a heart condition, yet Laverne was at Connor's playing with the rambunctious Trent while her own mother watched the baby.

In my heart I knew that some of the babies would be dead and most would be very ill by the time I spoke at the Parliament. Would I hurt my chance with what I was going to write? Would I be aborted before I had chance to give birth?

"How do I do this, God?" I asked my own god, Hanuman, who once was the great god Shiva living atop Mount Kailash. When he looked down and saw what humanity was doing to humanity, he began to cry. Where his tears fell, trees grew. From these trees came the rudraksha beads that my students and I wear around our necks and wrists. We call them the "crying beads." Shiva saw that humility was missing from the earth and took the form of a monkey, vowing to serve the world and to show that a great god can be humble enough to be a monkey and to serve where needed.

I sat next to this heartbroken young woman and watched her serve little Toby, who was kissing her cheek with big wet sounds.

"My God," I repeated, "don't let me ruin this opportunity." I found myself in a place of rage and didn't know how to get out of it. The worst part was that I wasn't sure that I wanted to stop my rage. Too many religious leaders refuse to give comfort to my people, many of whom are the street people of this world. Where was the compassion of my Christ, who had told me to teach all ways, for all ways were His?

"Ma, Ma, come back," I heard Laverne call. "Ma, you'll be able to do it. Just take us all in your heart. Remember what Tran used to tell you."

My eyes began to tear up at the thought of little Tran pulling the oxygen tube from his nose and saying, as he tried to put it in mine, "One for you Ma, and one for Tran." One breath for Ma and one breath for Tran. Even though he'd been buried for a few months and his pain and suffering were over, I was still hearing his words. "One for you Ma, and one for Tran."

Deena, who spoke Haitian as fluently as English, said in her high-pitched voice, "Ma, tell them about me and how I died." The nursery became silent. I couldn't move. I sat across from her and said, "OK, baby, I'll get there and speak about how you lived and how you died."

She turned away from me and said to one of my students, "Would you mind rubbing my feet a little harder?" Her feet were swollen badly due to her nonfunctioning kidneys. Deena forgave the world her suffering. I wondered if I could find the same forgiveness that I helped little Deena have.

The months flew by, the excitement was building. The phone calls went back and forth to Chicago. I was to be in a Plenary Session with Brother David Steindl-Rast and some other important people. I was offered my own workshop and was asked to be one of the main speakers at the memorial service for my dear friend Father Bede Griffiths. The most important function I would be attending would be the three-day Assembly of two hundred fifty religious leaders where global problems would be aired. Here was my chance. But most important of all, I would have a chance to speak with His Holiness, the Dalai Lama. If I could persuade him to address AIDS and all its problems, the world just might listen.

The month before the Parliament I was traveling around the country with my children and grandchildren speaking about and taking care of my heroes with AIDS. Arriving in Chicago, we entered the hotel lobby of the Palmer House and were at once impressed by the range of dress and costumes representing the various cultures of the world. For the first time since my visions of the Christ and the visitation of my Guru, I, Ma, did not look strange and out of place; I was just another woman in a sari with a dot on my forehead. The Palmer House, with its hundreds and hundreds of spiritual leaders, would be my home for the next ten days.

At first it was like a huge playground. I put my hands together and pranammed to everyone I saw. To my happy surprise they all answered in their own way, some bowing, some smiling, and others pranamming in return.

The next evening the leaders gathered together before joining the procession into the main ballroom. I was meeting so many people; my eyes were spinning round and round. I was carrying a large picture album of my people in different stages of AIDS. I showed them to everyone who would listen and to some who wouldn't.

The Native Americans were wearing their finery. People were asking to take pictures with them. Arlo Guthrie and I walked over to his friend Thomas, the chief of the Hopis, feeling the situation was a little degrading to him. Arlo introduced us. "Thomas, this is my Guru who works with people with AIDS." Thomas placed his hands on my head and gave me a blessing from the Great Spirit. He said we had a hard job ahead of us; no one wanted to hear about the Native Americans or persons with AIDS. I kissed his wrinkled cheek and said, "We will see."

In the ballroom I felt so choked up. There we were, all together. "Please, dear God, let's listen to each other."

Before leaving on my summer trip I had spent a lot of time with Sydney in the Palm Beach County Home. Sydney was blind from AIDS, and he suffered with a terrible wart condition that was spreading all over his body. His throat was a mass of red warts, bleeding and filled with pus. He had gone blind from CMV, one of the many opportunistic illnesses that afflict AIDS patients.

"Ma," he said, "be kind to everyone and be stern at the same time. Tell them all about us." "OK, Sidney, I'll try." When the pain got too bad, Sydney hid behind his blindness and blocked us all out. He was struggling to stay with his thoughts. "Ma, please do something. Don't lose it, girl. Remember there are hundreds, if not thousands, counting on you."

And so I sat in that ballroom thinking of everyone I had lost; they were all sitting there with me. Local and Parliament dignitaries spoke eloquently welcoming us. A few of the world's problems were mentioned. "OK," I said to myself, "take it easy, girl. This is just the first night." I repeated these words over and over, like a mantra.

The next morning, I looked out my hotel window and addressed the rising sun. "Please let this be a day of understanding. Let us all rise in unity in the love of the one God and his Word."

It was my turn to be on the stage in front of thousands of people. I was scheduled to read two poems, one about my river, the Ganga, and one called "On the Wings of a Butterfly." The presenters would be given a certain amount of time, and no more. Brother David went first. Before reading from his paper he talked in a beautiful way about God and humankind. A Native American demonstrated the heartbeat of Mother Earth. They were both so beautiful and right on. And then it was my turn.

"Ma, I am here," said my little dead Deena and Trent and Tran. "Ma, don't forget me." Whose voice was that? My God, it was Scott, the blind young man who had asked me if he could find God in the dark. I had held him close and told him, "In the light or dark, you have already found Him, son."

I greeted the audience and began to speak about Scott and Deena. I didn't stop and, to the credit of the Parliament people and the lady who had selected me to speak, I was allowed to continue.

After a little while I read my poetry. There was a silence when I finished. Then, everyone stood up and applauded. I put on my glasses and saw on many of the leaders' faces the tears that fell unashamedly from their eyes. I felt humbled by my own words; I knew I had gotten something across. Then I heard the sound of my Lord Christ's voice: "Not enough. It is not enough. These are only tears of the moment. There must be tears in all moments." I knew on that stage in front of all the leaders and their disciples that I needed to talk a lot more, and during that week in Chicago I spoke at every opportunity and met the leaders one by one.

I was impressed when I saw the size of the room where I would be giving my main presentation on Wednesday afternoon, and I was surprised to see the place packed. There was standing room only and very little of that. Behind me were posters showing some of my people; many in the audience stared at them for a long time. The photos weren't very pretty; they were very beautiful.

At the end of my talk, there were many questions, the main one being how I avoid burning out. "I drink as I pour," I told them. But I didn't want the questions to be about me. I wanted them to be about my people—human beings who were suffering and alone, children under twenty dying without the mothers who gave them birth.

"Now, what's next?" I asked God as I prayed that night, the night before the Assembly was to begin. "From your heart; talk from your heart." This was the Christ of my early spiritual journey. He came to me in 1972 and has never left me. This was not the voice of brimstone and fire; this was the gentle Jesus lying in his Mother's arms at the end of his crucifixion. My children, my men, and my women are being crucified now, only unlike the Virgin Mother, many of their mothers refuse to hold them while they are dying. And yet I've met so many parents who have stood by their offspring right to the end. They are the true leaders of the world.

We, who had been chosen to be in the Assembly, were seated seven to a table with a Parliament person running the show. This was fine with me; I would finally be able to make my point. "Three days sitting here may not be so bad," I thought.

"Will all the Catholics please stand," asked the president of the Parliament. I stood up. Yashoda, who has been taking care of me for the past twenty years, whispered in a high screech, "Sit down, Ma." She pulled on my sari.

"Who here are Hindus?" said the President. I, of course, stood again. I love Hanuman and I follow the Hindu path of unity. By now I had caught the eye of other spiritual leaders. I just smiled, holding tight to my sari.

"Who here is of the Jewish faith?" Why, of course I was Jewish. My Jewish name is Sheyndele. By this time Shodie had given up. I stood up for all the religions called out by the president, a man I had met during the first night and whom I loved. He gave me a look across the room that I could see even without my glasses. I wasn't trying to be funny. I love all ways and all ways are the Christ, and I had to honor the God inside myself. Anyway, my people with AIDS are of all different faiths and religions.

The Assembly met for three days. In the intermission during the first day, Brother Wayne Teasdale brought me over to a very handsome, imposing man. I saw at once that this was a man of God. He was sitting with a number of Sikhs dressed all in white, looking spotless and very pretty in their turbans. "You come with me after the Assembly," said the big man. "Sure," I answered, knowing I would love to get to know these people.

"Who was that?" I asked Wayne as we were walking away. Wayne whispered "Yogi Bhajan." We then tried to locate Swami Satchitananda and Professor Diana Eck. Diana's book about my beloved city, Banaras, had become my spiritual bible. I had just met her, and I loved her immediately. We found Swami, who remembered me from twenty years before. I kissed his feet, and we hugged.

After the Assembly adjourned for the day, Wayne, Yashoda, and I went off with Yogi Bhajan and his entourage. We entered his suite and, to my surprise, we were treated the way my chelas, my students, treat people; we were fed and made to feel honored. This man was indeed Yogi Bhajan, also known as the Siri Singh Sahib, the leader of Sikh Dharma. His beautiful wife, Bibiji, was at his side. We had a good time, but I saw that this regal man was taking on a great deal of the world's pain. I asked for a few private moments with him and his wife.

I learned that he had just had a double bypass heart operation and had come to the Parliament against the advice of his doctors. I was appalled at the way he was carrying on. I told him so, and he duly ignored me, but not before he and I became great friends. I loved his vision for world peace and his vision of a task force that would carry on the work of the Parliament. He loved my vision for my people with AIDS; I wanted the world leaders to practice the compassion and mercy of their various gods and to hold the people of this holocaust to their breasts. We talked for a long time, the Sikhs and the yogis coming together for the benefit of world peace and understanding.

The last day of the Assembly dawned wet and foggy. It was cold, and I felt that the wind beating against my hotel window was trying to tell me to be true to myself and to my people. After all, wasn't this the same town that had hosted the Parliament a hundred years before when Swami Vivekananda spoke of world peace and understanding? Yogi Bhajan didn't want to wait another hundred years, and neither did I.

I let the sound of the wind enter my heart, and I walked to the Parliament with a sturdier step. I felt like a warrior of god.

Back in the Assembly, cards were displayed on the walls summarizing the subjects we had talked about during the past three days. I watched as the Dalai Lama entered, and I pranammed to this great man. He pranammed back.

My new friend, Samdhong Rinpoche, had introduced me to His Holiness the previous day. I had screamed for my photo album and Arlo had come running out of nowhere with my pictures. His Holiness laughed as he listened to my Brooklyn accent. He looked at each photo asking how old my people were and when they had died. We hung out right there in front of everyone for a long time. "Please, Your Holiness, do something," I begged without shame. He touched my face with a caress I can still feel to this day and said, "Yes."

I scanned the lists on the walls looking for the words "AIDS" and "HIV." I was open and vulnerable; little six-year-old Zack had just died that morning and my heart hurt deep inside. Nowhere did I see those words, and I was furious.

We sat down and people raised their hands to ask questions of the President. The Global Ethic was to be signed. I was OK with it as long as the words "for all people in spite of their sexual orientation" were added to it.

Yogi Bhajan got the mike and said in his powerful voice, "Sign it already. We will figure it all out later. Just let us all sign it now. Let us forget our differences. We are all here under our God. Sign the declaration!" We all applauded, and I said, "No one is perfect. How can we expect the document to be perfect."

Diana Eck, whom I had given the name "Ganga Ma" the night before, said, "Why don't we say instead of a document *for* a global ethic, *toward* a global ethic?" It was the right thing to say, and it calmed everyone, that is everyone but me with my dead weighing like a heavy stone in my heart.

Yea! I got the mike, "Your Holiness," I said, walking toward him, "I am Ma and I have no shame crying in front of you. On the way here I received a message that a little boy of six had just died. I am now begging—" The gavel went down, stunning me.

"With all due respect, Ma, you are out of order."

"Sir," I said with tears falling down my face, tears I had not shed for twelve years since this plague started, tears that have stayed in my heart causing a huge river of grief to well inside of me. "Sir," I said refusing to give up the mike. I looked at the Dalai Lama, who was urging me with his hands, eyes, and heart to go on. "Sir," I repeated, sounding like a whine to my own ears.

"Sir, I am not out of order. I am about AIDS. I am about the thousands of women, men, and children dying alone in the hospitals and hospices in every city, in every country around the world. I have no shame or embarrassment to get down on my knees and reveal to you my broken heart. Please listen, you who lead, please tell those who follow about AIDS." I was too choked up to continue, but I couldn't let go of the mike. It was my weapon of nonviolence.

That night, in front of thousands of people in Grant Park, His Holiness spoke eloquently about AIDS. I swear to this day he was looking for me in the crowd. His eyes locked on mine; I pranammed and bowed my head. I knew that one great spiritual leader had heard me. As his people were being slaughtered in Tibet, he had the patience and holiness to hear about mine.

The next day I had a very private meeting with His Holiness. Once again he caressed my face, and he said I was a very strong woman with a big heart. He took my hands and assured me that I wasn't alone.

I thanked him and went into the lobby where many came up to me to thank me for my enlightening talk about AIDS. This time I heard my own voice saying "Not enough, not enough."

It took me three hours to leave the hotel and the Parliament. It will take me forever to forget my little Deena, Trent, Sydney, and the hundreds of others who have died in my arms. And when forever is finished, I shall never forget those heroes who fought so gallantly without violence, carrying the mightiest weapon of them all—love.

The Parliament was wonderful. So many people worked so hard for so many years to make it happen. But it is not enough! There must be another one and another until all the pain of the world is over. Yogi Bhajan's dream is to carry it on, and so is mine.

13

Sharing Our Visions:
An Open Letter

BURTON PRETTY ON TOP

First of all I would like to tell you that I feel very honored to be part of this gathering of religious leaders that attended this world gathering. As you know I didn't anticipate as much participation as I was involved with at the Parliament. I was simply content with being there, present, for the religious gathering, to learn from other people and to show the respect and sensitivity to others that I would hope would be shown to Native American Spirituality and Native American traditions.

As a traditionalist, as a Native American spiritual leader among my Crow people and being recognized as a spiritual leader by other tribes across America, I have a big responsibility. The responsibility is "walking a hard walk" because in order to be a good leader you have to be a good listener. My grandfather, the one who raised me from the time I was three until the time I was eighteen, brought me up to show respect not only for myself and the Creator, but for all of my brothers and sisters. That's how my grandfather taught me. To respect all my brothers and sisters and to love them because in loving them, he told me, I was loving the Creator himself because the Creator's Spirit is within all human beings, not one color but all colors on the face of this earth. My grandfather was a very wise man and I learned from him quite a bit. A lot of the stuff that I experience today, a lot of the stuff that I encounter, was previously mentioned to me by my grandfather, not only him but also other Elders of the Crow Tribe.

Among the Crow nation Elders are the teachers of our people. They share their stories and through those stories our children learn who they are as people of the Crow nation. Through them we learn who we are, and what we're about, and what our roots are. So through those stories there is a lesson to be taught. This kind of reminds me of going back to Biblical times—how this man who was nailed to the cross often taught the people in parables and stories. Through those stories there was always a message. That is how the Native American tradition is among the Crow nation and how it is passed on from generation to generation. Those stories were handed on by the Elders to the people and from the people to the children, etc. There are a lot of similarities between Native American traditions and the Jewish faith, the Hebrew faith. Also the man who was nailed to the cross came from a tribal group of people with set laws and regulations. He came from a tribe, the Hebrews, that had a culture that was very strong with a belief in God. It's identical to the culture I belong to. I came from a tribal group, the Crow nation. I belong to a culture that has a very strong faith in God. We knew of God and his presence among us long, long before this man, Columbus, ever set foot on this continent. We as indigenous people knew of God and his presence among us, not only in the human form but in many, many forms, in all that God has created, in everything that God has his fingerprints on. Our belief is that God's Spirit is in everything he has created, not only human beings but also the rocks and the trees and the grasses of the meadows, everything. In the air that we breathe, the water that we drink, the fire, the sacred fire, and the earth, all of these have God's Spirit in them. That is why we have this interconnection with everything that God has created. Our belief is that everything is good, everything is holy.

A little bit about my personal background. My English name is Burton Pretty on Top. My Indian name, which was given to me at the age of three years old by my great, great grandfather, was his name, his Indian name, that he passed on to me. When I was three years old my great grandfather was eighty-six and when he gave me his name it was at the end of his life; he knew that his time was coming to pass from this world to the other world, the spirit world. When my grandfather took me to my great grandfather for the purpose giving me an Indian name my great grandfather, instead of picking a name out for me, gave me his own. The Indian name I use today on the Crow reservation at our ceremonies, whether it be a social or a spiritual ceremony and whenever I am among my own people, the Crow people, is *bia iiku ku saxxin,* which means "Flirts with Women." It has nothing to do with my life, or my upbringing. My great grandfather was given that name because he was a tall, good-looking young man, and had many, many girlfriends before he got married. That name was, I guess, quite appropriate to give to him. When I was a little boy he gave me that name and within a month he passed away.

As a spiritual leader I have also been given another name. Within our tradition, the Crow tradition, we don't just give names for the sake of giving names. It's like doing an honor, and with that honor you are given a name associated with that thing that you were able to accomplish. My other name was given to me just recently in 1990. Following the Native American spirituality and Crow tradition is a hard walk. I have fasted without food and water. I have gone up the sacred mountains on our reservation nine times. I felt the calling that I climb those sacred peaks, those mountains, and I fasted from food and water for three or four days. Often after going through that suffering I came back among my people again. Each time when I went up and when I came back off the mountain on that vision quest, I went into the sweat lodge. In the Crow tradition, we use the sweat lodge as a purification.

Those times when I went up those peaks on a vision quest it wasn't what I personally chose to do, it was something that I felt, a yearning. I felt a calling within myself that I needed to do what I had to do. I know that people cannot understand this way. I know that when I share these stories with people they often say, "What's he talking about?" I hope that you will understand that when I share this story with you it comes from my heart. Those times that I felt the calling inside me I would be at peace with myself only when I answered that calling. Those times that I climbed those sacred peaks it was done with that purpose, and that mind—as part of my work. This is how I show the Creator that I love him very, very much. He is a part of me and I am a part of him. Ever since I was a little boy I knew this. As far back as I can remember, when I was two years old—maybe three years old—I knew of God and his presence inside me. It was a very powerful feeling. I don't want you to think that I am conceited, that I am brash, that I am bold. I'm not really. But I am sharing with you what I feel inside me and sometimes when you share the feelings inside you expose yourself to people. When I do this it is from my heart that I speak.

I am not saying that I am anyone special, in fact I think that I am the least of God's human beings because I am probably the weakest of his children of all colors. I'm afraid of the dark. I believe in ghosts; I know that they exist. I lie sometimes. I have weakness in my life that I have to deal with. Sometimes I'm conceited and my ego gets in my way sometimes I stumble over that badly but each time I stumble I get up and I walk. I am happy that I have been able to eliminate alcohol from my walk. I used alcohol when I was very young, fresh out of high school, from about eighteen, until the time I was about twenty-seven. I used alcohol, not extensively either; it was mainly beer. I drank beer and got into a lot of fights because I wasn't able to handle the racism that

I was confronted with outside the reservation when I went to college. I was confronted with racism and when the non-Indian people looked at me for the color of my skin telling me that I was weaker than they are and less than what they are I got very angry. As a young man I got into many fights. I was an athlete in high school. I made all-conference football, basketball, track, and through that I was given a scholarship for college. I know that you have to experience life and you have to be fully human and I've done all those things. Today I am able to deal with racism in a much better way and I've been able to—knock on wood—I've been able to handle the alcohol, eliminate it from my life. It's been seventeen years now. I don't miss it, I don't want it, I don't need it. I wish that other people, not only Native American people but also other people who have the disease of alcoholism, would be able to confront it and handle it the way God has helped me with mine.

I want you to know that I am very weak; I have many faults I'm imperfect; I know that. I am also happy that the Creator that made all of us knows all of this and he still chooses to use me. And that to me is the ultimate love that he has for all of us: this unconditional love that he has for the human race. In spite of the who he is and what he is about, I love him and am using him. But you know I love him so much that when I suffer, I suffer for him. I know that he did it for us. And I do it for the children. I do it for the human race. When I suffer on top of those mountains without food and water, for three days and three nights, or four days and four nights, I suffer to my ultimate. I feel that I am going to faint from lack of food and water and at those times when my stomach is on fire I cry, I cry like a little baby. I've seen things up there in the mountains. I've heard things that I haven't fully shared with people. If I were to share with people fully what I've heard, people wouldn't believe me anyway, they'd think I was lying. I've entered into the spirit world. I've been there and I've come back to this world. It was a very powerful experience, that moment.

When I was in the spirit world, one of our last great chiefs, Plenty Coup, who died in 1932 and was our last Chief of the Crows, came and spoke to me and gave me some teachings. And through Plenty Coup, in that spirit world I was given a new name. That new name was "Two Mornings." That is the name that was bestowed on me in that dream, in that vision. When I came back into this world I shared that story with my Elders on the Crow reservation. They interpret dreams for us. But you know what, our Elders could not interpret that dream, nor could they put the connection for me in a form that I could understand. All they said was that "Two Mornings" is a very powerful name. Among the Crow nation, they said, no one has ever had that name before, we know of no one within our history, no individual has ever had that name, "Two Mornings." But they said that by receiving it from the spirit world, it is very powerful indeed.

There was another person among us in that sweat lodge, that purification when I came off the mountain, a Catholic priest, Father Charlie Robinson. I've know Father Charlie for sixteen or seventeen years. It was Father Charlie that interpreted the dream for me, among the other Elders that were there. He said, "Burton, that name that you shared with us, can I share with you my interpretation of what I saw?" And I said, "Yes." And the Elders all said, "Yes, go ahead and speak." Then Father Charlie said:

> You know that when Jesus was nailed to that cross as was foretold by the prophets he died on that cross and they took him off that cross put him in a big tomb. It was foretold that he would be in that tomb for three days and after three days he would come back to life again and ascend into heaven. And you know that name, 'Two Mornings,' there is a connection with this story because when Jesus was in the tomb for three days, if you think about it, in between the three days there were two mornings. Therefore I feel that this name, 'Two Mornings,' is an Indian name, a Crow name for the one that was nailed to the cross, that man that we call Jesus Christ.

That's the interpretation that Father Charlie has given to me. The Elders have also accepted this interpretation. So "Two Mornings" was given to me in 1990 on top of the same peaks in the *awa kia we pia* mountains in Montana where Plenty Coup himself, the one who came and spoke to me, fasted when he was a young man and became a prophet and a leader for our people.

It is a very short time that we are here and I know that our bodies that we are using are for a short time. I have had out-of-the-body experiences, which show me that this body is just temporary in this world. There is a much larger world that's in the spirit world and there is a time we will enter into this world. I know that my body is just something that really doesn't belong to me. I look at my body and I know that I need to take care of it.

When I think about these things I think about the Parliament of World's Religions, I think about the World Day of Prayer for Peace that was called by Pope John Paul II in 1986. I think about those times. The reason I put those pieces together is so that you and I and all the people that were there at the Parliament, in Chicago, were there for a purpose. We were there for a reason and that reason was not a coincidence. We were put there by design. God had forechosen the people that were present there. He had chosen that location where we would gather together. And this is why we were there. It was not coincidence. It was preplanned; prepicked individuals were present.

The challenge now for us is this: can we go out with respect and learn from each other? We have to understand that all colors are good; the Black, the Yellow, the Red, and the White. These are things that we have to understand. That my color, the Red, does not make me any better or worse. The spiritual people, the leaders, must also rise up today, they must rise up and take ownership of the direction of this earth and the future of generations to come. I think that we as spiritual leaders, religious leaders, have sat back too long and let the political leaders take ownership and power. We just need to look around the country and look at the desecration of the human race and also the destruction of things, the atmosphere, the environment and of all of God's creation. We have to go back to our roots.

Each religion that God has given to us is good, they are all holy because they came form him. I see a tree, that tree I see is Jesus Christ. Just like a tree it comes up as one out of the ground and has many limbs, and those limbs that I see, those branches that I see within that one tree are the many religions of the world. Going down from the limbs, to the branches, to the tree itself and looking down that tree and into the ground and mother earth and the roots of that particular tree that I see is God himself. All religions have to understand that we are here together. We must get along. We belong to the same tree. There is enough destruction going on today. Enough of this. Separations must end, they must cease.

We have to understand that God brought us together for a purpose. That purpose is to form a new community of God's people, to start afresh and anew for the next seven generations to come into this world. All spiritual beings have the same values and knowledge but we have to put the pieces together to light the world so that the darkness that is present among all peoples will be extinguished. We need to have a world where people have a right to their own language, their own identity, their own culture. No one culture has a right to rule over another culture, and to exterminate another culture. This basic human right that God has given to us must be recognized.

The struggle is not only for the indigenous peoples but the struggle is for all the people of the world. As a Native American person and spiritual leader I have often heard the cry of the poor. Because I am poor myself. I live with them. I live among them. I am one of them. What we lack in material things, in the want for food, God has replaced with a spiritual wisdom, a spiritual strength. This is the true calling that God has bestowed on the human race. A basic understanding of each other in the world is needed, we must eliminate bigotry and racism. We must educate and enlighten our loved ones to unite all people together. We must learn from our history. History can be a teaching, history can be healing if we are honest with each other and confront the issues together. We need to eliminate or avoid the past mistakes that we as the human race have made instead of doing it over and over and over again. Today in 1994 we still have racism, oppression, and exploitation of the native people and of other cultures. You know that Evil has a plan too, a plan to create chaos and confusion. This plan is working successfully today in 1994 because a lot of us are caught up in racism and negativity. That is why the society we live in today is so confused.

But you know, the human race needs to wake up and go back to the Elders' teachings, respect yourself first and others and God and most importantly, pray. Pray to him, the one that created all of us, Our Father, Our One Father. The Crow word that we use for God is *Ak ba dat dia* which means the Creator of All Things. For me, morning is the time to greet the Spirit, God. That is when I walk and I talk with him. Sometimes I pray that the world will be one family.

I feel that as a Native American spiritual leader I must preserve the mountains, not for me, but for God and the future generations to come. Not only just the Crow Nation, I'm talking about the whole world. Because the mountain belongs to him and earth belongs to him. God the Creator of all things. Issues of separation must stop. I'm not Indian, you are not white, we are a spirit of God. The order of things is to bring humankind together for the fulfillment of the divine order. Creating that new world, a new state of beingness, of fulfillment.

You know as a Native American spiritual leader believing in the traditional ways I am also a Christian because for me there is no separation. My native spirituality and my Christianity are equally important and can be blended together into one. I'm like that tree that I talked about. From the Elders the teaching is that the mornings are the times the spirit teaches many, many things of wisdom to all of his children. When I am surrounded by the many mountains on a vision quest in the clear air, high up on those peaks, this is where I'm safe, this is where I'm strong and at peace with my Father and all things. I know that the Creator is within me because I can feel the oneness in special moments. I love him so very much. We, the human race, are to make a difference. Each and every one of us has a sacred responsibility for that unity, that new community of God's people. Our actions of the past caused the death and destruction of lives and of cultures and of our basic love for each other.

I have a warning, that not all of the human race have this joyous vibration that we feel as spirit because their bodies are unclean, their spirits are unclean. They are out to destroy this earth and they do have an effect on the outcome. We need to look around and open our hearts, our eyes, and our minds. When we do this we become aware that Christ has reappeared, yes, Christ has reappeared, in many forms; in the youth of our people; in the poor of our people. Christ is there, take the time to recognize him. Take that moment and you will see him. But not if we shut up our ears and our hearts to the struggle. Once we are comfortable with our lives we do not hear that small whisper, we do not hear the cry of the poor. We no longer see the destruction. These are simple truths that I am sharing with you. I know that violence in today's world, violence and destruction, are self-perpetuating. Perhaps the fault is ours, partly ours at least. As spiritual people we need to look into ourselves, take a personal inventory of ourselves, asking and challenging ourselves, what are we doing about it? That's the responsibility that we have. God has given us that task to bring about his good news. It is recognizable in all religions, not just the Christian faith, but in all religions because all the religions of the world belong to him.

We consider the United States of America our holy ground and we consider earth as our mother. So with the United States considered as holy ground, this is our promised land, for our people, for the indigenous people, the Crow nation. All that we ask of our brothers and our sisters is, please respect and be sensitive with our traditions, and of our spirituality. Please don't deny me my right to live my life, my uniqueness, as a Crow individual. And the spiritual wisdom that God has given to me, please don't deny me that right either. Accept and respect as we have accepted other religions that have come to this world, the United States. They have come here as visitors and we have taken them in and we have shown them respect. We have lived together with them and in spite of the genocide that we have experienced in the United States we are still in a situation where we as indigenous people are willing to forgive.

People are familiar with the genocide of Jewish people at the hands of Hitler. And are often reminded of that infamous genocide of human people. But another genocide that people don't really understand nor do they learn about in U.S. history, is the genocide, the holocaust of the Native American people in this world that we consider as holy land for us. In the 1500s, when the Europeans arrived there were close to 80 million inhabitants in the Americas and fifty years later there were only 10 million left. In Mexico alone the population dropped from 25 million to 1 million. The West needs to meditate deeply on these facts and on the suffering and injustice that they represent. From the blood of the martyrs of these lands of the Americas there is emerging today those liberation movements in the south of North America. In 1992 I was involved with a gathering in of indigenous people in Managua, Nicaragua. That very powerful gathering of indigenous people was at the time of the remembrance of the 500th anniversary of this individual who got lost and wound up on this continent, this man that they call Columbus. He did not discover America; rather he was lost and he wound up over here and we took him in, we saved him. In spite of the friendship we showed to him and the trust we showed him he took some of our people back to Europe. Those people, members of our people, were never seen again because he took them back as slaves.

I have to be very honest with you. I am sharing with you from my heart. I am sharing with you my concerns as a native American spiritual leader. I am sharing and being very honest with you. I hope that you understand where I am coming from, that you feel what I am feeling. Do you feel the hurt that I feel? Do you feel the oppression that I feel? I hope that you do. Because only then can we do things to make things better on this earth. Issues need to be confronted. Spirituality with power, Native Americans have that. We must rise up, and with this resurrection of Jesus Christ comes the resurrection of the indigenous people, yet we invite the conquerors to be transformed.

Today in America, at this Parliament of World's Religions and the gathering, we need to be honest, very, very honest with each other and take the time to listen to one another and only then can we do some good because without that honesty with each other we are limited to nothing more than the niceties that we have shared with each other. For us to accomplish something good on behalf of the human race, those niceties have to become real within society itself. We must live it daily and all people have to live it—we, meaning the spiritual leaders, religious people. Not talk about it only, or preach about it but do it with our actions. With our sincere and utmost actions. So you see without implementation, that gathering in Chicago, that week and weekend, would be no more than just a vacation for all of us. I would hope and pray that gathering is much more than that because God put us together for a purpose, a reason. It was not coincidence that God brought us all together in Chicago. It was to form a new community of God's people. To start afresh, anew, for the next generations to come into this world. I still suffer today. I still feel the hurt of my people. Yet I struggle not only with the indigenous people but also with the people of the world itself, because to me there is no separation. There is no separation, with God.

We are a poor people the Native Americans, we live on reservations. If we were to judge ourselves with Western culture, the materialistic world we live in, we're poor. We live in homes that are old, the plumbing sometimes does not work. We struggle to put food on our tables, because unemployment is so high. We are an oppressed people. As a Roman Catholic, when I see a priest living in modern house, having three square meals a day, a vehicle to drive around, without any worry about paying for anything or supporting any one and then preaching to us about the simplicity of St. Francis, it doesn't make sense. When I see a Roman Catholic bishop drive around in a very expensive, $20-$30,000 vehicle, living in those cathedrals with the marble trimmings, is that what its all about? Is that what Jesus Christ is about? Lets open our eyes and try to see what Jesus Christ sees and what he's feeling.

I'm sorry if I offended you. I have done my part. I have prayed at the beginning of this letter, I have prayed while I was doing it, and I am praying now and I am speaking from my heart. At the Parliament of Worlds Religions I felt that there were many new people within the group that were trying very insensitively to distribute manuscripts of their own teachings to others. I almost felt that they were trying to convert other people, religious people, to their way. I felt pressured by others who came to me and gave me handouts and questioned me about their faith and inviting me to their faith. If it is done in a very sensitive way then it is good but there were times when I felt that I was pushed and pressed, pressured, that they were trying to force their religion on me, on my faith, on my understanding of my culture. We as Native American people are taught to respect other peoples of all colors and to be sensitive with those people. That sensitivity was not shown in Chicago. We must do things right in the correct way. The meaning and purpose was there for us but we need to do it in a correct way.

I'm a little tired now. I hope that if I offended you, that you will forgive me. I did not attack you personally, but rather I brought up issues that needed to be said. There was a person that was given the Nobel Peace Prize in 1992 when I was in Nicaragua. This Native American lady who was given the Peace Prize, Roberta Manchu, the 1992 Nobel Peace prize winner had made a statement that was very powerful for me as a Native American person. She said, "We [native people] have lived a long darkness, a long night, much genocide and many massacres have occurred since 1492 and nevertheless we have always had hope of moving forward. If history were to judge, who stands more in need of evangelization—the missionaries or the indigenous?" When I was in

Nicaragua, I looked at this Mayan saying that was on the wall of a church. It was in Spanish but the translation was next to it in English. This Mayan saying spoke about the people who had come from Europe, the Spanish people, conquering the indigenous people. It said, "You have come to our land, you have taken our fruit, you have cut off the branches, you have burned the tree, but you could not kill the roots." In this way, the indigenous people of this land continue to live to this day.

So I pray with you as a brother. Let us pray that the future generations of this world, as yet unborn, will reap the benefits of what we are attempting to do at this time in our lives; that they will see the difference that we started in the World Parliament of Religions. When we are in the spirit world we can look back and say, "Yes, we truly did our part, with love, and respect and sensitivity. We did it because of our love for Christ, and the Creator of us all, and because of our love for the human race."

I will close for now and say that I love you, I mean that with all sincerity. I say, *ka la chick de awa gah wic,* which means "May you have many good days ahead of you in this world," and in parting *ba gu bia,* which very simply means, "I will see you again, my brother."

* 14

Socially Engaged Christianity: One Example of Contemplation and Action

GEORGE F. CAIRNS

Dear Brothers and Sisters. It is so good to be here with you. It is at times like this that we can have hope for the future. It is at times like this that we can experience our place in the web of all creation. We nurture one another with our shared lives.

I've been asked to speak with you about matters that are delicate and difficult to describe with words. Talking about experiences that are of the heart is both joyful and painful. Words must be chosen with great care. Please excuse my clumsiness. As a follower of Christ, I only hope that what I say may help build bridges and not create brokenness.

God has been so good to me. Through God's grace the kindnesses of people from several traditions have enriched my journey. Sharing the work of healing the earth with my Native American sisters and brothers and celebrating this healing has been a time of powerful spiritual experience. I have seen the eagles come to the ceremonies.

Buddhist and Hindu friends have taught me the importance of silence and how the heart may open in the space between the thoughts that seem ever-present to me. Later, friends in the Christian tradition introduced me to centering prayer, which helped me to deepen my journey and to see the interconnectedness of these practices. Sufi and Jewish friends taught me about the importance of breath and its intimate relationship with spirit. People of color, feminists, and womanist sisters

Presentation at the 1993 Parliament of the World's Religions Plenary Session—The Inner Life and Life in the Community, September 1, 1993.

and brothers have helped to lift the burdens of my youth. Without God's lure through these people, I would not have entered seminary.

The homeless people on the streets of Chicago have also been my teachers. They have helped me detoxify elements of the Christian tradition that have helped me reenter the Church. Tonight I would like to talk with you about a ministry with the so-called outcasts of our society that we at Peoples Church engage in.

First of all let me describe the context that we are working in. Studs Terkel calls the Uptown neighborhood of Chicago "the United Nations of the have-nots." On the lakefront people are living in $1500/month apartments; within two blocks people are sleeping on the streets. It is an extremely diverse community—in the neighborhood high school over sixty languages are spoken. For the past twenty-five years the adjoining neighborhoods of Edgewater and Uptown have been one of the primary places in the city where chronically mentally ill people have been "dumped" by an inadequate community mental health system. There is also a Clan and Nazi party presence there.

I could not do this work alone. There are a number of us who work together in the Urban Mission Program at Peoples Church. Reverend Marguerite Voelkel, the senior pastor at Peoples Church, has been a constant companion on this journey. Other spiritually gifted colleagues in ministry have joined with us. We have many friends who contribute funds and "hands-on" help.

Another source of support and inspiration for me and my wife is a covenantal and ecumenical Christian-base community, Shalom Ministries, that has as its focus cross-cultural ministry. Two Shalom principles that I will share with you tonight grow out of the experience of this community and have been written down by Dr. Claude Marie Barbour, a professor of mission at Catholic Theological Union and at McCormick Theological Seminary, who is the founder of the community. These are not some abstract set of ideas—they provide those of us who try to live them out with both a challenge and a sense of excitement.

We are deeply guided by a theological principle called *Mission-in-Reverse*. I attempt, with my total presence, to be with others as they discover new possibilities and to choose to remove stumbling blocks that prevent them and me from becoming fully human persons. It means that I endeavor, in the most authentic way I can, to encourage the other person to be my teacher.

What this means in practical terms is that I am a presence on the streets and in other public places, always trying to respect the other persons's moves towards engagement or disengagement. This had led in some very interesting directions. First of all, you need to understand that I wear this clerical collar while on the streets—I have come to regard this as becoming a walking Rorschach ink blot test—people project onto me their feelings about the church, and for many poor and marginalized people this has meant the projection of their anger and hurt at what they see that the church, as an instrument of the dominant culture, has done to them. To work on the streets is always walking a razor's edge. The "betweenness" of who I believe myself to be and how others encounter me seems amazingly similar to my experiences in centering prayer. Everyone on the street is expected to have an agenda for manipulation. At first, when I did not act like other "street preachers" people made up stories trying to figure out who I was. For a while the word was out that I was a "Narc," an undercover police officer. This is not a good reputation to have. It can get you hurt. Later, one guy asked me if I used to ride motorcycles and I told him "yes." Although I am a Protestant minister I have become named by my teachers as Father George the biker, hoodlum priest.

I hold up this bag. It is my office. In it I carry Bibles, rosaries, prayer cards, and other items that my friends might find helpful. I have been asked to provide the Christian sacraments and Bible study. I have been asked to provide direction to the nearest synagogue or Catholic Church. I have been asked to help native American friends reconnect with traditional ways. One man asked me to help him find an AA group that would respect his Islamic beliefs. I always try to help the person to the next step. We are in a dance and they have the lead. I have faith that God is providing the tune. I ask myself, "If Jesus were here, what would he do?"

The second Shalom principle is that the place to engage in ministry is at the *grass roots* (or the *base community*). As I have walked the streets of Uptown and talked with the people there, I have coevolved with three of these grassroots communities: people who live in a SRO (Single Room Occupancy) hotel, chronically mentally ill people who live in one of several "halfway" houses, and a board and care hotel where many chronically mentally ill people live. In many ways none of these three communities understood that they constituted a community to begin with. But as we came together and shared our lives, we became a community. In our country—particularly in the inner city—this is an unusually difficult task, given the fragmentation of our society. Simply maintaining a collective memory of ourselves is difficult. Several people in our small communities have died or been killed over a short period of time. New people with new issues are constantly joining with us. Over the past year or two more and more people with AIDS are with us as they become materially impoverished by our health-care system.

I frequently stop for a bit of silence, ask God to help me open my heart, and then move on. The unexpected encounters on the street and in the hotels resonate with these brief periods of prayer to provide grace-filled moments. I know that this spiritual path of deepening relationships is central to many of our traditions. Living the life of service is a transformative path for me as well as for others. In our Christian tradition this path of service sometimes provides moments of agape love—the deepest joining in relationship that I have experienced. At heart, I know that serving another person allows me to catch a glimpse of the face of God—and for me this is a profound means of personal transformation. Our hope is to offer this path so that other persons and ultimately our culture itself may be transformed.

Let me close with a quote from Jeremiah 29:7: "but seek the shalom, the peace and justice of the city, where I have sent you into exile, and pray to the Lord on its behalf, for in its shalom, its peace and justice, you will find your shalom, your peace and justice." Shalom, my friends.

15

The Qur'anic Formula:
To Save Humankind

IRFAN KHAN

> 1. By the (passage of) time. 2. Verily man is in (the way of) loss. 3. However, the case of those is quite different who believe and do righteous deeds and counsel each other unto the Truth (and doing of mutual duties) and counsel each other to be steadfast. (The Qur'an, Surah #103)

1. The *Tawhidic*[1] Concept of One Community[2]:

The Qur'an asserts that before its revelation to Muhammad, prophets and messengers of God were sent throughout the world. They received similar revelation and conveyed to their people(s) essentially the same message that this Divine Book delivers to humankind today. Two questions arise: what was this message and what was the goal toward which the efforts of these prophets were directed? What was the Divine purpose in sending these prophets and messengers? The Qur'an makes it clear that the strivings of these prophets were directed toward turning the divided human family into one community of God's servants, after the primordial *one community* became divided by mutual exploitation and corruptions.[3] The prophets of God were striving against *shirk,* i.e., lordship of other than God. Originally the Lordship of One God made

---

1. *Tawhid* is the principle that One God alone is worthy of worship and there should be no lordship of Man over Man. All are servants *('ibad)* of One God only.
2. For the occurrence of "One Community," i.e., *unmah wahidah* in the Qur'an, please see the following nine explicit references: It is hard to count large number of implicit references of this theme in the Qur'an. 2:213; 5:48; 10:19; 11:118; 16:93; 32:92–93; 23:51–53; 43:8; 43:33.
3. Just consider 2:13, which is further explained in 10:19 and 11:118.

humankind *one community*, but when some human beings virtually became lords of other human beings, division resulted. Human beings becoming fellow servants of God involved sustainability and thereby led to economic and social justice. As co-*ibad* (fellow servants), fellow human beings were mutually *concerned* with each other; they had mutual *respect* and *regard* while *sharing* their resources together.

They knew that when God blessed them with some of His favors in, seemingly, an inproportionate way He was only testing them.[4] He gave to some of His servants more material resources, because He wanted to see how far they could succeed in using these resources for the benefit of those *fellow* human beings (i.e., their co-*ibad*), who were in need of these. The same was true of His other special favors like political power or prestige in society or some other kind of authority or position, or even ability or skill. In fact, whatever God placed at humankind's disposal on earth, human beings are responsible for its proper care and use.[5] Natural resources and human potentialities should not be wasted and proper care should be taken for their best possible development. On the Day of Judgment we will stand before God to account for our performance, e.g., how we used the resources at our disposal and how successfully we did our duty to our fellow beings. The prophets of God encouraged their people to correct themselves (i.e., to repent) and seek His forgiveness. They said to the unjust people that God is very forgiving but if they did not repent His punishment might follow and then no one would be able to help them. He alone is the Creator, Sustainer and Sovereign of all—*everyone else is His servant.*

2. The Epistemic Dimension of *Tawhid*

In the above we outlined the social implications of the *tawhidic* message. But the prophetic movement had another equally important concern. The *tawhidic* mission of the prophets aimed at giving humans their true *freedom* and *dignity*. The prophets and messengers of God liberated human minds and spirits from the slavery of their leaders—including the mental slavery of so-called religious leaders. The prophets emphasized the use of reason; they taught the people to use their intellectual powers and never to follow their tradition or their leaders blindly.[6]

---

4. See how 89:15–16 is being further explained through 90:17–20.

5. Just consider 2:28–29.

6. Please consider mainly 2:165–76; 9:31–33 and 32:9. Also consider very frequent use of *aql* (reason) and *tafakkur* (reflective thinking) in the Qur'an.

Prophets of God were exceptional persons. They had a direct communication with God, receiving Revealed Guidance in Divine Words, and it was in its light that they encountered the prevailing situation. With the cooperation of their believing community they applied the *RGDW* to human life. They explained this Divine Text to their people *in their own words*. In spite of the fact that prophets were human beings, there was a sense in which they were above mistakes. They were working under direct Divine Supervision. Whenever it was needed God would intervene and correct them, so that what they would deliver to their people was free of any error.

There were unjust, cunning leaders who could even misuse peoples' religious concerns and who exploited their illiterate masses that blindly followed them. Contrary to them, the prophets of God helped the people in thinking rationally and in purifying themselves. Of course, the greatest help came from the Divine Text (RGDW) itself. The inspiration that the believers received as they built their direct relationship with the Book was instrumental for their intellectual liberation. As they followed the prophetic guidance reflecting over the Divine Words that he recited to them, they developed in themselves an ability to think clearly with their own minds. Thereafter all their confusions were dispelled.

3. However, in Leading the Evolution of Human Society God Has Been Working on Two Planes.

God, Who was leading a gradual moral and spiritual development of humanity by sending His prophets and messengers according to a systematic plan, was also leading the intellectual evolution of humanity through the scientific and technological progress as well as through the developments in philosophy, literature and fine arts. In a way this was preparing human minds to understand and interpret Revealed Guidance in Divine Words just as it was creating in human beings ability and skill to put into practice the program of action that would emerge from this study.

4. Unlike Angels Men Create Corruption and Cause Bloodshed! What is the Divine Wisdom in Creating Such a Creature?

In the light of the above the story of human creation as related in the Qur'an can be well understood.[7] Human beings are persons. They have

---

7. The story is discussed at length in 2:30–39 and 7:11–35. But it is also mentioned at 15:26–44; 17:61–65; 18:50; 20:115–23; and 38:71–85.

reason, freedom of will, and moral consciousness. Among creations of God, persons have a status that is higher than that of nonpersons. However, an angel is another kind of person. Unlike us, angels never fail to do their duty to God. They never disobey Him—never commit a sin. They do not have those impulses that motivate humans to commit sin. Obviously there is something in the nature of Man due to which all this progress in science and culture became possible—something that earlier, angels and jinn (the two other kinds of persons the Qur'an mentions), could not achieve. Human beings have such potentialities and their desires go on increasing indefinitely. However, it was due to their goodness, but lack of knowledge of Divine Wisdom in the creation of humankind, that angels were so worried about human corruption and bloodshed on earth. They realized their mistake when God showed them the Divine Wisdom in humankind's creation. There was a demonstration to this effect in which Adam also participated.

As God was sending His prophets for the guidance of human beings, He was giving them full freedom to believe or disbelieve. When the prophets of God reminded the people, quite often the unjust people, instead of repenting and correcting their ways, they stood against the prophetic movement that was a threat to their corrupt authority.[8] The Qur'an offers many examples including that of Jesus and Moses. They would even plan to crush their movement, killing the people who stood with Truth and Justice. The Qur'an points out that God could have fulfilled His purpose (i.e., that humans become one family of His servants) without all these hurdles. But this is not what His Wisdom demanded.[9]

In the above situation the Divine Policy was that He would not take immediate action against the unjust people. He rather reminded/ warned them repeatedly and gave them time to correct themselves. Of course, at its right time the Divine Help came to the prophets and their truthful followers. The unjust people were defeated and the followers of the prophets had a free hand to build the *One Community,* becoming servants of their true Lord and establishing a society with sustainability, justice and peace.[10] It was through the two kinds of situations (both

---

8. This was very clearly the case with Jesus and Moses as the Qur'an relates their story see, e.g., 3:51–54 and 40:25–28.

9. See, e.g., 2:253.

10. Concerning the followers of Jesus the Qur'an mentions explicitly that they became victorious with Divine Help (61:14). Earlier there is a promise from God to Jesus that his followers will always have an upper hand over those who disbelieve him. Support of God to followers of Moses and their subsequent victory is mentioned at many places at the Qur'an, e.g., 2:49–50; 10:89–93.

before and after their freedom—whether favorable or unfavorable), which the believers encountered, that their moral and spiritual development took place. During various stages of the *tawhidic* movement, God was with the believers guiding them through their journey, helping their spiritual and moral development and listening to their prayers. At all times He was watching how wisely and sincerely they would act.

From the Divine point of view the significance of this world lies basically in its being a testing place. Immense possibilities of progress and true happiness will open to us in the Hereafter if we have received our forgiveness and guidance earlier. It is only in the present life that humans are blessed with guidance and the process of their purification is initiated. Again, it is in the present life that efforts are made to remind people and make them realize their mistakes.

5. How Are the Hereafter and the Present Phase of Life Mutually Related?

The efforts of those who sincerely believe in the Hereafter in this life are actually directed toward turning this world into a paradise. But these noble souls will attain a paradise for themselves in the Hereafter. Here in this life they will have to pass through various kinds of hardships and test situations.

The belief in the Hereafter helps to ameliorate the life of this world, as if the betterment of this world was the end. One who seeks the rewards of the Hereafter will have an enlightened self-interest. Such persons will virtually try to put into action the Marxist maxim: "from everyone according to one's abilities to everyone according to his/her needs." They will be concerned with their co-*ibad* (fellow human being) and will try to do their best share.

[Listening to the Divine Call (the one in RGDW) virtuous people started arraying behind the prophets of God. These people care for human values and were concerned with human beings. Their strivings were directed toward the creation of an ideal world. According to the Qur'an, a counter movement is also started by Satan. His antihumanistic movement soon gained momentum. Around the other pole gathered persons who had their vested interests with the unjust system. I am referring to those who do not repent in spite of all efforts for this purpose. They became so blind in the pursuit of their selfish desires that they did not see their own long term gains in the Hereafter. They rationalized all their wrongdoings and did not hesitate in acting inhumanely against the prophets and their virtuous followers who were advised to return good for evil. However, the unjust powers even planned the eradication of the movement of the virtuous people.]

6. In the Light of the Above Elaborations the Meanings of the Surah #103 of the Qur'an Should Become Quite Clear.

The first *ayah* (verse) is apparently a swearing refers to the missions of the prophets of God in history whose stories are repeatedly related in the Qur'an.[11] The *ayah* wants the readers to learn a lesson from these stories and do it before it is too late. Time is running out!

Then the lesson is stated in *ayah* two and three. The second *ayah* states that today also some persons were heading toward destruction—the way the addressees of the prophets (who instead of correcting themselves stood against the prophetic movements) were acting.

The third *ayah* says something about the future—as compared to the first and second *ayahs* that were speaking of past and present. All of a sudden the gloomy tone of the earlier part of the *surah* is changed. The *ayah* presents a bright future for humanity. The *ayah*, in fact, answers the questions: how will the purpose of humanity's creation be fulfilled and how will human beings attain *al-Falah* (true happiness/success)? Even a cursory look at the overall wordings of the *surah* will make it clear that the gloomy tone of the earlier part of the *surah* was intended only to be a warning.

The following is a brief explanation of the four-point formula for the success of humankind *(al-Falah)* which the *surah* presents:

(1) The first requirement is *iman* or belief, that is, commitment to *tawhid* which is briefly explained above in section one and two. Thus the *surah* is inviting all human beings to respond positively to the call of the prophets.

[However, mainly to all those who already possess a sense of belonging to the prophets this *surah* would suggest that they must develop true *iman* (belief) within themselves. All the followers of the prophets are called to become *One Community* of God's servants, and salient features of this community are also underlined. My own suggestion is that those who profess to be followers of the prophets of God develop a step by step process to attain this oneness.]

---

11. See, for example, 7:59–171; 10:71–93 and 11:25–110.

(2) The second requirement is *al-salihat* or righteous action.

That is, the commitment or faith must find its expression in practical action. The word that is used for righteous actions is *salihat,* that is, healthy action—those actions that lead to peaceful and healthy development of the human world. This would include proper use and care of the earth's resources.

Now the *surah* adds that though the above two steps are necessarily required they are not sufficient. A mutual support system is also a necessity for the future progress, even continuance, of the *One Community.*

(3) It is required that if some individuals of this community fall short of their duty then others remind them.

(4) Likewise it is required that when some individuals are put to the test (e.g., face hardship in the way of Truth and Justice) then others should give moral support.

Part IV

· · · · · · · · · ·

MODELS FOR
THE FUTURE

✳

* 16

The Parliament Experience: 1993 and Beyond

JIM KENNEY

This article is an account of an idea and an organization in process, in conflict, and in resolution. The Parliament of the World's Religions was a groundbreaking event. The events that preceded it, and those that have followed, have powerful significance for the continuing efforts of the international interreligious community. This article addresses both. The theme that shapes this retrospective is interreligious encounter and action, at the international level. The author's hope is that we all can and will learn from the past.

As the year 1993 approached, the members of the Council for a Parliament of the World's Religions (CPWR), whose lives had come—through the preceding five years—to revolve around the Parliament, lived in hope, exulted in the possibilities, and feared the worst. We had come together in service to a project that seemed to promise so much and seemed so likely to come to nothing. Conventional wisdom suggested that an undertaking of this sort and of this scope could only fail. The religions of the world were simply too diverse, too disparate in their visions of the ultimate, and too various in their address to human possibility and human action.

As the work progressed, an even more challenging question emerged, "What, after all, is religion?" What should be our standard? Which traditions, which organizations, which groups, and which individuals should be included? Which should be excluded? That was our first encounter with the argument about exclusivity. Soon enough, we began to worry about the deeper significance of inclusivity. Had our outreach extended far enough? Would all the world's religious traditions, and all the world's spiritual paths be involved? We understood all too well that that would not be possible. But had we done enough? We were concerned as well about representation, about the democratic process, so often absent from the deliberations of the world's great religious traditions and institutions. Again the questions arose, had we done enough? Who should attend? What kind of Parliament would it be? What kind of gathering ought it to be? Whom should we invite? Who should participate? Who should not? On and on we agonized.

The Council finally arrived at some essential protocols. We would make the effort to reach out as broadly as possible. All who responded to the call for a Parliament of the World's Religions would be invited. With the understanding that all participants must agree to abide by the principles of civilized interreligious dialogue the Parliament would, in effect, welcome all comers.

As the dust of indecision began to settle, we came slowly to understand that the 1993 Parliament would be an unprecedented event. The invitations had finally gone out, the responses had come in, slowly at first, and then in a flood. We had invited and drawn in some of the best and brightest participants in international interreligious dialogue, and some of the most committed, engaged, and creative of the world's "religionists."

They gathered and they celebrated. They came together in extraordinary variety: Buddhists and Christians, Hindus and Jews, Muslims and Zoroastrians, Jains and Sikhs, Indigenous peoples, Pagans, and New Agers. They came together to celebrate a remarkable idea: that somehow there is harmony in our incredible diversity.

The animating theme and abiding message of the 1993 Parliament (and the key to its success) was simply this: that the world's religions should gather to proclaim their respective visions, to acknowledge each other, and to celebrate together the values they share and their common commitment to addressing the critical issues confronting humankind at the threshold of the twenty-first century.

Identity, Dialogue, and the Critical Issues

At least three major themes resonated throughout the planning stages, were addressed in the more than seven hundred presentations that textured the event, and brought together the 8,700 persons who attended. For some, the Parliament meant the vital opportunity to present or re-present the ideals and realities of their traditions to an uninformed, skeptical, and sometimes hostile world. Many of the planet's most ancient and venerable religions are little understood outside their native lands. Many of the newer faiths and spiritual paths are unfamiliar to all but a few. The question of religious identity thus became one of the essential focal points of the process. Who are we? How do we believe and how do we practice? How do we address the transcendent? What is our hope for the future? What message do we have to share with the world?

For others, the lure of the Parliament was the opportunity it offered to listen and to share, to engage in serious dialogue with other faiths, other cultures, and other paths. Dialogue, of course, demands not only understanding but also the willingness to be changed, and a great many of those in attendance brought that kind of openness to Chicago. What do we all have in common? How and why do we differ? How can we move from tolerance to understanding, and from understanding to mutual respect and even admiration? How do we move from admiration to cooperation? How can we help one another to grow? What can our community-based interfaith efforts hope to accomplish? As these questions emerged and developed, the Parliament began to take on a new internal life.

The third, and for some, the most important dynamic that shaped the process was the encounter of religion with the critical issues that confront the human community at the threshold of the twenty-first century. Can religion, can the religions, make a difference? This theme found expression in countless programs and informal conversations throughout the week, but it was most powerfully addressed in a plenary session entitled, "What Shall We Do?" Dr. Gerald O. Barney offered a profoundly sobering and yet surprisingly energizing account of what is sometimes termed "the world problematique." His presentation ended with four questions addressed to the planet's religious and spiritual leaders:

What Are the Traditional Teachings—
and the Range of Other Opinions—within
Your Faith on the Following Issues:

(1) How to meet the legitimate needs of the growing human community without destroying the planet's ability to support the community of all life;

(2) The meaning of "progress" and how it is to be achieved;

(3) A proper relationship with those who differ in race, gender, culture, politics, or faith;

(4) The possibility of criticism, correction, reinterpretation, and even rejection of ancient traditional assumptions and "truth" in light of new understandings of revelation.

These questions, which echoed down the corridors of the Parliament for the remainder of the week, lie at the heart of what may well be the most essential dialogue of our time. That dialogue has only begun. At every level—from conversations in tiny congregations to national and even global initiatives undertaken by interfaith organizations and by the religious communities themselves—these challenges continue to provide a hopeful and creative framework for inquiry and action. And they have informed the continuing work of the CPWR as it has struggled to find a vision.

Beyond 1993

The message and the spirit of the 1993 Parliament were clear enough. But the follow-up wasn't to be so simple. There must somewhere be a gem of folk wisdom that describes what the Council for a Parliament of the World's Religions went through in the year that followed the event. We exulted. We commiserated. Then we began to divide.

Some held that the legacy of the 1993 Parliament demanded a new and concerted effort to bring the world's religions together. Others insisted that the field of interreligious dialogue was already overcrowded. The resources, they argued, are limited, and the role of the CPWR had been played out. How would we proceed?

It was clearly time for a consultation, a time to engage in conversation with some of the major players in the 1993 event. And so, the Council invited a wide spectrum of Parliament participants to come to Chicago to discuss the future of the Parliament, its international role, and its future course.

That consultation, held in September 1994 proved to be a major turning point for the CPWR. Members of the Assembly of Religious and Spiritual Leaders met with other Parliament participants in a two-day meeting. The focus of that meeting was the future of the Council's international effort. It proved to be a diverse and wonderful gathering, with voices raised both in approbation and in critique. Finally, a common theme emerged. The CPWR should craft an international initiative. The 1993 Parliament had had, at the very least, a spirit. Somehow, that spirit should not die. Somehow, it should yield up a new legacy of interreligious cooperation and, above all, action.

The consultation urged that a special meeting be held, bringing together a small group of representatives of the 1993 Assembly of Religious and Spiritual Leaders and others. This task force should be challenged to craft a truly "international" and "interreligious" initiative. The CPWR should present a new and concrete plan to make the world a better place.

That meeting took place in Chicago in November 1994. The group that gathered included some key members of the 1993 Assembly, as well as representatives of the Chicago interreligious community. What follows is a summary of the action plan that emerged from their discussions as well as an outline of the program that the CPWR's International Initiative has put into place for the further design and implementation of that plan.

In the next several years, there will be no shortage of such action plans. The current volume chronicles the progress of one effort to make a difference in the world, and this article describes a single course of inquiry, debate, and action. Those who are committed to the idea that religion, so often "the source of the problem," can somehow become a wellspring of solutions might well give some consideration to the ideas and structures that follow.

The International Initiative

The CPWR has crafted a three-fold International Initiative. The plan is complex and, at the same time, wonderfully simple. It may or may not come to fruition, but it represents a new beginning. In a sense, this plan does not belong in this volume. It's simply to new and too untested. In another sense, however, it gives this volume its heart and its hope.

Whatever happens with the International Initiative of the CPWR, it should be and will be remembered as one of the first and finest of the new efforts essayed at the threshold of the twenty-first century. The relation between religion, spirituality, and the "critical issues" is the animating theme of the work of the Council. Readers should consider what follows as an initial attempt to give shape and focus to a work in which we should all be involved.

The International Initiative
Has Three Essential Components:

1. Parliaments of the World's Religions

The aim of the CPWR is not to create permanent institutions, but rather to nurture and to spread the spirit of the 1993 event in a movement that will encourage local regions to develop interreligious understanding and collaboration. The CPWR is committed to furthering the understanding of religion as a major resource in the address to the problems that now confront the human community. The CPWR also recognizes the need for and is committed to furthering the development of personal spiritual growth. To this end:

- The CPWR will facilitate the convening of a new Parliament of the World's Religions, every five years, each in an appropriate site, around the world.

- The CPWR will convene a new Assembly of Religious and Spiritual Leaders—two to three years before, as well as during—each Parliament.

2. Toward a Global Ethic

At the 1993 Parliament, the Assembly of Religious and Spiritual Leaders gave overwhelming assent to a groundbreaking document, *Toward a Global Ethic: An Initial Declaration*. The CPWR is committed to further dissemination, discussion, and critique of that document, as a basis for increasing mutual understanding of the shared moral ground of the world's religious and spiritual communities, and cooperation for the common good. No "final" version of the document can or should be produced. Rather, the process will continue to move "toward a global ethic."

- The CPWR will disseminate the document as widely as possible, encouraging discussion and critique.

- The Council will work to establish cooperative working relationships with international interreligious groups now engaged in the effort to promote understanding of the ethical "common ground" of the world's religions.

- The CPWR will work to link all discussions emerging from consideration of the document to the ongoing program for the creation of Periodic Parliaments.

3. Projects 2000

The heart of the International Initiative's "Projects 2000" plan is cooperation with another international organization. Dr. Gerald Barney set the tone for the 1993 Parliament's focus on the critical issues that now confront the human community. The International Initiative has made the commitment to full cooperation with Dr. Barney and the Millennium Institute of Washington, D.C. in focusing worldwide attention on the "millennial moment (1999–2001) as a unique opportunity for inspiring individuals, groups, nations, and religious communities to make strategic "millennial threshold" gifts that will make a long-term difference to the planetary community.

Herein lies a major complication for any international organization wishing to focus on the coming millennium. The year 2000 is, after all, a Christian date, commemorating an event celebrated only by Christians. How can the Millennium Institute and the CPWR call on the nations and the religions of the world to offer "gifts" in response to a Christian event?

The essence, perhaps, of interreligious "coming together" lies in recognition of what all religions and all people have in common. The year 2000 represents a major turning of a calendar arguably shared by most of the peoples of the world. The CPWR and the Millennium Institute have collaborated in the effort to ascertain whether or not the world's cultures will come together in acknowledgment of the coming millennium. The clear answer is "yes."

In the year 2000, through the efforts of Dr. Barney and the Millennium Institute, nations and religions of the world will gather at Thingvellír, Iceland, to celebrate a new vision of humankind and a new understanding of humanness. They will gather to announce their gifts to the world community. In 2000, the vision of the Millennium Institute and the vision of the International Initiative of the CPWR may just coalesce in a new celebration of the future of the planetary community.

The Millennium Institute is dedicated to securing the commitment of the nations of the world to making real gifts to a world in travail.

Projects 2000 represents the commitment of CPWR to encouraging and facilitating equivalent gifts by the world's religions and religious communities.

- The CPWR will invite the world's religious communities (from worldwide organizations to local congregations) to create their own projects in service to the world. Such projects might include (but not be limited to): compilation of the traditions "best" and "most relevant" teachings with regard to social service and the future of the planetary community; conflict resolution; education; service to women, children, and the poor; hunger relief; disease prevention; ecological preservation; promotion of ethics and social justice; and spiritual renewal.

- The CPWR will work with the Millennium Institute to facilitate the participation of religious leaders, religious communities, and other groups in the special Global Event—to be held at Thingvellír, Iceland, in the year 2000—at which they will join with heads of state to announce their contributions to a world in travail.

It's rare indeed that persons living in an age in which a major paradigm shift occurs have the opportunity to observe, to comment, and to critique that shift. The Parliament endeavor is animated by and itself will help to animate that shift. The effort suggests and demands a significant transformation of our worldview, and, so, it invites critique and comment. This article is a simple offering. It's a description of the efforts of a tiny group dedicated to making a big difference. By the time this article and its companion articles reach you, much will have happened. But your reactions will always matter. We live in a time of change, an age of the change of models, and the change of standards. Our choices, however, shape the world. We can learn from what has gone before. We can be energized by what is taking form. We can find hope in the promise of a past reappraised and a future in transformation.

17

Toward a Global Ethic:
An Initial Declaration:
Its Making and Its Future

THOMAS A. BAIMA

The purpose here is to examine, affirm and, where necessary, to challenge the document now known as *Toward a Global Ethic: An Initial Declaration,* (see Appendix A) so that we can, as the title implies, move toward an ethical formulation that is truly global. For us to do that, we will need to know something of the textual history of these documents and the process that produced them. What is *Toward a Global Ethic: An Initial Declaration* and how shall we use it?

The material begins with Dr. Hans Küng and his recent writings about ethics in the global community. Dr. Kung has prepared a presentation that he gave an UNESCO February 7 to 10, 1989, which in some sense could be called the predecessor document of *Toward a Global Ethic: An Initial Declaration.* The following month, on March 10, he delivered a series of lectures at the University of Chicago. At that meeting he suggested that the matter of ethics should be taken up by the 1993 Parliament of the World's Religions when it convened in Chicago. It was April 28, 1989, when Ronald Kidd, then the administrator for the Council of a Parliament of the World's Religions, issued an invitation to Dr. Küng to collaborate with the Council on the development of an ethics document. Dr. Küng himself had continued to write on the subject, publishing a major piece in April 1990, in *Concilium* and in early 1991 publishing his book, *Global Responsibility,* in English. On February 27, 1992, Dr. Daniel Gómez-Ibáñez, the Executive Director of the

---

Presented at the Global Ethics Seminar, on September 14, 1995, at the Catholic Theological Union, Chicago.

Council, spoke with Dr. Küng and together they reached an agreement that Dr. Küng would produce the basic paper that the Parliament would use in the development of A *Global Ethic*.

It was at this point also that a basic difference of opinion surfaced between the expectations that the Council had and in those that Dr. Küng had. The Council maintained that such an ethical statement needed to be brief and powerful. The original suggestion was to keep it to one page in length so that its precepts could actually be memorized as people sought to incorporate them into their daily living. Dr. Küng disagreed and maintained that thoroughness was the primary value, that the declaration needed to have a certain depth so that it would not be dismissed. This disagreement was never resolved. But rather than an either/or solution, the Council chose to adopt a both/and solution.

At that point, Dr. Küng's insistence on a longer text began what I would call the Tubingen dialogues. He consulted with a number of his colleagues to compose the principles by which one would address this subject. All were scholars in the field of religion, working in academic settings. He consulted with persons who are outstanding in their fields, some of the best-known scholars in history and literature of religion and theology. In the summer of 1992, he devoted his summer teaching seminars to the question of A *Global Ethic* and those seminars wrote and refined what would come to be the first draft of the document. A nomenclature problem arrives here as we try to follow the textual development. Dr. Küng throughout his work refers to the long document by the title, The Declaration, whereas the Council of a Parliament of the World's Religions had reserved that title for the short text. I will therefore adopt the terms "long text" for what Dr. Küng wrote and "short text" for what I wrote.

On July 14, 1992, he communicated with a number of correspondent scholars throughout the world who offered critiques for the development of this first text. It was then on October 23, 1992, that the second draft of the long text was transmitted to Dr. Daniel Gómez-Ibáñez and the Council for a Parliament of the World's Religions. The plan at that point was to forward the long text to religious leaders outside the academic community to broaden the base of interreligious dialogue that was producing this document. The Council for a Parliament of the World's Religions' Planning Committee, which had the responsibility of overseeing the preparation for the Assembly of Religious and Spiritual Leaders, chaired by Ms. Helen Spector, communicated the second draft to members of The Council for a Parliament of the World's Religions' Research Committee and the individual host committees who forwarded it to their own international scholars and leaders in their religious traditions. Over a hundred persons were involved in this consultation. Many communicated their comments about the text to the planning committee. Several of the respondents introduced proposals for additions of new sections to the text and even of new concepts. The long text was criticized as too Western and too academic in nature and a call was made for the inclusion of Asian religious thought structures and manners of presentation.

It was on the basis of this consultation that the planning committee considered what to do next. We were confronted with a document that, in no way, met our original goal of a short, powerful statement that could be read aloud and easily reported to the secular media. On the other hand, we were also presented with a work of considerable depth, of fine scholarship that had emerged out of an academic conversation with some of the finest professors of religion that could be assembled. The matter was referred to the Council for a Parliament of the World's Religions' Public Information Committee who, with the assistance of our public relations consultants, Hill and Knowlton, reached the following recommendation: accept both the Council's goals and Dr. Küng's goals as separate, parallel endeavors. Revise the long text for its own sake and develop a short text here in Chicago. While this conversation was going on in PIC, the Research Committee was conducting its own review of the long text. Dr. Jeffrey Carlson led a group of forty scholars and professors from universities and seminaries in Chicago in this review. They agreed with the text's basic form and content and offered some editorial suggestions on how to sharpen some of its language for a Chicago audience.

In the meantime the Planning Committee received the recommendation of PIC on the development of a short text and set about with the drafting. Four proposals were returned to the Planning Committee at this point. The first came from the Islamic Host Group. The second was from Rabbi Herman Schaalman. The third I wrote and the fourth came from the Brahma Kumaris. Both the Muslim and Rabbi Schaalman's text were drawn directly from the Küng document in a summary fashion. The Brahma Kumaris's text was, in fact, an already published document from an earlier study of global cooperation that the Brahma Kumaris World Spiritual University had undertaken. My text introduced the new development of naming the pains and agonies the world was experiencing, which called forth the need for the global ethic. It was organized in the form of denouncing vice and extolling virtues. In that early form, it concluded with the four ethical norms identified by Dr. Küng in his long text.

There was great discussion about these texts in the Planning Committee. Because the Brahma Kumaris's text had already been published elsewhere, it was decided that we must set that aside. Whatever document was issued by the Parliament had to be its own creation. This left the committee with the decision on whether the short text should summarize the Küng document or go beyond it. The committee chose to do the latter and my text was selected as the basis then for an actual drafting effort. Comparison with the Brahma Kumaris's text, however, had exposed the problem of Western versus Eastern language. The four universal precepts in Dr. Küng's text, in fact, are four of the Ten Commandments. Some had the feeling that our declaration would then appear to be an abbreviation of Western morality that would play very negatively in the U.S. press. We envisioned headlines like "God gives ten commandments, Parliament accepts four, rejects six."

It was Pastor Dirk Ficca who suggested that the style of presentation found in the Brahma Kumaris's text, which was a listing of precepts such as one would find where a person takes on a precept as a personal responsibility in their life, might be a moral helpful way of presenting the ideas we were struggling with. To this end, I was charged with doing the first draft of the short text. I returned to Küng's long text and began looking for preceptorial statements. I also worked, in a large message, from the analysis that was done by Brahma Kumaris's Brother Jagdish Chandar Hsassija, who had identified in Küng's long text, eighteen ethical norms. I reviewed and reorganized the material, and then presented it to the planning committee as a two-page declaration. This was written in the form of the eighteen precepts of a global ethic. Actually through seven drafts the numbers of precepts fluctuated between seventeen and twenty and we rewrote and recombined sentences.

By this time there was agreement on the basic content of this declaration. We were, however, presented with another media problem. If we presented the short text in the form of a list, people would be inclined to check off the ones they agreed with and focus on the ones that they might have worded differently. The list seemed to invite too much editing on the first reading. At this point Dr. Daniel Gómez-Ibáñez volunteered to rewrite my text in prose fashion, much after the fashion in which UN declarations are written. In the eighth draft of the short text, we presented two alterative endings of the document to the Planning Committee. One was the precept text that I had written. The other was a text in which Dr. Gómez-Ibáñez had rewritten the list of seventeen precepts into a prose form with some slight rearrangement of the order. It was at that point that he added a sentence, "We are interdependent," which had been implicit in the precepts, but which brought clear enunciation to this concept. Having thus articulated the concept of interdependence, he completely rewrote the precepts to expose this second foundation. This came to be the eighth draft. Since the purpose was media accessibility, upon the review of the two options, the Planning Committee chose to use the prose text as the basic document, since it was judged that this would be the most acceptable to the media.

As you can imagine, that was the point when the real "nitpicking" began. Dr. Gómez-Ibáñez, Ms. Yael Wurmfeld and I then cloistered ourselves in several long meetings and line by line went over revising the short text. We were then confronted with what to call it. CPWR felt very strongly that it had to be The Declaration so that the media would give it the proper attention. We therefore named our short Text *The Declaration of a Global Ethic,* and renamed Dr. Küng's text *Commentary on The Declaration of a Global Ethic.* With the comments of Dr. Carlson's group completed, we packaged all of this material up and forward it to Dr. Küng on July 17, 1993.

Dr. Küng found the suggestions and improvements that CPWR called for in his long text to be pleasantly positive. He set about reworking the entire document to include these suggestions and he also integrated language from our short text into his final draft. Dr. Küng was persuaded, in principle, that we needed a media piece. However, he rejected the condemnations in our short text. He wrote his own summary document, which he called *An Appeal for a Global Ethic* with the stated goal to invite the people to read the longer text. It was a very pleasing document and introduced the style of affirmation and declaration as its outline, "We affirm, We declare." He completed his work on the final draft and forwarded it to the Parliament along with his appeal.

The planning committee was very impressed with his revision of the long text. We were not, however impressed with *An Appeal.* We again showed it to the Public Information Committee, which unanimously concluded that it would not make it into the American media. Dr. Küng had criticized our naming the short text *The Declaration* and his long text *The Commentary* because that would suggest that the longer text derived from the first, which was not the case; in fact exactly the opposite was true. Again, the PIC offered us what we considered to be a win/win solution. We would retain our short text under the name of *The Declaration of a Global Ethic* and would retitle Küng's long text *The Principles of a Global Ethic,* which would then suggest that *The Principles'* text was foundational and that *The Declaration* was drawn from it.

Daniel Gómez-Ibáñez and I then reedited the short text to include the very helpful language of affirmation and declaration from Dr.

Küng's short *Appeal*. With these final revisions to the short text and with some style changes to the English translation of the long text, we published *A Global Ethic*, which contained two documents within it, *The Declaration* and *The Principles*.

Now that we had the final draft, the plan had been to send it out for prior endorsement by Presidents and prominent spiritual and religious leaders who would attend the Assembly. Unfortunately, the clock had run out and this was not possible. The original hope was to bring the document already signed into the Assembly where it could be discussed and provoke actual dialogue around the tables without the burden of editing the text, but just the opportunity to encounter one another face-to-face around these provocative issues. The closing ceremony would then have included a ceremonial signing of the document, but by people who would have already given their assent before coming to the Parliament.

Sadly, time did not permit us to reach that agreement before the Parliament and so a portion of the Assembly was, in a certain sense, a failure. The meeting degenerated into arguing over sentence structure and where pronouns were. The document was leaked to the press prematurely, which damaged some of the public relations effect. Because we lack the prior endorsements, we were left working in an Assembly that had no rules of order capable of managing a discussion around amendment. At the end, we could agree on only one amendment—to change the title in such away it would indicate the provisionalness of the document. This was done and the document was amended to read *Toward a Global Ethic: An Initial Declaration*.

And that brings us back to our task here.

A first step was taken last year at the World Mission Institute where critical analyses of the document were offered. Unfortunately, the expected recording of this session failed for technical reasons. But there was general agreement that two conversations need to proceed.

First, there are questions of methodology. Dr. Aziza Alhibri stated this well when she said, "This is a document produced in the West, using Western academic categories, through a Western committee process." While this has value, it would be good to see what additional methodologies and processes could contribute to this dialogue. Clearly, we in the West cannot organize or manage this conversation. But we can call for it to take place.

But there is a second set of issues that require attention. These are the issues of content. *A Global Ethic* identified about eighteen points of ethical agreement. We need to test those points to find the actual depth and breadth of agreement.

For example: Do we agree with the precept of nonviolence or is it really agreement on nonaggression? When we say, "Thou shalt not kill," what are the exceptions—Criminals, unjust aggressors, the mental defective at the end of life, the developing child? What does this precept mean to Christians, Jains, Hindus, Muslims or Buddhists?

This second conversation requires a faithfulness in reporting the traditional teaching and contemporary interpretation so that we can adequately compare meanings. This must be done by the religions themselves, not by others describing them.

This Global Ethic Seminar sponsored by the Center for Global Missions is one place where this second discussion of content will take place. In doing so, you provide a valuable next step in the development of an ethical consensus that is truly global.

It may take years, but I have a dream for this process. I really believe that if we can identify the depth and breadth of convergence that already exists in ethics, we will discover the basis for promoting the common good in a pluralistic society. Clearly unlimited individualism or the groupism of political correctness is not the path. Mutual, agreed upon parameters of respect will only come from the religions. This seminar is a step in that direction. As we say in my own Catholic Christian tradition, may God who has begun this good work bring it to completion.

18

The Peace Council:
An Initiative Inspired
by the Parliament

DANIEL GÓMEZ-IBÁÑEZ

The peoples of the earth desperately need to rediscover a way of living based on genuine understanding and a wholehearted acceptance of the interdependence of all life and our universal responsibility for the well-being of everyone. These two insights of interdependence and universal responsibility themselves rest on the deeper perception of community as the ultimate expression of reality and how religions, cultures, nations, and groups should live and interact in a creative way. This book has rightly identified its importance, recognizing its explicit historical emergence at the Parliament. These transformative insights are the shared legacy of the great-faith traditions. They must now guide the lives of individuals, communities, organizations, corporations, nations, and other groups.

At the historic Parliament hundreds of religious and spiritual leaders from around the globe demonstrated the active role of faith in guiding people to live responsibly and sustainably together on Earth. They discussed the critical issues of peace and survival, and endorsed the common principles contained in *Toward a Global Ethic*. They were not afraid to acknowledge the shortcomings, misuses, and abuses of religion in the past, and they urgently called for a continuing effort to work together. They wished to emphasize and show that service grounded in wisdom and compassion can direct the world through the torrents of ignorance and hatred, leading it into the safe harbor of social, economic, and environmental sanity. We propose the Peace Council as an answer to the many calls at the Parliament for an organization or network concerned with the critical issues of the twenty-first century. This organization is firmly committed to effective action.

The Nature of the Peace Council

The Peace Council's membership is comprised of twenty-five spiritual leaders, men and women who live the ways of peace. Their lives embody the qualities of kindness, simplicity, generosity, understanding, and compassion. They are grounded in the spiritual wisdom of their traditions. At the same time they are aware of, and participate fully in, the contemporary world. Each of these leaders has found ways to serve the needs of others in his or her own community.

They are persons of great moral standing in their respective communities and beyond. All of them are actively engaged in social action, often evidencing exceptional courage, endurance, and strength. They are respected for what they do, stand for, and how they live, not because they hold high offices, although some serve in that way.

These spiritual leaders are convinced with us that what they can accomplish together is considerable. They are committed to sharing their knowledge, networks, and influence. Together they are willing to speak and act collectively with vigor and clarity on the critical issues that transcend cultural and religious boundaries. More importantly, they wish to exemplify practical ways of living harmoniously together in the larger understanding of community: the Earth Community.

We believe this Peace Council will be effective because it will meet and act in a spirit of love and mutual acceptance. The Council's programs are based on the principles of interdependence and universal responsibility. Its activities are rooted in respect for diversity and a commitment to better mutual understanding, to socially beneficial, peace-fostering, and Earth-friendly ways of life. The Peace Council incarnates and practices the principles of the Parliament's Global Ethic.

Mission and Goals

Our hope, in the years ahead, is that the Peace Council will enflesh "peace" as a way of living together. Peacefulness or peacemaking, in this view, includes a commitment to social, economic, and environmental justice with its requisite responsibility.

Our goals include:

(1) To promote peaceful, ethical and sustainable living.
(2) To increase awareness of the interdependence of all life, and to promote the values of universal responsibility.
(3) To influence attitudes, values and behavior on a broad scale.

(4) To provide a voice of conscience for the planet, emphasizing the links between peace and social, economic, and ecological responsibility, seeing these as part of the more comprehensive scope of universal responsibility.

(5) To bring an end to religiously justified conflict and warfare.

(6) To increase understanding, respect, and cooperation between people who differ in religion, culture, nationality, race, or economic status.

(7) To provide a framework for spiritual leaders to work together.

Methods, Activities, and Initiatives

The Council hopes to accomplish these purposes through practical actions and inspiring leadership. Effective public education and media relations will be an important component of the Council's work. Public interest in the Council's activities will be enhanced by the stature of its members and by the perceived fact that they are indeed working together.

The Peace Council is involved in the following activities:

A Forum for Spiritual Leaders
- Periodic meetings at which members of the Peace Council can work together, get to know one another as friends and colleagues, and establish networks and initiatives.

A Voice for Peace
- Reevaluation of religious teachings or interpretations that appear to condone or inspire mistrust or hatred. Rejection of violent extremism and the misuse of sacred teachings.
- Clear statements on the importance of interfaith harmony and acceptance.

Peacemaking
- Dramatic and well-publicized instances of dialogue and collaboration between members of different religious communities.
- Repeated, insistent, and collective calls for peace, for economic and social justice, and for wise environmental stewardship. These include inspiring and symbolic actions by leaders of religious communities whose members are in conflict.
- Where conflicts are in progress, close cooperation with local groups to encourage religious leaders (whose followers are justifying their

violence on religious grounds) to meet, to engage in dialogue, and to call on their followers to renounce violence.

- Interfaith "pilgrimages" or missions of spiritual leaders to places or regions in need, in close cooperation with local groups in those places.
- Collaboration in conflict mediation—making the "good offices" of religion available to existing international (intergovernmental) organizations and quasi-public conflict mediation groups.
- Private mediation, where practicable, between groups in conflict.
- Public or private search for workable alternatives to conflict.
- Quiet diplomacy, including confidential (nonpublicized) message carrying between the leaders of warring factions (or between parties that find themselves close to blows) who are willing to participate in this quiet diplomatic activity.

Peace Yearbook
- We propose that the Peace Council publish a *Peace Yearbook* that would include an audit of conflicts and potential conflicts—not only wars but also other threats to the community of living beings—and a record of peace initiatives. It would profile winners of international peace awards, such as the Nobel Peace Prize, the Friedenprieis des Deutschen Buchhandels, the Right Livelihood Award, the Matsunaga Institute of Peace Award, the Niwano Peace Prize, the UNESCO Prize for Peace Education, the Wateler Vredesprijs, and others. It should also include recommendations on future initiatives and essays on integrated approaches to sustainable and ethical living.

Dialogues on Critical Issues
- Promotion of interfaith dialogue on the critical issues of living together in the world.
- Encouragement of groups organizing grassroots dialogues on peaceful living.
- Promotion by individual Council members of dialogue within their own religious communities—intrafaith dialogue—on the critical issues, and dialogue between religion and science, government, business, and other professions.

The Peace Council is in its infancy, and there will be many challenges ahead, but we feel a sense of genuine confidence that if we harness the spirit of the Parliament that gave birth to the Council we will succeed in creating a new chapter in humankind's history, one in which war, injustice, disease and hunger are no more, and universal community is finally realized.

19

The Chicago Model

DIRK FICCA

In 1893 the whole world came to Chicago for the World's Columbia Exposition. In conjunction with the Exposition, a World's Parliament of Religions was held, the first public meeting ever of representatives of the world's religions. Men and women from forty-one religions and denominations met together, making the birth of interreligious dialogue in the modern world.

One hundred years later, that historic event was commemorated with the 1993 Parliament of the World's Religions, also held in Chicago. Over 7,000 religious and spiritual leaders and others gathered to address the role of religion and spirituality in resolving the critical issues facing humankind as we move into the next century.

Beyond hosting the 1993 event, one intent of its organizing body, the Council for a Parliament of the World's Religions (CPWR), was to use the event as a catalyst to promote greater interreligious dialogue and cooperation locally. For today, the whole world lives in metropolitan Chicago. Today in metropolitan Chicago, there are more Buddhists (120,000) than Episcopalians (50,000), more Muslims (300,000) than Jews (260,000). Among the Christian community there are distinctions between Protestants (1,300,000), Roman Catholics (2,300,000) and Orthodox (250,000), further differentiated by race and ethnicity. A large population of Hindus (80,000) worships at eighteen temples, while Zoroastrians (500) gather at their single center. There are also active and practicing communities of Bahà'ì's (2,000), Sikhs (2,500), Jains (1,000), Native Americans (15,000), and Unitarian Universalists (5,000), as well as persons of indigenous religions, and a host of ecumenical, interfaith and interreligious, and nonsectarian, organizations.

Yet, in spite of this incredible diversity, Chicago is one of the only major metropolitan communities in North America without an ongoing, metropolitanwide interreligious network or forum to help people of diverse traditions to talk and work together. So, following the 1993 Parliament, CPWR launched the Metropolitan Chicago Interreligious Initiative (MCII) in an effort to organize such a locally based interreligious infrastructure. Still in its initial phases, the MCII is in the process of demonstrating the possibilities for dialogue and cooperation through interreligious forums, encounters, and pilot project. A series of hundreds of interviews with key religious and spiritual leaders from around the metropolitan community has resulted in a framework for encouraging dialogue and cooperation is emerging.

Though it may sound like splitting hairs or merely semantics, the first key to this framework that has been discovered is to be seeking after religious and spiritual *harmony, not unity.*

The "melting pot" approach to religious and spiritual diversity—and racial and cultural diversity for that matter—is no longer a viable vision. The attempt to "boil everyone down" to their common denominators ultimately means everyone compromises and no one is satisfied. This is especially true of religion and spirituality, where the distinctness and uniqueness of many, if not most, traditions precludes "unity" as an option.

Harmony is a different matter. Harmony has to do with respectful, even appreciative and working relationships between religious and spiritual communities *as they are,* with each community freely maintaining their own integrity and particularity. No one has to sacrifice their identity in order to talk and work with others.

The second key that has been discovered is that a dialogue and cooperation work best on the basis of *convergence, rather than consensus.*

Parallel to the problem of achieving unity, very few religious and spiritual communities can come to consensus on a religious, moral, ethical, or social agenda. This is a problem not only with relations *between* diverse religious and spiritual traditions, but nearly as often with relations between various constituent groups or movements *within* a particular tradition.

But there are *points* of convergence, of shared interest or self-interest, of common purpose or cause, that can be the basis for dialogue and cooperation, without necessarily agreeing at most or all other points. From the interview process, seven points of convergence spanning the diversity of religion and spirituality found in metropolitan Chicago have surfaced.

- respect for *religious and spiritual identity;*
- awareness and appreciation of *religious and spiritual diversity;*

- *interreligious dialogue* for the purpose of mutual understanding and personal growth;
- rooted in faith and spirituality, collaborative *service* in response to pressing human needs;
- *community-capacity building* through advocacy, community development and public policy;
- *conflict resolution* between religious and spiritual communities or other types of communities, especially when rooted in racism or religious intolerance;
- bringing the *voice of religion and spirituality* to bear on matters of common social, moral, ethical and civic concern.

The significance of these two lessons cannot be underestimated. Notions of unity and consensus as the goals would have been major impediments to interreligious relations in metropolitan Chicago. Feedback from key religious and spiritual leaders is that an approach emphasizing harmony and convergence are the keys to opening the door to greater interreligious dialogue and cooperation.

From this follows the third lesson, that the MCII will seek to foster greater interreligious dialogue and cooperation as a *facilitator, not as a membership organization*. For nearly every community has a problem joining an interreligious organization with "everyone else religious and spiritual" in the metropolitan community. In all probability, such an organization would eventually either have to cater to the established, mainline religious and spiritual communities, or end up being constituted primarily by the smaller communities who now find themselves on the fringe.

In a facilitator model, on the other hand, an individual religious or spiritual community does not have to join anything, with anyone. This approach emphasizes relationships and collaborative projects where each community can choose with what other communities it wants to be in dialogue, and with what other communities it wants to collaborate.

All of this fits with the sense of mission for the MCII that has also emerged from this overall process:

- To *deepen respect for and strengthen* the life and vitality of individual religious and spiritual community;
- To *build positive relationships* between diverse religious and spiritual communities;
- To empower the collective religious and spiritual community in *bringing the force for good* found within religion and spirituality

to bear on the challenges and opportunities of the metropolitan community.

This mission puts the MCII in a position to relate to each and every religious and spiritual community at their level of comfort and interest, while promoting the positive and potentially transformative impact of the collective religious and spiritual community on the quality of life of the broader metropolitan community. If this approach succeeds, metropolitan Chicago won't have to wait another one hundred years to celebrate and foster the hope, spirit, and contribution that is made possible by interreligious dialogue and cooperation.

20

Religions on the Eve of the Twenty-First Century

EWERT COUSINS

All the religions—and all the peoples of the world—are undergoing the most radical, far-reaching, and challenging transformation in history. The stakes are high: the very survival of life on our planet—either chaos and destruction, or creative transformation and the birth of a new consciousness. Forces, which have been at work for centuries, have in our day reached a crescendo that has the power to draw the human race into a global network and the religions of the world into a global spiritual community.

The forces that are bringing about our present transformation have been global from the start. It is imperative, then, that we make an attempt to see our history as a global history. In order to do this, we must disengage ourselves from any particular culture or religion, situating ourselves at a viewing point from which we can see clearly both cultures and religions in a universal perspective. In doing this we will be like the astronauts who traveled into outer space and looked back on the earth. What they saw overwhelmed them! For the first time in history, humans actually saw the earth as a whole. They saw the earth's clouds, oceans, and continents, it is true, but not as discrete elements; nor did they behold merely a limited horizon as when standing on the earth's surface. Rather they saw the earth as an interrelated, organic whole—a single globe of remarkable beauty and unity. It is striking that

This article contains the substance of the talk given by the author at the Parliament of the World's Religions, September , 1993. Major portions of this article have appeared in his book *Christ of the 21st Century*(see note 3 below) and in his article "Judaism-Christianity-Islam: Facing Modernity Together," *Journal of Ecumenical Studies*, 30:3–4 (Summer-Fall, 1993), 417–26.

at the very moment in history when culture is becoming globalized, we have obtained our first sense impression of the earth as a single globe. This image of the beautiful blue globe, shining against the back background of the universe, moving in its orbit in space can concretely symbolize the emergence of global consciousness on the eve of the twenty-first century.

The Axial Period

From our astronaut's position, let us look back in history to another period when the world religions were fundamentally shaped into their present form. If we look at the earth from our distant vantage point during the first millennium B.C.E., we would observe a remarkable phenomenon. From the period between 800–200 B.C.E., peaking about 500 B.C.E., a striking transformation of consciousness occurred around the earth in three geographic regions, apparently without the influence of one on the other. If we look at China, we will see two great teachers, Lao-tze and Confucius, from whose wisdom emerged the schools of Chinese philosophy. In India the cosmic, ritualistic Hinduism of the Vedas was being transformed by the Upanishads, while the Buddha and Mahavira ushered in two new religious traditions. If we turn our gaze farther west, we observe a similar development in the eastern Mediterranean region. In Israel the Jewish prophets—Elijah, Isaiah, and Jeremiah—called forth from their people a new moral awareness. In Greece Western philosophy was born. The pre-Socratic cosmologists sought a rational explanation for the universe, while Socrates awakened the moral consciousness of the Athenians. Plato and Aristotle then developed metaphysical systems.

It was Karl Jaspers, the German philosopher, who forty-six years ago pointed out the significance of this phenomenon in his book *The Origin and Goal of History*.[1] He called this period from 800–200 B.C.E. the Axial Period because "it gave birth to everything which, since then, man has been able to be." It is here in this period "that we meet with the most deepcut dividing line in history. Man, as we know him today, came into being. For short, we may style this the 'Axial Period.'"[2] Although the leaders who effected this change were philosophers and

---

1. Karl Jaspers, *Vom Ursprung udn Ziel der Geschichte* (Zurich: Artemis, 1949), pp. 19–43.
2. Ibid., p. 19; trans. Michael Bullock, *The Origin and Goal of History* (New Haven: Yale University Press, 1953), p. 1. For the ongoing academic discussion of Jaspers' position on the Axial Period, see *Wisdom, Revelation, and Doubt: Perspectives on the First Millennium B.C., Daedalus* (Spring, 1975); and *The Origins and Diversity of Axial Age Civilizations*, ed. S. N. Eisenstadt (New York: State University of New York Press, 1989).

religious teachers, the change was so radical that it affected all aspects of culture, for it transformed consciousness itself. It was within the horizons of this form of consciousness that the great civilizations of Asia, the Middle East, and Europe developed. Although within these horizons many developments occurred through the subsequent centuries, the horizons themselves did not change. It was this form of consciousness that was spread to other regions through migration and explorations, thus becoming the dominant, though not exclusive, form of consciousness in the world. To this day, whether we have been born and raised in the culture of China, India, Europe, or the Americas, we bear the structure of consciousness that was shaped in this Axial Period.

What is this structure of consciousness and how does it differ from pre-Axial consciousness? Prior to the Axial Period the dominant form of consciousness was cosmic, collective, tribal, mythic, and ritualistic. This is the characteristic form of consciousness of primal peoples. Between these traditional cultures and the Axial Period there emerged great empires in Egypt, China, and Mesopotamia, but these did not yet produce the full consciousness of the Axial Period.

The consciousness of the tribal cultures was intimately related to the cosmos and to the fertility cycles of nature. Thus there was established a rich and creative harmony between primal peoples and the world of nature, a harmony that was explored, expressed, and celebrated in myth and ritual. Just as they felt themselves part of nature, so they experienced themselves as part of the tribe. It was precisely the web of interrelationships within the tribe that sustained them psychologically, energizing all aspects of their lives. To be separated from the tribe threatened them with death, not only physical but psychological as well. However, their relation to the collectivity often did not extend beyond their own tribe, for they often looked upon other tribes as hostile. Yet within their tribe they felt organically related to their group as a whole, to the life cycles of birth and death and to nature and the cosmos.

The Axial Period ushered in a radically new form of consciousness. Whereas primal consciousness was tribal, Axial consciousness was individual. "Know thyself" became the watchword of Greece; the Upanishads identified the *atman,* the transcendent center of the self. The Buddha charted the way of individual enlightenment; the Jewish prophets awakened individual moral responsibility. This sense of individual identity and responsibility, as distinct from the tribe and from nature, are the most characteristic marks of Axial consciousness. From this flow other characteristics: consciousness that is self-reflective, analytic, and that can be applied to nature in the form of scientific theories, to society in the form of social critique, to knowledge in the form of philosophy, and to religion in the form of mapping an individual spiritual journey. This self-reflective, analytic, critical consciousness stood in sharp contrast to primal mythic and ritualistic consciousness. When self-reflective logos emerged in the Axial Period, it tended to oppose the traditional mythos. Of course, mythic and ritualistic forms of consciousness survive in the post-Axial Period even to this day, but they are often submerged, surfacing chiefly in dreams, literature, and art.

Although Axial consciousness brought many benefits, it involved loss as well. It severed the harmony with nature and the tribe. Axial persons were in possession of their own identity, it is true, but they had lost their organic relation to nature and community. They now ran the risk of being alienated from the matrix of being and life. With their new powers, they could criticize the social structure and by analysis discover the abstract laws of science and metaphysics, but they might find themselves mere spectators of a drama of which in reality they were an integral part.

The emergence of Axial consciousness was decisive for religions, since it marked the divide in history where the major religions emerged and separated themselves from their primal antecedents. The great religions of the world as we know them today are the product of the Axial Period. Hinduism, Buddhism, Taoism, Confucianism, and Judaism took shape in their classical form during this period; and Judaism provided the base for the later emergence of Christianity and Islam. The common structures of consciousness found in these religions are characteristic of the general transformation of consciousness effected in the Axial Period.

Axial and Primal Spirituality

The move into Axial consciousness released enormous spiritual energy. It opened up the individual spiritual path, especially the inner way in which the new subjectivity became the avenue into the transcendent. It allowed the deeper self to sort out the difference between the illusion of the phenomenal world and the authentic vision of reality. On the ethical level it allowed individual moral conscience to take a critical stand against the collectivity. And it made possible a link between the moral and the spiritual aspects of the self, so that a path could be chartered through virtues toward the ultimate goal of the spiritual quest.

One of the most distinctive forms of spirituality that became available in the Axial Period was monasticism. Although it had roots in the earlier Hindu tradition, it emerged in a clearly defined way in Buddhism and Jainism at the peak of the Axial Period and later developed in Christianity. Monasticism did not exist among primal peoples because their consciousness was not oriented to sustain it. Axial consciousness was grounded in a distinct center of individuality necessary to produce the monk as a religious type. For the monks and nuns themselves take a radical stand as marginal persons, separating themselves from family and community, stripping themselves of material goods by practicing poverty and withdrawing from the fertility cycles by celibacy—as wandering beggars or as members of monastic communities who share their sense of radicalness.

Although Axial consciousness opened many possibilities, it tended to close off others and to produce some negative results. The release of spiritual energy thrust the Axial person in the direction of the spirit and away from the earth, away from the life cycles and the harmony with nature that the primal peoples experienced and that they made the basis of their spirituality. In some traditions this emergence of spiritual energy caused a radical split between the phenomenal world and true reality, between matter and spirit, between earth and heaven. Although in a number of traditions this separation was not central, nevertheless the emergence of Axial consciousness, with its strong sense of subjectivity, made that separation not only possible, but a risk and a threat. From the time of the Axial Period, the spiritual path tended to lead away from the earth and towards the heavenly realms above.

Note that I am placing the radical transformation of consciousness in the first millennium B.C.E. and not at the rise of Western science in the Renaissance and the Age of Enlightenment. It is, of course, true that Western science was innovative, even radical. Yet I believe that it developed within the horizons of Axial consciousness and represents one of its possible trajectories. In fact, at the same time that science enlarged the understanding of matter, it progressively narrowed Western Axial consciousness by employing exclusively a mechanical model and by limiting human knowledge to what can be grasped only by an empirical method. In Western science the earlier Axial split between matter and spirit was intensified. Descartes ignored spirit and saw mind as a detached observer of mechanical forces. Although this paradigm yielded enormous knowledge of the physical world, its narrow perspective only added to the fragmentation latent in the original Axial transformation.

The Second Axial Period

If we shift our gaze from the first millennium B.C.E. to the eve of the twenty-first century, we can discern another transformation of consciousness. It is so profound and far-reaching that I call it the Second Axial Period.[3] Like the first it is happening simultaneously around the earth, and like the first it will shape the horizon of consciousness for future centuries. Not surprisingly, too, it will have great significance for world religions, which were constituted in the First Axial Period. However, the new form of consciousness is different from that of the First Axial Period. Then it was individual consciousness, now it is global consciousness.

In order to understand better the forces at work in the Second Axial Period, I would like to draw from the thought of the paleontologist Pierre Teilhard de Chardin.[4] In the light of his research in evolution, he charted the development of consciousness from its roots in the geosphere and biosphere and into the future. In a process that he calls "planetization," he observed that a shift in the forces of evolution had occurred over the past hundred years. This shift is from divergence to convergence. When human beings first appeared on this planet, they clustered together in family and tribal units, forming their own group identity and separating themselves from other tribes. In this way humans diverged, creating separate nations and a rich variety of cultures. However, the spherical shape of the earth prevented unlimited divergence. With the increase in population and the rapid development of communication, groups could no longer remain apart. After dominating the process for millennia, the forces of divergence have been superceded by those of convergence. This shift to convergence is drawing the various cultures into a single planetized community. Although we have been conditioned by thousands of years of divergence, we now have no other course open to us but to cooperate creatively with the forces of convergence as these are drawing us toward global consciousness.[5]

According to Teilhard this new global consciousness will not level all differences among peoples; rather it will generate what he calls creative unions in which diversity is not erased but intensified. His understanding of creative unions is based on his general theory of evolution and

---

3. For a more comprehensive treatment of my concept of the Second Axial Period, see my book *Christ of the 21st Century* (Rockport, MA: Element, 1992).

4. Pierre Teilhard de Chardin, *Le Phénomène humain* (Paris: Editions du Seuil, 1955); see also *L'Activation de l'énergie* (Paris, Editions du Seuil, 1962) and *L'Energie humaine* (Paris; Editions du Seuil, 1962). For a more detailed study of Teilhard's thought in relation to the second Axial Period, see my paper "Teilhard de Chardin and the Religious Phenomenon," delivered in Paris at the International Symposium on the Occasion of the Centenary of the Birth of Teilhard de Chardin, organized by UNESCO, September 16–18, 1981, UNESCO Document Code: SS.82/WS/36.

5. Teilhard, *Le Phénomène humain*, pp. 268–69.

the dynamic that he observes throughout the universe. From the geosphere to the biosphere to the realm of consciousness, a single process is at work, which he articulates as the law of "complexity-consciousness" and "union differentiates." "In any domain," he says, "whether it be the cells of a body, the members of a society or the elements of a spiritual synthesis—*union differentiates.*"[6] From subatomic particles to global consciousness, individual elements unite in what Teilhard calls center to center unions. By touching each other at the creative core of their being, they release new energy that leads to more complex units. Greater complexity leads to greater interiority that, in turn, leads to more creative unions. Throughout the process, the individual elements do not lose their identity, but rather deepen and fulfill it through union. "Following the confluent orbits of their center," he says, "the grains of consciousness do not tend to lose their outlines and blend, but, on the contrary, to accentuate the depth and incommunicability of their *egos*. The more 'other' they become in conjunction, the more they find themselves as 'self.'"[7] At this point of history, because of the shift from divergence to convergence, the forces of planetization are bringing about an unprecedented complexification of consciousness through the convergence of cultures and religions.

In the light of Teilhard's thought, then, we can better understand the meeting of religions on the eve of the twenty-first century. The world religions are the product of the First Axial Period and the forces of divergence. Although in the first millennium B.C.E., there was a common transformation of consciousness, it occurred in diverse geographical regions within already differentiated cultures. In each case the religion was shaped by this differentiation in its origin, and developed along differentiated lines. This produced a remarkable richness of spiritual wisdom, of spiritual energies and of religious-cultural forms to express, preserve, and transmit this heritage. Now that the forces of divergence have shifted to convergence, the religions must meet each other in center to center unions, discovering what is most authentic in each other, releasing creative energy toward a more complexified form of religious consciousness.

Such a creative encounter has been called the "dialogic dialogue" to distinguish it from the dialectic dialogue in which one tries to refute the

---

6. Ibid., p. 292; trans. Bernard Wall, *The Phenomenon of Man* (New York: Harper and Row, 1965), p. 262.
7. Teilhard, *Le Phénomène humain*, p. 262.

claims of the other.[8] This dialogic dialogue has three phases: (1) The partners meet each other in an atmosphere of mutual understanding, ready to alter misconceptions about each other and eager to appreciate the values of the other. (2) The partners are mutually enriched, by passing over into the consciousness of the other so that each can experience the other's values from within the other's perspective. This can be enormously enriching, for often the partners discover in another tradition values that are submerged or only inchoate in their own. It is important at this point to respect the automony of the other tradition: in Teilhard's terms, to achieve union in which differences are valued as a basis of creativity. (3) If such a creative union is achieved, then the religions will have moved into the complexified form of consciousness that will be characteristic of the twenty-first century. This will be complexified global consciousness, not a mere universal, undifferentiated, abstract consciousness. It will be global through the global convergence of cultures and religions and complexified by the dynamics of dialogic dialogue.

This global consciousness, complexified through the meeting of cultures and religions, is only one characteristic of the Second Axial Period. The consciousness of this period is global in another sense: namely, in rediscovering its roots in the earth. At the very moment when the various cultures and religions are meeting each other and creating a new global community, our life on the planet is being threatened. The very tools that we have used to bring about this convergence—industrialization and technology—are undercutting the biological support system that sustains life on our planet. The future of consciousness, even life on the earth, is shrouded in a cloud of uncertainty by the pollution of our environment, the depletion of natural resources, the unjust distribution of wealth, the stockpiling of nuclear weapons. Unless the human community reverses these destructive forces, we may not see the twenty-first century. The human race as a whole—all the diverse cultures and the religions—must face these problems squarely. In this Second Axial Period we must rediscover the dimensions of consciousness of the spirituality of the primal peoples of the pre-Axial Period.

As we saw, this consciousness was collective and cosmic, rooted in the earth and the life cycles. We must rapidly appropriate that form of consciousness or perish from the earth. However, I am not suggesting a romantic attempt to live in the past, rather that the evolution of

---

8. On the concept of a dialogic dialogue, see Raimundo Panikkar, *Myth, Faith and Hermeneutics* (New York: Paulist Press, 1979), pp. 241–45; see also *The Intrareligious Dialogue* (New York: Paulist Press, 1978).

consciousness proceeds by way of recapitulation. Having developed self-reflective, analytic, critical consciousness in the First Axial Period, we must now, while retaining these values, reappropriate and integrate into that consciousness the collective and cosmic dimensions of the pre-Axial consciousness.

We must recapture the unity of tribal consciousness by seeing humanity as a single tribe. And we must see this single tribe related organically to the total cosmos. This means that the consciousness of the twenty-first century will be global from two perspectives: (1) from a horizontal perspective, cultures and religions must meet each other on the surface of the globe, entering into creative encounters that will produce a complexified collective consciousness; (2) from a vertical perspective, they must plunge their roots deep into the earth in order to provide a stable and secure base for future development. This new global consciousness must be organically ecological, supported by structures that will insure justice and peace. The voices of the oppressed must be heard and heeded: the poor, women, racial and ethnic minorities. These groups, along with the earth itself, can be looked upon as the prophets and teachers of the Second Axial Period. This emerging twofold global consciousness is not only a creative possibility to enhance the twenty-first century; it is also, and more importantly, an absolute necessity if we are to survive.

The Task of Religions

What does this mean for religions on the eve of the twenty-first century? It means that they have a double task: to enter creatively into the dialogue of religions and to channel their energies into solving the common human problems that threaten our future on the earth. It means that they must strip away negative and limiting attitudes towards other religions. They must avoid both a narrow fundamentalism and a bland universalism. They must be true to their spiritual heritage, for this is the source of their power and their gift to the world. They must make every effort to ground themselves in their own traditions and at the same time to open themselves to other traditions. In concert with the other religions they should commit themselves to creating the new complexified global consciousness we have been exploring.

But to meet, even creatively, on the spiritual level is not enough. They must channel their spiritual resources toward the solution of global problems. For the most part, this calls for a transformation of the religions. Having been formed in the First Axial Period, the religions bear the mark of Axial consciousness: in turning toward the spiritual ascent away from the material. The religions must rediscover the material dimension of existence and its spiritual significance. In this they can learn from the secular: that justice and peace are human values that must be cherished and pragmatically cultivated. But they must not adopt an exclusively secular attitude, for their unique contribution is to tap their reservoirs of spiritual energy and channel this into developing secular enterprises that are genuinely human. It is in this larger context that I believe the other religions the world, on the eve of the twenty-first century, must face together the challenges of the Second Axial Period.

Part V

VISIONS
FOR THE FUTURE

21

The Planetary Parliament

BEATRICE BRUTEAU

Time was when we were all afraid of each other's religion. Our gods forbade us to have any "strange gods" around, lest we start to prefer them to the gods of our ancestors, of our particular ethnic group. We had special names for the people who worshiped the "strange gods." We called them "idolators," "unbelievers," "heathen," "barbarians," "savages." We did not enter their houses of worship or permit them to enter ours. We did not study their beliefs because we knew—each of us in our particular religions—that we had the only true religion and therefore the others had to be immature, mistaken, or deceived by evil spirits. The others were superstitious and primitive, whereas we were mature and civilized, enlightened, had received God's true revelation, were specially chosen and commissioned.

Of course, this was a very long time ago. Today we can look back on those times with indulgent chuckles over the foolishness of our childhood. Today we talk with each other as adults, with respect and eagerness to learn, to exchange insights, share and forward our common human enterprises of reaching the highest values of truth and goodness. A futuristic fantasy? Not entirely.

The facts of life have forced us into this situation. The planet has suddenly unified. We are not living in our protected corners of the landscape anymore. Our economic lives are irrecoverably intermingled in a global marketplace. Our events are public property through the instantaneous media of information and comment. We criticize one another's domestic arrangements, and occasionally we come to one another's rescue. The Earth has entered on a great conversation in which all parties have a right to speak. We have become a planetary parliament.

A Good Conversation

This "parliament" needs to be a genuine "talking together," in which there is both authentic speaking and open-minded listening. Both our listening and our speaking need to be conducted in such a way as to protect and promote the further free speaking and open listening of all the other parties. We must listen with a sincere intent to learn, to be open to receiving something of value, something that we do not yet know and that we can perhaps to some extent accept. We must say what we judge will be "hearable" by those to whom we speak, respecting their intelligence and experience and avoiding forcing our language and world-model assumptions on them, as far as we can, while at the same time honoring their reciprocal efforts to open themselves to us and learn from us. No honest conversation can take place unless all parties believe in the value of what each has to say.

As the recent Parliament of the World's Religions made manifest, we are being drawn into an interconnective relation with all our neighbors in which communication is central. It is a huge conversation, a planetary conversation. We want it to be a good conversation, both pleasant and productive. We can get some tips on how to do this from people who use conversation to help stimulate their creative efforts, the Media Lab scientists and inventors at the Massachusetts Institute of Technology, who have developed what they call the "hallmarks of a good conversation."

The heart of a good conversation is *interactivity,* everyone participating, both initiating and reacting to what others have initiated. The more creative the responsive interaction is, the more successful the conversation. If everyone simply comes out the same, the conversation has been a failure. Sometimes, though, we can't satisfy our colleagues in the conversation, can't give them an answer that puts the conversation forward. In that case, the disappointed party can help by being understanding and trying to move in another and perhaps more fruitful way. We need to resolve not to give up on a conversation, to conclude that it is no use, that we can never reach a meeting of minds. We are all human beings, and we are intelligent and creative people. If we continue to try to come together, we will eventually find ways to do it.

Views at variance can be presented in such a way as to offer respectful arguments and positive alternatives for consideration, while showing that the position of one's opposite number has been correctly understood, not caricatured. We must never compare the popular level of one religion with the academic or spiritually sophisticated level of another. The corresponding side of this is that when we are criticized and alternatives or correctives or expansions proposed to us, we must not harden our hearts or resist listening, or try to excuse ourselves from taking these words seriously by attributing either ignorance or ill will to their sources.

It behoves all parties to make their interventions in such ways as to preserve the conversational viability of all other members. No one participant should assume leadership or speak from a position that supposes all others are to be compared with that view, or presume to set the agenda. If all try to adhere in a general way to the "thread" of the interchange, while allowing for improvisation and unpremeditated development, then the conversation becomes creative and fruitful. Giving ourselves trustingly to the creative potential and dynamism of the conversation itself, following where it leads, without trying to control it, can enable the conversation to lead into wonderful, unexpected spaces. This perhaps implies that all parties see the conversation itself as a religious act and religious experience, something that can be made significant in each of their particular views, as a way in which the insight with which their tradition has been gifted is continuing to develop.

This expansive and depth-opening creativity and religious significance can be enhanced by encouraging a more or less indefinite scope for the exchanges. There are, fortunately, all sorts of resources that can be called upon as relevant to this subject of the ultimate meaning of our lives. We may not know ahead of time from what strange source a new inspiration will appear. At the same time, we have gathered together on the basis of some contexts in common, some "environment" that we share. Starting from this very general but unifying foundation, and reverting to it from time to time, can help to build up the organic usefulness of what we are doing. By entering into the conversation at all, we have committed ourselves to confidence in both our unity, our commonness, our shared reality, and our variations, our differences, our polarities. It is the creative interaction of both these dimensions that supports the value of the ongoing conversation.

This last is the final clue to what makes a good conversation. We can say different things at different times. The same question doesn't always have to get the same answer from any of us. Perhaps it won't stay the "same" question throughout this, our shared living together. Perhaps everything will change and grow for all of us. For the conversation itself is alive, and if we have given ourselves to it sincerely, it is a living vehicle for the religious values we all seek.[1]

---

1. See "the hallmarks of good conversation in Steward Brand, *The Media Lab: Inventing the Future at MIT* (New York: Viking, 1987), pp. 46–50, 183.

Similarity, Complementarity, Implementarity

The Dalai Lama, speaking at Berea College in 1994, in the context of cross-cultural understanding and world peace, pointed out the strength of our similarities on which we can build further understandings and sympathies. "We are all human beings," he said. As human beings we share many fundamental experiences, such as the desire to live in peace and modest comfort, health, and opportunity to learn; such as the need to love and be loved, to find values in life, and to create; such as fears of the unknown, of pains and sorrow for ourselves and loved ones, resistance to injustice and cruelty; such as wonder before the scales—great and small—and the intricacies of the universe and eagerness to understand this marvel and play our role in it well; such as commitment to our families and our respective cultures, which we believe have done worthwhile things that should be carried on; such as a sense of something that calls forth our religious feelings, sets us on a spiritual quest, and commits to go beyond ourselves.

Recognizing that we all, as human beings, must experience these aspects of our life, though each in our own way, we feel a spirit of kinship among us, we begin to draw together. We sympathize with one another, knowing that what we feel, the other feels, and what the other longs for, we long for too. This feeling of commonness provides a minimum of understanding, takes away some of the strangeness, and thus constitutes a foundation for the beginning of trust. With even a little trust to build on, we can make a start.

If we strengthen ourselves with the thought of similarity, if we take our stand there and look out upon our intercultural world from there, then we are in position to assess and appreciate our variations, be honest about them, and seek positive values in their reflections on one another. One of the ways we can identify positive outcomes from the relations of our several religions to one another is in terms of their complementarity to one another. This means that where one is weak another is strong, what one lacks another supplies; if many views are possible, those views not developed in one tradition may be worked out in others. The connotation is mutual aid and support rather than exclusion or opposition. The word itself suggests that by doing this, we will cover all the possible views, but this is, we may be fairly sure, not so. We have in fact no idea of what a "complete" view would be. Even with all the traditions we have, we must cover only a very small part of what the total truth is. Perhaps this is why Swami Vivekananda urged us to create more religions, to find further ways of exploring the Great Mystery.

Nevertheless, there are ways of relating the existing traditions to one another by seeing how all parties can be saying valuable things that do not necessarily exclude one another. An example of this might be the way a basic polarity—the forms and the formless—is dealt with (in general, or characteristically, or even sterotypically) by "the East" and "the West." If we apply the polarity to God (the Absolute) and the World as Formless and forms respectively, then we say that as a general cultural characteristic, the East makes much of the Formless, while the West has developed the Forms. Sometimes this polarity is seen as Spirit and Matter, or Otherworldly/This worldly. Eastern traditions have a vast vocabulary and technical treasure for states of consciousness and ways of exploring, purifying, and elevating consciousness. Western technology, on the other hand, has discovered and invented an enormous world of material meaning and machinery. Despite the liability to abuse either way, both of these have contributed to the good of us all. And if we consider the Total Real to include both, then we can feel that between us, we have done worthwhile things as human beings confronted with the mystery of existence.

Trading places, now, and interpreting the Formless in terms of one God, one truth, and the Forms as multiple images of God and varieties of theologies and philosophies, the West is seen as championing the Formless, while the East takes up appreciation for the many Forms. Of course, the key to finding this kind of complementarity advantageous is the willingness to regard both sides of the polarity as valuable— good and true. But that in itself is problematical. Many parties to the conversation wish to adhere to only one side of the complementarity, denying the reality or the value of the other. Perhaps this comes in part from the belief that if one side is chosen the other must be denied, that it is not possible for both to have value simultaneously.

If so, this difficulty may be got at by examining our thoughts about the Absolute and the Relative. What we do simplistically is to identify the Absolute in itself with our particular way of approaching it. We tend to believe that if some other way is "just as good as" the way our people do it, then all truth dissolves in Relativism and the Absolute is absolutely lost. I would argue that this is not so, since in fact, as everyone admits, the Absolute cannot be contained by any particular finite way of expressing It, by any relative view; all relative views necessarily, therefore equally, fall short of the Infinite. But, that does not mean that they fail altogether. On the contrary, we do touch, receive, live in the Absolute through the mediation of our particular way of doing it. All the great traditions possess sufficient means to lead their devotees into fulfillment.

Putting these two truths together should enable us to see that we always have both the Absolute and the Relative. The fact that we touch the Absolute in a Relative way does not mean that we do not touch the Absolute. Reality is absolute and makes itself available Relatively. The conclusion might well be that the **more** Relative ways we can sustain, the deeper will be our contact, just as seeing a three-dimensional object from various points of view will give a more realistic opinion on it than looking from only one perspective. If we begin to think that this makes sense, then we will be developing our conversation in complementary terms.

A third possibility leads us into even deeper intimacy, and perhaps— if we are right about the conversation itself being a religious event, medium of revelation, enlightenment—into still deeper truth and reality. Michael von Bruck, dealing with the theological polarity personal/impersonal, admits the question, Which view is the more comprehensive of the two? And then he asks, Or is it possible to integrate them? Not merely by complementarity, he answers, for that is still hindered by a static two-ness: each view remains itself, does not really cross over into the other. He proposes that we try to come to see such pairs of views in terms of *implementarity,* that is, as *implying* one another.[2]

This means that any of us who begin with one aspect of the religious experience, can, by persistence in depth, come to realization of the value in another—as, for instance, if we begin with a personal experience, it will lead us, if we follow it far enough, to the impersonal. Conversely, when we attain the impersonal, it will lead us again to a higher "personal" than the one we had rejected, and this again to a higher "impersonal," and so on. This is dynamic and experiential rather than theoretical.

Perhaps this is why many people feel that it is the monastics[3] who can make the best first approaches to this important planetary parliament of religions. They are the ones who deal with these issues experientially, in the reality of their daily lives, their lived experience, as distinguished from theologians, who represent their received traditions, the codified

2. Michael von Bruck, *The Unity of Reality: God, God-Experience, and Meditation in the Hindu-Christian Dialogue* (New York: Paulist, 1991), pp. 201–2.
3. Monastic Interreligious Dialogue is the North American branch of the international Aide Intermonastère, an initiative of the worldwide Benedictine confederacy, headquartered in Paris, which promotes exchanges between Benedictine monastics and their opposite numbers in other religions. Recently Tibetan Buddhist monks have been visiting the United States and Americans are visiting Buddhist and Hindu sites in India. Joint Hindu/Christian conferences are also under way. The MID publishes a Bulletin, obtainable from Brother Harold, OCSO, Abbey of Gethsemani, Trappist, KY 40051.

doctrines, and the deductions that can be made therefrom. What the monastics, and especially the mystics, actually report from their experience often contradicts—or at least exceeds—what the theologians would permit from their rational work with the conceptual schemes.

Where the theologian finds an excluded middle, the mystic revels in a mutual indwelling. "That's not possible!" says the theologian. "You can't have it both ways." "I know," replies the mystic, "but that's the way it is!"

This very suggestion and experience itself is already verified in several traditions. For instance, Ramakrishna clearly insisted that God is simultaneously Formless and expressed in the multitude of blissful Forms, and that both the personal worship and the impersonal realization were correct and led to one another. Dōgen saw Enlightenment and Practice as thoroughly indwelling one another: practice of enlightenment without beginning, enlightenment of practice without end.[4] The Christian Gospel speaks of the Father (the Invisible) in the Son (the Exegete) and the Son in the Father, as well as the Deity in the worshiper and vice versa, all in "reciprocal immanence."[5]

The Symbiotic Model: Communication and Community

Interaction and mutual immanence are key features of a good model for our planetary parliament. Since we must all live together anyway, why not make *symbiosis,* mutually beneficial "living together," our conscious intent?

Religions can initially get together on the development of more just, humane, and ecologically sensitive ways of living together on our shared planet. Global Education Associates is coordinating "Project Global 2000," a partnership of fifteen international nongovernmental organizations and UN agencies that are collaborating in programs and creative initiatives through six Councils: Religion, Education, Youth, Health, Communication, and Business. The idea back of the partnership is the symbiotic one that by sharing knowledge, skills, materials, and information networks, much more can be accomplished than by any of the partners working alone.

The Religion Council is currently [Summer 1994] working on "Religion and World Order," which is concerned with global governance as we begin to look seriously and practically at the twenty-first century.

---

4. Hee-Jin Kim, *Dogen Kigen, Mystical Reality* (Tucson: Univ. of Arizona, 1987), p. 61.
5. Bruno Barnhart, *The Good Wine: Reading John from the Center* (New York: Paulist, 1993), p. 320.

The World Conference on Religion and Peace and UNESCO are among the partners for this enterprise. Needed are a *global ethic* and the development of systems that can respond effectively to the rapidly emerging new conditions of our symbiotic dynamic itself.[6]

President Vaclav Havel of the Czech Republic goes even further. In a speech in Philadelphia in July 1994, he urged that the global community must find a new common set of transcendent values to replace the traditional beliefs that many people can no longer support and to prevent the reversion of other types to "the ancient certainties of their tribe, with the cultural conflicts to which that could give rise.

This shows a recognition of another segment of our human household, those who do not subscribe to any of the existing religions or spiritual traditions. They may make some of the most creative contributions, for they may be most intensely aware of the fact that we are departing a finished era and are entering a new one whose character is not yet clear—and indeed cannot be clear yet, for it remains to be created by us.

President Havel's further suggestions show another important recognition that we must engage explicitly, and that is to count *science* among the organized efforts to make sense of, and to find value in, our experience of ourselves and the rest of our world. As science tries to find, on the one hand, the ultimate foundation of all things, and on the other hand, holistic views comprehensive enough to include and integrate everything that we (so far) know to exist, it begins "producing ideas that in a certain sense allow it to transcend its own limits."[7]

Among the comprehensive views, or general models, available, we might look at this notion of *symbiosis,* interpreted as mutualism and as system. Components of a certain level of organization come together and share their functional abilities in a common context, all of them interacting—everyone contributing, everyone receiving, everyone adjusting according to their integration of everyone else's inputs. The consequence of this dynamic is that a new form *emerges* as the pattern of all their combined individual behaviors, but *transcending* any of them singly. It is not the result of adding them together, and certainly not of limiting or reducing any of them. Rather, the new reality arises precisely

---

6. *Breakthrough News,* organ of Global Education Associates, Summer 1994, p. 10. Proceedings of the Religion and Global Governance Symposium, February 4, 1994, sponsored by the Religion Council of Project Global 2000, are available from GEA, New York. A multireligion conference is to be held in 1995 to share research; to produce a multireligious document, and to further cooperation between religious networks and the other agencies.

7. Nicholas Wade, "Method and Madness: A Fable for Fleas," *The New York Times Magazine,* Sunday, August 14, 1994, p. 18, quotations from President Havel.

from the highly individual and characteristic behaviors of the components in their *interaction*. If the components do *not* keep their respective proper uniqueness, their distinctness from their colleagues, then the symbiosis fails. There is no genuine togetherness but only a juxtaposition, and therefore no emergent, no growth, no creativity, no novelty, no advance.

A fine example of such a symbiotic advance in the world is the origin of eukaryotic (nucleated) cells from the symbiotic union of prokaryotic cells (no nuclei—such as bacteria). Under pressure from the newly generated free oxygen in the atmosphere—gift of the newly operating photosynthesis with the help of chlorophyll—different types of cells clubbed together, smaller ones inside larger ones, and survived. Not only survived, but made something completely new, a much bigger and much more complex kind of cell, with differentiated functions inside it carried out by the "foreign" cells the big cell had ingested. And not only did they survive the oxygen, they found ways to use it that give them much more energy and a greatly expanded life.[8] All the more complex life forms on the planet were built up from these enterprising cells, from their daring sharing, those who could resist the oxygen sheltering those who could use the oxygen, each helping each. Our own bodies are made of eukaryotic cells in which the original symbiosis is still going on.

By analogy we can see the same sort of thing going on at all levels of cosmic organization, from the quarks composing the nucleons to individual animals composing societies and all kinds of beings composing ecosystems. It seems to be one of the most universal method patterns under our observation. Diversity is not only preserved but protected and enhanced, while union by *interaction* brings forth a new level of reality with hitherto unknown properties and powers, a new level that **transcends** the properties and the complexity and the integration of its components.

If we are interested in looking for a way to understand ourselves as meaningfully embedded in something greater than ourselves, and if we are open to accepting suggestion from our scientific views of the cosmos, then this sort of thing may be such an opportunity. Perhaps, among other ways of honoring the Transcendent, we may admit this cosmic symbol of it and by adding this universal icon to those we already treasure, draw into our conversation those to whom the traditional symbols do not speak. And perhaps we may do a further thing. Perhaps we may use the model of symbiosis for the interaction of our planetary parliament.

---

8. See Lynn Margulis, *Early Life* (Boston: Jones & Bartlett, 1984), pp. 17, 75, 80, 85–86, 97.

There are surely values that all our religions rank very high, values that relate to improvement of human life; growth in consciousness, sensitivity, virtue; therefore commitment to the human community and the wider life community, to *wholeness,* indeed to living together. And it is evident that such community life achieves wholeness only through *communication,* through sharing of characteristically human goods: ideas, feelings, beliefs, aspirations. It is this communication that is the *interaction* by which our particular level of organization in the cosmos is reaching out to compose the next grander level. It is precisely our communication community that constitutes our wholeness, and outside which none of us can exist as human, perhaps cannot exist at all.

It is clear that communication is intensifying among us by leaps and bounds. Ability to improve and expand communication is becoming an explicit value. Communication is finding new channels and new media. All levels of social organization are coming to be able to be in direct contact with one another, local to local, local to provincial to national to regional to global. The more the communication grows, the more mutual understanding has a chance, among responsible parties and among grassroots citizens, who recognize and respond to the common themes in human life everywhere.

This is the new frontier in the interactions among all human minds. In another simile, we may be said to be like neurons stretching out their dendrites to make further contacts with still other neurons, thousands and thousands of contacts, which constitute intelligence, consciousness, knowledge, feelings, and values. Our joined minds have girdled the Earth, have made a network over the planet. The network is growing finer details locally and more holistic self-realizations globally. We are beginning to identify primarily as Earthlings, Terrans, Gaians. It is a tremendous moment in our history.

History continues on the move. It is dynamism that is its essence. It is the dynamic of the community that makes the community, the interactivity of communicating. A dynamic system like this is always incomplete, always a little off balance, a little inconsistent, always striving, looking ahead. That's what makes it go. It's like a melody, leading on to the next note. It doesn't measure itself by finally coming to a halt in some expected achievement. It delights in the movement. All this applies to our religions.

"Were religious consciousness static," says Raimon Panikkar, "our task would be only to unfold what was already there nicely 'folded.'. . . [But] *growth* is perhaps the most pertinent category to express [the actual] situation, which is more than simple development or explication. In growth there is continuity as well as novelty, development as well as a real assimilation of something that was outside and is now incorporated, made one body. In growth, there is freedom. . . . I repeat: Growth means continuity and development, but it also implies transformation and revolution. . . . We do not know where we are going. Yet in this common ignorance genuinely religious people experience real fellowship and fraternal communion."[9]

As our parliamentary interaction coaxes us into such growth, we will help one another mature. We may hope that each tradition will find that its own revelation, insight, or enlightenment urges it to see value in the community and in its communication. This can include those who stand creatively outside the received traditions. Each of us can perhaps say, from our own point of view: Nurturing this community in the sincerity and generosity of its intercommunications is a value that our view supports. Helping one another in this intercommunication, why should we not reach further values that each of our traditions or views will acclaim as the fulfillment of its own ideas and aspirations? Why not, indeed? As we ease into this confiding conversation on which we are launched, let us all hope that it may be so, and open ourselves to the intercommunication that may make it so.

---

9. Raimon Panikkar, *The Intra-Religious Dialogue* (New York: Paulist, 1978), pp. 70–72.

22

The Role of Religions in the Twenty-First Century

THOMAS BERRY

If the finest consequence of the First Parliament of Religions, held in 1893, was the recovery of a profound sense of the divine in the human soul through the leadership of Swami Vivekananda, the finest consequence of the second Parliament of religions, held in 1993, should be the recovery of an exalted sense of the divine in the grandeur of the natural world. Vivekananda himself recognized that the locus for the meeting of the divine and the human must take place in the natural world if it is to survive in the human soul.

This concern for the visible world about us came to expression in only a few of the papers given at the Parliament but there can be little doubt that the main issue confronting the future in all aspects of the human venture will be achieving a viable relationship between humans and the natural life systems of the planet. Just now the human is a devastating presence on the planet. While ostensibly humans are acting for their own benefit, they are in reality ruining the conditions for their own survival and well-being. This applies both to the physical and the spiritual survival of the human, since the inner world of the soul needs to be activated by experience of the outer world in all its grandeur.

The pathos of the present is that the human community has lost its capacity to interact creatively with the other components of the planet Earth. This includes the landscape of the planet; the nurturing qualities of the air, the water and the soil; the energy flow that enables the dynamic powers of the Earth to continue their functioning; the life systems that are integrated with each other in an immense complex of patterns beyond all human understanding.

While humans have never had any comprehensive understanding of the mysteries manifest in the world about them, they have in former times developed, through their religious traditions, a capacity for being a creative presence within the ever-renewing sequence of life upon the Earth. In these closing years of the twentieth century we seem to have lost this capacity. We have instead become a deleterious presence throughout the planet. We thought that we were improving the human situation although in reality we were devastating the human along with all the other components of the Earth community.

Just now we begin to realize what we have done. We begin to realize that a degraded outer world leads immediately to a degraded inner world. A recovery of the sublime meaning of the universe could lead first of all to a greater intimacy of the human with the manifestation of the divine in the natural world; then to a greater intimacy of the different religions among themselves.

It becomes increasingly clear that humans have a common origin and a common destiny with every other component of the Earth community. We live on the same planet. We breathe the same air. We drink the same water. We share the same sunlight. We are nourished by the same soil. In all these ways we share in a common spiritual mode of being as well as in a common physical sustenance.

The integrity of the natural world as a condition for the integrity of the inner spiritual world needs an emphasis just now because the relationship of humans with the natural world has deteriorated in a devastating manner between the earlier Parliament and this more recent parliament. Disassociation of the human from the larger community of nature is by far the most significant change in human existence since the earlier Parliament. It is also the most significant change in the biosystems of the planet and in the chemistry of the planet. We might even say that we are terminating the Cenozoic (the last sixty-five million year) period in the history of the Earth.

The only future really possible for humans or for the planet is for a transition into an Ecozoic Era, an era when humans would be present to the planet in a mutually enhancing manner. This would introduce not simply a new era in human affairs but a new era of the planet itself. To bring about this new geobiological period is the condition for any integral functioning of the planet in any phase of its activities whether this be economic or cultural or religious.

Religion, we must remember, is born out of the sense of wonder and awe and majesty and fearsomeness of the universe itself. The great decline in religion in industrialized countries can be attributed in large part to the lost experience of the grandeur of the natural world due to our newly acquired technological control over the functioning of the planet. Presently we are completely encompassed by the world of human artifice.

This alienation from the natural world sets us off from the immediacy with the natural world that we observe with indigenous peoples the world over. In their immediacy with the wonders of the world about them these earlier peoples have an intimate presence to the sacred as manifest throughout the planet. The world is attractive and yet threatening, benign yet fearsome. Divine Powers enable the fruits and berries and nuts and various forms of vegetation to come forth. These same powers bring the monsoon rains and the withering desert winds, the arctic chill, temperate warmth, and tropical heat.

All these experiences evoke in the human soul a sense of mystery and admiration, veneration and worship. This is something beyond what is sometimes designated as nature worship. The worship of the divine as manifested in nature is in accord with the teaching of all the spiritual traditions of the world, especially with the teaching of Saint Paul in the first chapter of his epistle to the Romans.

Humans feel a need to integrate with these forces in order to survive and in order to fulfill their human role in the order of things for there is ever-present in the human soul a certain anxiety due to the limited understanding of humans, the fragility of human powers, and a consciousness that if we fail in the fulfillment of our obligations in the order of the universe then the Earth will not provide the necessities that enable life to survive in any integral manner.

The very purpose of our religious rituals is to enable us to enter into the dramatic manifestation of the divine in a sacred world. This is why we have bodies capable of movement, sight, and hearing and all our other senses, especially our capacities for ritual. Through our sacred ceremonies we enter into the primordial liturgy of the universe itself.

The earliest responses of humanity to the encircling world grew more elaborate as the great ritual civilizations came into being some three thousand years ago in the Hindu, Buddhist, Chinese, Mediterranean, and Central American modes of religious expression. India and the Middle East became especially prolific in their religious creativity. By this integration of human affairs with the regularities observed in the sequence of natural phenomena, humans obtained the spiritual power needed to confront the challenging nature of earthly life.

Restoration of this sense of the natural world as divine manifestation has a special urgency because of the devastation that we are presently causing to the natural world. Only the religious forces of the world with their sense of the sacred can evoke the psychic energies needed to transform a declining Cenozoic Era into the emerging Ecozoic Era. That the natural world is in its declining phase is evident from the judgment of the foremost biologists of our times. When Peter Raven addressed a professional society of scientists under the title "We Are Killing Our World," this was not simply a biological statement, it was also a religious statement; for life and death are religious issues, especially when it is a question of life or death for the Earth itself in many of its major life systems.

For the first time in human history we are concerned with the weakening of the ozone layer, with the extinction of species on such a scale, and with the degradation of the planet itself. While there is no question of extinguishing life in any comprehensive manner, we are extinguishing life on a scale unknown to the planet since the decline of the Mesozoic era some sixty-five million years ago. It was during the later years of this Cenozoic period that humans and all our human values, our thought and our religious awareness came into being. These insights and these values cannot survive on a devastated planet. To save the planet is to save ourselves.

In the emerging future the Great Work of every human profession and institution will be to bring the Ecozoic Era into being when humans would be present to the earth in a mutually enhancing manner. In this context the religions will recognize that the natural world has from its beginning been a mystical as well as a physical reality. As the primary manifestation of the divine, the natural world is the primary sacred scripture and the primary sacred community. There could be no verbal scriptures unless there were first the cosmic scriptures. There can be no human community apart from the Earth community.

This sense of the sacred character of the universe has been lost to many peoples of the scientific-industrial world because the scientists told us that the universe they discovered was a random process without meaning or direction, a universe known only by quantitative measurement. In this manner they stole the universe from us. In taking away our universe they took away our immediacy with divine presence throughout the visible world. Yet they could take the world from us only because we had ourselves already abandoned the world. We were ready to believe what we were told.

The Economists told us that a violent plundering of the earth, as so much indifferent matter, was to better our human existence. The Philosophical Realists told us that any appreciation of the mystical dimension of nature was a sentimental romanticism. The Political People told us that the way to controlling power in the world was by first conquering and devastating our own territory and then exploiting the territory of other people.

Whatever the situation in the past, an exciting future is opening up before us as the various religious traditions recover their integral relation with the dynamic forces of the earth. Since the gathering of religions in Assisi some years ago the religions of the world have begun a new period in their own activities. A new hope arises on the North American continent, as the new farming methods enable the land to recover its fertility, as the grasslands begin to be cared for by such persons as Wes Jackson and Don Geiger. So throughout the various other continents similar movements are emerging. There is Wangari Matthai in Kenya with her program for replanting the trees. There is the Chipko movement in India and the work of Vandana Shiva, an economist who is providing a critique of the past in India and providing directions for the future. There is Aida Valasquez playing a significant role in the ecological movement in the Philippines. There is John Seed in Australia. Everywhere persons with a profoundly religious dedication are arising. Throughout the world the forests begin to be protected by the Nature Conservancy. Mikhail Gorbachev is leading the Green Cross Foundation to assist the less wealthy nations to conserve their natural endowment.

The plundering of the forests raises increasing protests as the eroded soil is once again cultivated through organic agriculture on community-supported farms, as the rivers of the world are defended against further destruction by dams, as the meadows and the wildflowers once again come into bloom, as the diminished shoals of marine life recover their abundance. As all these things begin to happen there is hope that the springtime of the Ecozoic Era will soon appear in all its splendor.

Already we are recovering our experience of the divine as a pervasive presence throughout the natural world. This new intimacy with the Earth is inspiring a new religious poetry in America in the work of Mary Oliver and a pervasive sense of the sacred appear in the poetry of Gary Snyder. In music there are composers such as Paul Winter who has brought the songs of other living beings into participation in our human compositions. There is Carman Moore whose Mass for the Twenty-First Century gives expression to this renewal of the ecosystems of the Earth. There are others too such as Maia Apprahamian who is composing a choral symphony in celebration of the Universe Story. A new cultural phase has begun throughout the world, an Ecozoic culture inspired by the religious sensitivities proper to the new era.

A more comprehensive social consciousness is appearing, a consciousness that we form a single sacred society with every other member of the entire earth community; with the mountains and rivers and valleys and grasslands as well as with all the various creatures that move over the land or fly through the heavens or swim through the sea. This new social consciousness is already dawning in human consciousness as we insist on environmental impact statements before we venture into any construction project that affects the functioning of the life systems of the region. Even a great river in Florida that was put into a concrete trench some years ago at a cost of thirty million dollars is now being set free again. The concrete basin into which it was channeled is being exploded to enable the river to spread out over its flood plain. This at an expense of over two hundred million dollars.

In the emerging Ecozoic Era we already experience the universe as a communion of subjects, not as a collection of objects. We are hearing the voices of all the living creatures. We recognize, understand, and respond to the voices of the crickets in the fields, the flowers in the meadows, the trees in the woodlands, and the birds all about us; all these voices resound within us in a universal chorus of delight in existence. For the first time in modern biological studies a scientist as competent as E. O. Wilson has written a study entitled *Biophilia,* with an emphasis on the feeling rapport of humans with the larger array of living beings.

In a manner that has not happened in recent times we in the industrial America are beginning to recognize that the human is a subsystem of the earth system, that our first obligation in any phase of our human lives is to preserve the integral function of the larger world that we depend on in an absolute manner. We were brought into being in and through the Earth. We survive through our intimate presence to the Earth. While this is true in economics, in governance, and in the healing sciences, it is also true in religious affairs, since we are members of a single sacred community that includes every component of the earthly reality.

New religious sensitivities emerge into being as we understand better the story of the universe that is now available to us through our scientific inquiry into the structure of the universe and the sequence of transformations that have brought the universe, the Earth, and all its living creatures into being. While this new story of the universe is strictly scientific in its data, it has a mythic dimension as narrative. This mythic dimension is what lifts this story out of a prosaic study of the data to an integral spiritual vision.

This story, a new creation narrative, enables us to enter into the deep mystery of creation with a new depth of understanding. It is our human version of the story that is told by every leaf on every tree, by the wind that blows across the fields in the evening, by the butterfly in its journey south to its winter habitat, by the mountains and rivers of all the continents of the Earth.

Through this story we understand with new insight just how every component member of the universe is integral with every other member of the universe community. We understand how each religious tradition emerges into being unique in its form and in the role that it fulfills. We learn from all our studies: to be is to be different. To be is to contribute something so precious that nothing before or afterwards will ever contribute that special glory to the created world.

Through this story we learn something about how the primordial mystery of the universe brought the planet Earth into being as the most blessed of all the planets that we know about. We learn how life emerged and took on such immense variety in its forms of expression. We learn too how we were brought into being and guided safely through the turbulent centuries. It is in our contemplation of how those tragic moments of disintegration in the course of the centuries were followed by immensely creative moments of renewal that we receive our great hope for the future. To initiate and guide this next creative moment of the great story of the Earth is the Great Work of the religions of the world as we move on into the future.

23

The Great Circle Dance of the Religions

BROTHER DAVID STEINDL-RAST, O.S.B.

The very fact that the World's religions gathered together for a Parliament must make us wonder. Their variety is bewildering. Do all these religions have anything in common? And, if so, what is it? Can one hope ever to understand a religious tradition that seems so vastly different from one's own? What can be expected from a gathering of this kind? We know of religious wars throughout history. Can we envisage a relationship between the world's religions that may serve as a basis for peace?

In an effort to tackle these questions, I must appeal to your personal experience. The subject matter demands this. One cannot talk about spiritual matters from an outsider's point of view and hope to say anything worthwhile. In what follows here I shall speak from my own experience; please check it against yours. If it doesn't correspond to what you know from experience, it won't be of use to you, no matter how true it may be objectively. Try to let what I am saying speak to your heart, not only to your head. It is my conviction that at the core of every religious tradition lies an experience that is accessible to all of us, if we open our hearts to it. The heart of every religion is the religion of the heart.

At this point it will help us to distinguish between Religion and the religions. Religions are the different sociological entities we find for instance represented at this Parliament. They are shaped by history, by economics, by politics, even by geography and they define themselves largely by what makes them different from one another. Religion, in contrast, unites. I spell it with a capital "R" and we'll use the term in the sense of "spirituality." Religion unites, because it is the homing instinct of the human heart.

"Heart" stands here for that core of our being where we are one with ourselves, one with all, one even with the divine ground of our being.

"Belonging" is therefore a key word for understanding the heart—the oneness of limitless belonging. A second key word is "meaning," for the heart is the organ for meaning. As the eye perceives light and the ear sound, the heart perceives meaning. Not in the sense of the meaning of a word that we might look up in a dictionary. Meaning rather as that which we have in mind when we call an experience deeply meaningful. Meaning in this sense is that within which we find rest.

The great teacher concerning the heart in Christian tradition is St. Augustine. That he was an African may well have something to do with his awareness of soul and heart. Living during the collapse of the Roman empire from the fourth to the fifth century—the collapse in fact of the known world of his time—he turned inward and discovered the heart. His *Confessions* have been called the first psychological autobiography. In Christian art he is depicted as lifting up a heart in his hand.

"In my heart of hearts," St. Augustine wrote, "God is closer to me than I am to myself." Paradoxically, he also wrote, "restless is our heart until it rests in you, O God." The first of these two quotations expresses our deepest belonging, the second our restless longing for ultimate meaning. T. S. Eliot touches the same paradox when he writes "home is where we start from," but also,

> We shall not cease from exploration
> And the end of all our exploring
> Will be to arrive where we started
> And know the place for the first time.

What we know at the end of our quest is the meaning of belonging. And the driving force of the spiritual quest is our longing to belong.

In order to check this out more concretely against your own experience, please try to remember now one of your most alive, most awake, most meaningful moments. Psychologists call these moments peak experiences; religious parlance speaks of mystical moments. The mystic experience is an (often sudden) awareness of being one with the Ultimate—a sense of limitless belonging—to God, if you wish to use this term. Suddenly, for a brief moment, you feel no longer "left out," as we so often do, no longer orphaned in the universe. It feels like a homecoming to where you belong.

We all have had these moments even if we shy away from calling them mystical. Rightly understood, the mystic is not a special kind of human being; rather, every human being is a special kind of mystic. At least, this is our calling. In peak experiences we glimpse what life could be like if humans were relating to one another and to all there is, not in an atmosphere of alienation, but out of a deep sense of belonging. All of us are challenged by the glimpses we catch in our best moments. Those who rise to that challenge become mystics.

Remember how these glimpses surprise us, when we least expect them? Thomas Menton suddenly felt one with all on a street corner in Louisville/Kentucky, when he had merely set out to go to the dentist. You may have felt this limitless belonging on a mountain top, or when listening to music. But you may just as likely have been surprised by it when you were stuck in rush-hour traffic or changing your baby's diapers. Whenever it hits us, we know: this is it!—this is the answer, as it were, to a question we keep carrying around with us, unable to put it into words and unable to drop it. We may not be able to put the answer into words either—who can put the meaning of a sunrise into words?—but we can rest in it. We have come home. We have found meaning.

If this description rings true to you from experience, we have found a launching pad for our exploration into the vast universe of religions. We have found our personal access to what all religions have in common. For, by their own testimony, the mystic experience lies at the core of every one of them. Every religious tradition starts from the mystical insight of its (known or unknown) founder. Every one of them has for its highest goal to lead its followers to mystical oneness with the Ultimate.

Attention to our moments of meaning, no matter how fleeting they might be, can lead us even further. They provide us with a brief taste of the nectar, the sweetness in the chalice of all the different religions blossoming like so many flowers in the garden of this world. Our moments of meaning provide us also with a pattern for understanding the differences between the world's religions and their mutual relationships. In order to explore this pattern we must look deeper. We need to look carefully at some subtle aspects of your experience to which you may not yet have paid attention.

Whenever we experience meaning in which our restlessness finds rest (at least for the moment), three aspects can be singled out, which I shall call Word, Silence, and Understanding. Let's start with the most obvious. When we have a meaningful encounter, read or see something deeply meaningful to us, we are apt to say, "this speaks to me." Whatever it is that has meaning for us tells us something, has a message for us, and under this aspect; I call it Word. Obviously, we are not talking here about a word from a vocabulary list. Word stands here in the widest sense for anything that embodies its meaning—for the candle, for instance, that you light on a festive table for a meal you share with a friend.

It is not difficult for us to see that there must be something that "has" meaning whenever we "find" meaning. Nor should it be too difficult to agree on calling this something Word. It gets a little more difficult when we turn to a second aspect of every meaningful experience, one to which we tend to pay less attention. I call this aspect Silence. An example may help us. We can quite readily distinguish between a mere exchange of words and a meaningful conversation. In a genuine conversation we share something that goes deeper than words: we allow the silence of the heart to come to word. In contrast to an exchange of words, a true dialogue between friends is rather an exchange of silence with silence by means of words.

We have experienced Word and Silence in this sense. By focusing our attention we are able to distinguish them as essential aspects of anything that is meaningful. But there is a third aspect to be explored: Understanding. To call something meaningful implies understanding. Yet, there can be Word that is not understood and the same holds true, all the more so, of Silence. Without Understanding neither Word nor Silence have meaning. What then is Understanding? We may think of it as a process: the process by which Silence comes to word and Word, by being understood, returns into Silence.

There is a curious idiom in American vernacular: when something, say a piece of music or a moving event (Word, that is,) becomes profoundly meaningful to us, we might say "this really sends me." Language gives us a hint here. When Word deeply touches us, it sends us, sends us into action. Paradoxically both is true: Word, when it is understood comes to rest in Silence; yet, this rest is not inactivity, rather it is a most dynamic doing. Thus, Understanding happens when we listen so readily to the Word that it moves us to action and so leads us back into the Silence out of which it came and into which it returns. It is by doing that we understand.

Since every religious tradition is an expression of the human heart's perennial quest for meaning, the three characteristic aspects of meaning, Word, Silence, and Understanding will also characterize the world's religions. All three will be present in every tradition, for they are essential for meaning, yet we might expect differences of emphasis. In the primal religions—African or Native American, for instance—our three aspects of meaning are still quite equally emphasized and interwoven with one another as myth, ritual, and right living. But as the Western traditions (Judaism, Christianity, and Islam), Buddhism and Hinduism grow out of the primal religious matrix, emphasis falls more strongly on Word, Silence, or Understanding respectively, although all three will always play their role in each tradition.

Allow me to start with my own, the Christian tradition to sketch a (necessarily rough) scheme that might help us to appreciate the diversity of religious traditions and to understand their relationships to each other. It doesn't take much to see how heavily in Christianity—indeed in the whole biblical tradition—the emphasis falls on the Word. God spoke and the world was created. This is a mythical way of expressing the world view of the Bible: everything that exists can be understood as Word of God. So central is this notion that one might rightly see Judaism, Christianity, and Islam, all three of them, contained as in a seed in the statement "God speaks."

One of the Hasidic tales told by Martin Buber clearly brings out the preeminence of Word in Western religious tradition. Of Rabbi Susya, one of the great Hasidic mystics, it is said that he was unable to quote the sermons of his teacher. The story explains this serious shortcoming in the following way. Rabbi Susya's teacher was in the habit of beginning his sermons by first reading a passage from Holy Scripture. He would start by unrolling the Torah scroll, saying "God spoke: . . ." and then begin to read. But at this point poor Rabbi Susya had already heard more than he could bear. He would carry on so wildly that they had to lead him out of the synagogue. There he would stand in the hallway or in the woodshed beating the walls and shouting "God spoke! God spoke!" that was enough for him. Martin Buber suggests that Rabbi Susya understood the meaning of God's Word more deeply than all those who could quote their teacher's sermons. "For with one word the world is created," he says, "and with one word the world is redeemed."

Where Word is so central, response will be given a high priority. Hence the emphasis on responding to God in the Western tradition of spirituality. "Living by the Word" is a whole world of prayer that springs typically from the biblical faith in God who speaks. And "Living by the Word" implies far more than the idea that God gives the word in the sense of a command and the faithful carry it out. That is merely the moral dimension of it. The full religious dimension implies that we are nourished "by every word that comes forth from the mouth of God." But let us take Word in its widest sense, here too.

Since every thing, every person, every situation comes from the God who speaks, the whole world is Word by which we can live. We need only "taste and see how good God is." We do this with all our senses. Through whatever we taste or touch, smell, hear, or see God's love can nourish us. For the one creating and redeeming Word is spelled out to us in ever new ways. God who is love, has nothing else to say in all eternity but "I love you!" And God says this in ever new ways through everything that comes into being. And we "eat it all up;" as we might say of a book, "I devoured it, cover to cover." We assimilate this food and it becomes our life. We live in its strength. We become Word.

So strong is this emphasis on Word in Christian spirituality that even some faithful Christians are hardly aware that there are within their own tradition other worlds of prayer to be explored. One of them is known as "Prayer of Silence." Here the Silence itself becomes our prayer. C. S. Lewis, is in accord with ancient Christian tradition when he speaks of God as an Abyss of Silence into which we can throw down our minds for ever and ever, never will we hear an echo coming back. Yet, this silent abyss is paradoxically also the divine womb from which the eternal Word comes forth. As an early Christian saying puts it: "Those who can hear God's Word can also hear God's Silence." The two are inseparable. There are more and more Christians today who spontaneously discover the Prayer of Silence. Sometimes they cannot account for their hunger for Silence, their deep desire simply to let themselves down into the quiet depth of God. Unaware that they have found their way into an ancient, timelessly valid realm of Christian prayer, they would be all the more surprised to learn that this could rightly be called the Buddhist dimension of the biblical tradition. Word and Silence are inseparable, as we have said. Just as Word is the core of Western tradition, however, Silence is the core of Buddhism.

Nowhere does this become more obvious than in the account of the Buddha's great wordless sermon. How can there be a sermon without words? The Buddha simply holds up a flower. Only one of his disciples understands, it is said. But how can that one prove without a word that he understood? He smiled, the story tells us. The Buddha smiles back and in the silence between them the tradition is passed on from the Buddha to his first successor, the disciple with the understanding smile. Ever since, we are told, the tradition of Buddhism is passed on in silence. To put it more correctly: what is handed on is Silence.

Not that Buddhists have no sacred Word, but the emphasis is all on the Silence. Their sacred Scriptures are so voluminous, in fact, that it takes a whole day merely to page through them. This is done ritually and with great reverence at least once a year in Buddhist monasteries. And yet, a good Buddhist will say of these Scriptures, "Burn them all!" No one will burn them, of course. That's also quite significant. But just the suggestion to burn them expresses the deep conviction that words must not get in the way of Silence. For the same reason Buddhists will even say, "If you meet the Buddha, kill him!" A Catholic Priest I knew caught on to the universal validity of this Buddhist insight and tried to tell his parishioners, "If you meet the Christ, kill him!" His sermon wasn't a complete success—understandably—although the same insight, less emphasized, can also be found in the Gospel according to John, for instance. We simply have to respect the fact that in their quest for meaning Christians are as tenaciously committed to the Word as Buddhists are to the Silence.

Yet, Word and Silence are not opposed to each other. We cannot say this too often. They are two inseparable aspects of Religion, of the human quest for meaning. That is why in spite of all the emphasis on Living by the Word the Prayer of Silence is equally close to the heart of Christian spirituality and gives Christians—from within, as it were—access to the very core of Buddhism. And since we discovered that, together with Word and Silence, Understanding is another dimension of meaning, we should not be surprised to find a whole other world of Christian prayer focused on Understanding. The technical term for it is "Contemplation in Action," but it could as appropriately be named Prayer of Understanding.

Contemplation is in the biblical tradition exemplified in Moses. Moses ascends the mountain to spend forty days and forty nights in the presence of God. There he is shown the vision of the temple. Coming down from the mountain, he brings with him not only the tablets of the Law, the plan according to which the people will be built into a temple of living stones; he brings also the design for the physical temple, the tabernacle, which is to be built exactly "according to the pattern" that was shown to him on the mountain. These two phases of contemplation belong inseparably together: the vision of the pattern and the action of building according to that pattern.

What distinguishes Contemplation in Action is that vision and action take place simultaneously. A teacher who lavishes love on a child understands God who is love simply by loving. The vision of God is given to her in and through her action. How else do we ever understand except by doing? As the saying goes: "I heard and I forgot; I saw and I remembered; I did and I understood." This is why we could call Contemplation in Action the Prayer of Understanding.

"Yoga is Understanding," says Swami Venkatesananda with deep insight into what makes Hinduism tick. Just as Jews, Christians, and Muslims in their quest for meaning focus on Word and Buddhists on Silence, so Hindus focus on Understanding. Remember what we said about Understanding as the process by which Silence comes to Word and Word finds home into Silence. This gives us a clue to the central intuition of Hinduism: Atman is Brahman—God manifest (Word) is God unmanifest (Silence)—and Brahman is Atman—the divine unmanifest (Silence) is the manifest divine (Word). To know that Word is

Silence and Silence is Word—distinct without separation, and inseparable, yet without confusion—this is Understanding.

The Sanscrit word "Yoga" and the English word "yoke" come from the same linguistic root, meaning "to join." Yoga in all its different forms—service, insight, devotion, etc.—is the action that yokes together Word and Silence by Understanding. And Hinduism knows that this Understanding comes only through doing. In the Bhagavadgita Prince Arjuna is confronted with a conundrum he cannot possibly unravel. Fate has placed him in a position where it is his duty to fight a just but cruel battle against his kinsmen and friends. How can a peace-loving Prince make sense of this situation? The god Vishnu, disguised as Krishna, Arjuna's charioteer, can give him only this advice: do your duty and in the doing you will understand.

We may read volumes and volumes on the art of swimming, yet we'll never understand what swimming is like unless we get wet. So we may read all the books ever written on the love of God and never understand loving unless we love. Countless loving people practice Contemplation in Action without having ever come across its name. What does it matter? By loving they understand God's love from within. Just as the Prayer of Silence may be called the Buddhist dimension of Christian spirituality, so Contemplation in Action is its Hindu dimension.

Admittedly, all this is presented from my own perspective, which is the Christian one. But what other option do I have? If I try to be completely detached from the religious quest for meaning, I have lost touch with the very reality I want to investigate. I would be like the boy who takes his tooth, after the dentist pulled it out, puts some sugar on it and wants to watch how it hurts. One cannot understand pain from the outside, nor joy, nor life, nor live Religion. There is nothing wrong with speaking from inside of one tradition, as long as we do not absolutize our particular perspective, but see it in its relationship to all others.

Remember what we said earlier about our peak moments, our glimpses of meaning, and our spontaneous exclamation, "This is it!" The Christian perspective betrays itself by emphasizing the first word of this little sentence: THIS is it! Enthusiasm for the discovery that "God speaks," that everything is Word of God, makes us exclaim again and again, "THIS is it!" and "THIS is it, whenever we are struck by another Word that reveals meaning. Not so Buddhism. Buddhism in turn is struck by the one Silence that comes to Word in so great a multitude and variety of words. "This is IT," Buddhism exclaims; and this and this and this, every one of all these words, is always IT, is always the one Silence. We need Hinduism to remind us that what really matters is that this IS it—that Word IS Silence and Silence IS Word—therein lies true Understanding. The perspectives complement one another.

By appreciating other perspectives, we learn to broaden our own, without losing it. In fact, our understanding of our own tradition is likely to deepen through contact with others. Christians, for instance, may see the mystery of the triune God reflected in the pattern of Word, Silence, and Understanding. God, whom Jesus calls "Father" can also be understood as that motherly womb of Silence from which the eternal Word is born, before all time, as by God's Self-Understanding, the Silence comes to Word. The Word, the Son, in turn, obediently carries out the Father's will and in doing so returns to God through that Understanding which is perfect love, the Holy Spirit.

From the Cappadocian Fathers, the great theologians of the fourth century to the Shakers in the nineteenth, Christian tradition has conceived these innertrinitarian relationships as a great circle dance. Christ, the great leader of the cosmic dance, leapt from the heavenly throne, "when all things were in deep silence," and, dancing, leads all creation in the power of the Holy Spirit back to God. One way of looking at the interrelationship of the world's religions from a Christian point of view sees them as mirroring on earth God's own great circle dance of Silence, Word, and Understanding.

Religion is not only the quest for meaning, it is also the celebration of meaning. We can think of this celebration as a great dance in which those who live by the Word hold hands with those who dive into the Silence and with those whose path is Understanding. There is something intriguing about the image of a circle dance. Just visualize it for a moment. As long as you stand outside of the circle, it will always seem to you that those nearest to you are going in one direction, those furthest away in exactly the opposite one. There is no way of overcoming this illusion except by getting into the circle. As soon as you hold hands and become one of the dancers, you realize that all are going in the same direction. We made a beginning of this at the Parliament of the World's Religions. My wish for all of us is that we may fully enter into this Great Circle Dance and dance on into the third millennium, celebrating in the midst of our precious diversity our unity.

24

Pluralism and Oppression: Dialogue between the Many Religions and the Many Poor

PAUL F. KNITTER

There are two world-spanning realities that confront and challenge the relevance of any religion in today's world: the many other religions and the many poor. The fact that there are so many ways in which one can be religious and seek after meaning and engagement in life, together with the fact that there are so many persons who are suffering dehumanizing poverty due to an unequal distribution of this world's goods—these two facts will challenge the resources and the responsibility of any religious community. For Christianity, the challenge is intensified because Christians have traditionally claimed that theirs was the only true religion (today, they are modifying that claim to "the best religion") and because they also affirm a Jewish notion of God as One who cares about and responds to the suffering of God's people due to injustice or slavery.

In other words, Christians, together with persons of all religious communities, today must respond to the realities of *pluralism and oppression*. Different though they indeed are, both of these challenges must receive the concern of believers, theologians, and religious leaders; both issues must be brought together and balanced. At present it seems that, for the most part, these two realities have been seen and dealt with as separate issues, without much to do with each other. What is now needed is a coordinated, joint response to these two different, but equally pressing, issues: religious diversity and global responsibility, or interreligious dialogue and socioecological liberation, or in more Christian terms, a theology of religions and a theology of liberation. To join these two areas of concern and commitment is not easy; the balance between them is not neat. In fact, I will suggest that such a balance will make uncomfortable, but fruitful, demands on all religious communities.

The complexity, and yet the promise, of coordinating and balancing a response to the many religions and the many victims is captured and clarified, in more philosophical or academic perspectives, in what I would like to call a Northern (or European/North American) postmodernism and a Southern (or Asian) postmodernism. One of the salient features of the postmodern consciousness that has pervaded much of Europe and North America is its affirmation of, and its delight in, pluralism and diversity. Cultures, religions, ethnic traditions, viewpoints, and interpretations are diverse; they can never be boiled down to one. There can never be any one, absolute culture or meaning or interpretation. Every truth claim is always "socially constructed" and therefore limited. No one truth claim can lord it over or absorb all the others. So let a thousand flowers bloom! *Diversity is dominant!*

Certainly an Asian perspective, especially as I have studied it in India, would affirm such religious or cultural diversity; Indians, like many Asians, have been living within cultural, religious, ethnic pluralism for centuries. But they would add to the Northern postmodern awareness something that Europeans and North Americans all too often ignore or sweep under their expensive rugs. Southern postmodernism recognizes *not just diversity but oppression.* Suffering—of people and of the planet—due to oppression and injustice is also part of their postmodern reality and awareness. In fact, what weighs more heavily in the individual and social experience of countries like India is oppression rather than diversity. In a Southern postmodern awareness, one can say that the suffering of *oppression,* not diversity, *is dominant.*

I write as a citizen of the United States and can testify that the message we North Americans and Europeans hear from countries of the South like India is bound to make us uncomfortable. It reminds us that so much of our delighting in diversity, so much of our interreligious dialogue, has perhaps been a distraction from what should be our concerns about the suffering and oppression so prevalent through the world. But also, and even more uncomfortably, a Southern postmodernism tells us that pluralism and oppression cannot be evenly and neatly balanced; it's not simply a matter of "both and." Rather, the balance will be one of "first this, then that"; first a concern for oppression, then a delighting in diversity.

In other words, a commitment to removing the suffering of people and sentient beings due to oppression must have a certain priority over our concerns for affirming and embracing religious diversity. In our dialogue, our first or our central concern must be to face, understand, and liberate the horrible reality of suffering due to oppression. Such a commitment to liberation, to ecohuman well-being, must be, therefore, the principal *context, content, and criteria* of truth in our interreligious dialogue. Interfaith encounters that do not in some way contain a concern for oppression cannot be authentic dialogues—at least at the moment, in the world as it is.

More precisely, to "balance" pluralism and oppression properly in our interreligious dialogues, we are going to have to afford the oppressed of the earth, and the oppressed earth itself, a priority, a place of preference, around our dialogue tables. Their concerns, their experience, their analysis will have to have what theologians call "a hermeneutical privilege"—a greater weight, a special role in the efforts of religions to understand each other and to come to shared affirmations of truth and value and action. I suggest therefore that the balance between pluralism and oppression is not an equal balancing. The reality of oppression must have a *priority in the contents* of our interfaith dialogue, and the voices of the oppressed peoples and oppressed earth must have a *"hermeneutical privilege" in our dialogical deliberations.*

Such a claim may sound extreme to many traditional practitioners of dialogue. I would now like to present three main reasons why I think such a claim must be taken seriously. The oppressed must be given a hermeneutical privilege in interreligious dialogue in order (1) to make dialogue possible, (2) to make dialogue authentic, and (3) to protect dialogue from exploitation by the powerful.

To Make Dialogue Possible

Let me begin with a sweeping statement: the world as it is really does not allow for authentic dialogue between persons of differing cultures and religions; unless this world is transformed, we cannot truly speak with each other. This statement is based on Jürgen Habermas's notion of "the ideal speech situation" necessary for any conversation. For any genuine exchange between really different persons to take place, all persons or groups have to have full and free access to the table of dialogue; all must be heard and be taken seriously (Habermas 1984, 19). In the words of the Second Vatican Council, for dialogue to work, it must be *par cum pari*—equal with equal (Decree on Ecumenism, #9). Gregory Baum states it more practically: "The conversation involving two or more participants is only fruitful if there exists a certain equality of power among them" (1987, 92).

But that's the problem. Given the inequalities in our world today and the way those inequalities are created and sustained by the structures of economic, political, and military power, there is no common table of discourse in our world where all have ready access, where each voice counts as much as the other, where each participant truly feels free and unthreatened to speak her/his mind. Between nations, and within nations, there are power structures and socioeconomic disparities that *do not allow* all to have equal voice.

What is needed, therefore, at least as a "propaedeutics" to dialogue, is a shared effort to create "ideal speech situations" in the world or in our own societies. And that means praxis—acting together. Naturally, this is not simply a process of first liberation, then conversation. And yet, a conscious, active awareness of the inequalities in our society and of the way some people are not taken as seriously as others must be part of our dialogical mentality; otherwise, our conversations will be seriously lamed.

And so, when we approach "the others" in dialogue, it is not sufficient to affirm and open ourselves to their *difference*. Besides affirming their difference, we must also affirm their *freedom and dignity*. And if such freedom and dignity are lacking, then we must act to make them possible. To delight in difference, but to be unconcerned about dignity, is to be only half-human in reaching out to the other. "The valuation of difference, which leads to sustained encounter and knowledge of the other, then, entails a praxis of resistance against anything that disempowers the other. . . . Liberating praxis therefore is not just a practice of 'the good' in face of intolerable evil; it is also a necessary condition for affirming something 'true' about the other's cultural difference" (Taylor 1991, 159–60).

For how can I respect and affirm someone else's otherness if that person is not allowed to be what she wills to be? Thus, another condition for the possibility of genuine discourse with another whose identity is dominated by structures of socioeconomic or racial or gender oppressions is first to resist actively and act to overcome the domination. "Celebrating difference" and "resisting domination," therefore, become integral elements in the same act of discourse; dialogue demands a commitment both to difference and to emancipation. "This brings the struggle for liberation and justice and the struggle for knowledge amid relativity much closer to one another than we often think" (Taylor 1991, 164; see also 157–59).

To Make Dialogue Authentic

For interreligious dialogue to be authentic it must include not only what the *religions are saying* but also what *people* in the world of today are *asking*. In other words, interfaith dialogue, like theology, must make connections between religious traditions and what theologians like to call "common human experience." In our present world, however, it is evident that for vast numbers of people, their most "common" experience is that of suffering and poverty due to oppression. Therefore, in our dialogue we must accord a privilege or primacy to the voices of these who are suffering; otherwise, our dialogue is not representative of, or responsive to, the world as it is. Rebecca Chopp has stated this with clarity and passion:

> To be poor is the representative human experience; only by standing with the poor and by focusing our interpretative lens through the poor may we, too, adequately experience and interpret history. (Chopp 1986, 48)
>
> Only by standing with those who suffer—the poor and the oppressed, the living and the dead—shall we see the reality of human existence. (Ibid 151, see also 122)

When we of the "established" classes or "developed" nations or "mainline" religions begin to listen to and take seriously the reality and the witness of the countless victims of oppression, something both frightening and marvelous can happen to us. Similar to the sudden or gradual awakening of a Zen experience, we find ourselves viewing the world differently. Our usual way of seeing ourselves and our nation and the community of nations is, "interrupted," maybe "subverted," perhaps even "ruptured." We become "enlightened" to the reality of domination and injustice and how this pervades so much of who we are as citizens, consumers, and religious beings (Tracy 1987, 71–72). As it is communicated to us through the bodies and voices of victims, "suffering . . . ruptures our categories, our experiences, our history; suffering demands a new paradigm of interpreting existence and Christian [also religious] witness. . . . This question, the question of suffering, functions . . . to demand new interpretations and understandings, new ways of conceiving and answering questions, new ways of ordering questions and concerns" (Chopp 1986, 120). This presence of the victims and their suffering in the interfaith dialogue will both rupture and reroute the conversation.

But I also dare to suggest that the reality of suffering communicated in the presence of victims can provide the interfaith dialogue with as "common" a ground as can be found in our pluralistic, multiperspectival, relative world. This is due not only to the *universality* of suffering— that is, to the fact that it is found throughout the world in similar forms and with similar causes; suffering can also provide common ground because of its *immediacy* to our experience. Yes, as postmodern scholars remind us, all experience is interpreted. But if there is any experience where the gap between the experience and the interpretation is as short or transparent as it can be, it is suffering. While interpretations about the cause or the remedy of suffering will abound, the sense or interpretation of suffering as a reality that calls us to some kind of resistance is, I dare say, almost given in the very experience of suffering itself. Suffering has a universality and immediacy that makes it the ideal, and necessary, site for establishing common ground for interreligious encounter. The immediacy of suffering is available to all cultures and all religions. The filter of interpretation, in other words, has a harder time coming up with divergent perspectives on the reality of suffering; suffering is too immediate to be suffocated under the pillow of a hundred interpretations.

Francis Schüssler-Fiorenza is cautious but clear in advancing the same claim: "Suffering brings us to the bedrock of human existence and cuts through the hermeneutical circle. . . . Suffering is, so to speak, at the seam between interpretation and reality" (1991, 135). It cuts through the hermeneutical circle by bringing the endless movement of interpretations to a temporary stop and enabling us to make truth claims that call us to action. Our interpretations of suffering are close enough to its reality to warrant our action or resistance.

If the reality of suffering is going to be part of the content of interfaith dialogue, the presence of sufferers or victims in the dialogue is necessary. This necessity can also be argued from the very nature of the hermeneutical task as understood by Western "masters of interpretation" such as Gadamer and Habermas. If there are no absolute foundations for truth, if truth is not given to us on an untarnished and untarnishable silver platter that is beyond all particular interpretations, if all we have are our differing, culturally limited perspectives on truth—then the path to truth must contain a broad conversation between our various perspectives. The conversation must be as inclusive, as broad as possible. We need, as the specialists tell us, a "wide reflective equilibrium" between as many viewpoints as possible (Fiorenza 1984, 301–311).

But the recognition that our conversation has to be *inclusive* leads us to the equally important, but unsettling, recognition that it has been *exclusive*. It is an undeniable, though often neglected, reality that a vast assemblage of human beings have either been excluded, or not able, to participate in the conversations and deliberations taking place in our academies, halls of governments, churches. They have been called the "wretched of the earth," the "underbelly of history." They are the people who, for a variety of reasons, have not counted or who simply have not been thought about, or if they have been thought about, have been either excluded or not taken seriously. Theirs have been the "defeated knowledges." And if they have been the victims of economic injustice, they have also suffered from "cognitive injustice" (Fiorenza 1991, 136).

If our conversations-toward-truth must include the genuinely other in order to be successful, then we have to be clear on where we find these "others": the other is not only the culturally, religiously, sexually, ethnically different, but also the socially and politically excluded. In fact, I am suggesting that these "others" have a primacy of inclusion, that they have a special voice in the conversation, that their experiences and witness have a "hermeneutical privilege" in searching for the true and the good.

This primacy is based, first of all, on the simple and unsettling fact that they have been excluded for so long; now "cognitive justice" must be done. The conversation is radically maimed, and our "rationality" is crucially deprived, if the voices of the voiceless are not brought into the conversation and given a first hearing. Only in this way can our conversation be sufficiently broad to be serious.

> Recognizing the voices of those absent from the conversation—often voiceless because of death, persistent hunger, or systematic distortion of their social and political life—is *the crucial way* by which the fullest breadth of conversation can occur, a breadth needed for the truth of reasoning to occur and be sustained (Taylor, 1990, 64, emphasis mine).

The voices of the excluded victims—including those who can speak for the victimized earth—have a privileged place in the discourse, therefore, not only because they are so different but because their difference is challenging and, as stated earlier, can rupture and reroute our awareness. "It becomes necessary to make the community of discourse as inclusive as possible. One cannot simply appeal to experiential evidence as the warrant for truth; one has to bring the interpretation of conflicting paradigms and traditions into dialogue and conversation with the neglected and often repressed voices of others" (Fiorenza 1991, 137).

But it is not just the *quantity* of the oppressed that privileges them in the dialogue. It is also the content or the *quality* of the experience of oppression that enables the oppressed to know things that the comfortable and powerful can never know by themselves. This has to do with the victims' "greater experience of negativity." Though negativity is certainly part of the life of every mortal, the oppressed experience it both in a quantity and quality that make their experience different from that of the economically well-off and the politically powerful. Victims, therefore, have "an insight born of radical negativity not experienced by the more elite, centrist groups" (Taylor 1990, 65). More concretely, the oppressed can offer insights into social and political realities that those in the center simply cannot have. Victims have "learned more about the culture of the powerful than the powerful know about those they subjugate" (Ibid). Such insights about the negativity of human existence and about our established culture are not just "interesting"; they are urgently essential if our conversations are going to have anything to do with addressing the ills of the world.

But just what is meant in assigning a "hermeneutical privilege" or a "priority" to the voices of the voiceless? Certainly, I am not suggesting that theirs are the only voices to be heard. A central concern for overcoming oppression and suffering does not deny, indeed it demands, that our conversations and efforts be and remain *plural*. The voices of the affluent, of the middle class, of mystics and artists must be heard together with the voices of the oppressed. Also, the priority and privilege given to victims does not mean that their views or claims are simply and always normative. Victims can also have distorted interpretations of their reality and dangerous plans to remedy it. There are no absolutely privileged seats, no final gavels, around the table of dialogue.

Attempting to describe the privileged place of victims, I would suggest that it means that no conversation can be considered complete or finished unless the voices of the suffering have been heard. Also, these voices must be heard, not only "first," but also "constantly" (Taylor 1990, 66) and seriously. To take them seriously, to be able really to listen to them, we will have to recognize that it will often be difficult to hear and to understand them and that we will have to overcome initial reactions of mistrust and avoidance. Speaking from his privileged place in academia, Tracy has recognized this:

> All the victims of our discourses and our history have begun to discover their own discourses in ways that our discourse finds difficult to hear, much less listen to. Their voices can seem strident and uncivil—in a word, other. And they are. We have all begun to sense the terror of that otherness. But only by beginning to listen to those other voices may we also begin to hear the otherness within our own discourse and within ourselves. What we might then begin to hear above our own chatter, are possibilities we have never dared to dream. (Tracy 1987, 79)

To Protect Dialogue from Exploitation by the Powerful

Some of the sharpest criticisms of the new call for a truly pluralistic dialogue between religions comes from those who use a political analysis of language and of discourse to show how proponents of dialogue can be, and have been, coopted by the economic-political powers. The basis for their cutting critique is quite simple: our interpretations, our language, do not simply *limit* our own grasp of truth, they can also *oppress* the ability of others to assert and live their own truths. Language is not only limiting; it is also self-serving of one group and oppressive of others. David Tracy has taken these admonitions seriously:

> Every discourse bears within itself the anonymous and repressed actuality of highly particular arrangements of power and knowledge. Every discourse, by operating under certain assumptions, necessarily excludes other assumptions. Above all, our discourses exclude those others who might disrupt the established hierarchies or challenge the prevailing hegemony of power. (1987, 79)

We might easily miss the deeper, all-pervasive content of what is here being recognized about language and interpretation. What we did not face in the immediate past (modernity) and what has become frighteningly clear today (one of the postmodern insights) is that such exclusion of others, such power-serving and self-serving acts, are not just an occasional "misuse" of language that can be removed much as we clear a frog out of our throat. Rather, we are speaking about "systemic distortions," pervasive tendencies within all use of language—a disease in our vocal cords! We cannot interpret and we cannot speak without hearing—and often responding to—the siren call of ideology, the inclination to use our "truth" for our own power or dominance:

> Ideologies are unconscious but systemically functioning attitudes, values, and beliefs produced by and in the material conditions of all uses of language, all analyses of truth, and all claims to knowledge. . . . Ideologies are carried in and by the very language we use to know any reality at all." (Tracy 1987, 77)

These systemic distortions of language can become systemic distortions of dialogue. Our noble, high-sounding programs for a genuinely pluralistic dialogue can be turned into mechanisms to "manage" those who are different from, and possibly a threat to, us. As Raymond Williams warns:

> A primary means by which privileged groups mask their hegemony is via a language of common contribution and co-operative shaping [a language of pluralism and dialogue]; to the extent that such groups can convince all partners in public dialogue that each voice contributes equally, to that extent does the conversation deflect attention from the unequal distribution of power underlying it. (Williams 1977, 112)

Practitioners of interreligious dialogue who are aware of the actual unequal distribution of power in our world and who want to defend dialogue against the infection of ideology call for a "hermeneutical suspicion" that must begin all our dialogues. Our first step is always to cast a suspicious eye on our knowledge and programs and calls to dialogue—and to face and ferret out where it is that our truth claims are power claims. Here, precisely here, is where the voices of the oppressed must play a privileged role in the dialogue: without their voices, we cannot carry out a heremeneutical suspicion of our own tradition or of our own contribution to the dialogue. Alone, by ourselves, we are self-serving selves. Aloysius Pieris, who practices dialogue in the midst of Asia's suffering and oppression, speaks clearly and to the point: "The people who can truly purify a religion of communalist ideology are not the theologians or the religious hierarchs, but only the conscienticized victims of that ideology" (Pieris 1989, 308–9). Only with the help of the oppressed can the oppressors truly face their own oppression.

We can prevent the cooptation of dialogue by making sure that in *all* of our interfaith encounters the poor and suffering and those caring for the suffering earth will be *present* and will have a *privileged place* in our conversations. In other words, we must recognize and insist not simply that "each voice contributes equally" but that some of us have a more urgent and a more helpful word to speak—namely, those who in the past have not spoken and who in the present are victims. If dialogue must always be *par cum pari* (equal with equal), there are also those who are *primi inter pares* (first among equals).

But if the suffering and the victimized are truly to exercise a heremeneutical privilege in our dialogues, it will not be sufficient for those with the power to simply *listen* to them; we will also have to *act* with and for them. Understanding what the suffering are saying, grasping the structures of oppression that keep them in bondage and that afflict our planet, is not simply a matter of "theory." It can come only from praxis. Our present-day world demands that those who engage in dialogue engage in some kind of liberative praxis. Without such praxis, we will not be able to "hear" the voices of the privileged victims; and our dialogue will be distorted or coopted.

> What is demanded . . . is an alternative practice, that is, gestures and acts of solidarity with movements that wrestle against those unjust structures. Such a practice would modify the consciousness of the participants and affect the reading of their own religious tradition. . . . A new practice [is] an indispensable dimension of the quest for theological [dialogical] truth. (Baum 1991, 13)

The conclusion of these reflections is that there is *not* a neat balance between pluralism and oppression. To recognize and affirm this imbalance is to recognize not a problem but an opportunity. By granting the oppressed of the earth, and the oppressed earth, a prior or privileged place in our dialogue, we will be able to make the pluralism of religions a source of enrichment and transformation for our world. The oppressed of the earth, in other words, can serve as the bridges between the many, differing religions of the earth. The oppressed can be the "mediators" who will help the differing religions to understand each other and to work together. By first listening to the oppressed of the world, the religions will be better able to listen to each other.

Works Cited

Baum, Gregory. 1987. "The Social Context of American Catholic Theology," in *Catholic Theology in North American Context: Current Issues in Theology* (CTSA Proceedings), George Kilkourse, ed. Macon: Mercer University Press.

Baum, Gregory. 1991. "Radical Pluralism and Liberation Theology," in *Radical Pluralism and Truth: David Tracy and the Hermeneutics of Religion*. Werner C. Jeanrond and Jennifer L. Rike, eds. New York: Crossroad, pp. 1–17.

Chopp, Rebecca S. 1986. *The Praxis of Suffering: An Interpretation of Liberation and Political Theologies*. Maryknoll: Orbis Books.

Fiorenza, Francis Schüssler, 1984. *Foundational Theology: Jesus and the Church*. New York: Crossroad.

Fiorenza, Francis Schüssler. 1991. "The Crisis of Hermeneutics and Christian Theology," in *Theology at the End of Modernity*, Sheila Greeve Davaney, ed. Philadelphia: Trinity Press International, pp. 117–40.

Habermas, Jürgen. 1984. *The Theory of Communicative Action*. Vol. 1. Thomas McCarthy, tr. Boston: Beacon Press.

Pieris, Aloysius. 1989. "Faith Communities and Communalism" *East Asian Pastoral Review*. Vol. 3–4, pp. 294–310.

Taylor, Mark Kline. 1990. *Remembering Esperanza: A Cultural-Political Theology for North American Praxis*. Maryknoll: Orbis Books.

Taylor, Mark Kline. "Religion, Cultural Pluralism, and Liberating Praxis: In Conversation with the Work of Langdon Gilkey," *Journal of Religion*, 71 (1991)

Tracy, 1987. *Plurality and Ambiguity: Hermeneutics, Religion, Hope*. New York: Harper & Row.

Williams, Raymond. 1977. *Marxism and Literature*. New York: Oxford University Press.

25

The Interspiritual Age: Global Spirituality in the Third Millennium

WAYNE TEASDALE

The Parliament of the World's Religions was a world historical event! A thousand years from now it will be regarded as the most creative event crowning the second millennium. Something radically new broke through at the Parliament. I experienced it as nothing less than a new, universally significant Pentecost. Although the participants were not of one mind, they were definitely of one *heart*. At the Parliament, a unifying consciousness emerged, not a consciousness that obliterates the rich diversity, but one that inspired in us the realization of and invitation to *community* among members of the different religions, etc.

The Parliament is a turning point in history because the possibility and experiential fact of this community emerged during this extraordinary event; it became explicit. A new model of how the religions relate to one another has surfaced, replacing the old model based on mutual suspicion, antagonism, competition, and conflict. This development is extremely important because it sets aside one of the chief sources of war in our historical experience.

The rise of community among cultures and religious traditions brings with it a deeply fruitful openness to learning from one another. It makes possible what we can call *interspirituality:* the assimilation of insights, values, and spiritual practices from the various religions and their application to one's own inner life and development. This phenomenon has truly revolutionary implications, especially for the real likelihood of a global culture and civilization forming that is unmistakably universal in a more than geographical sense.

The community of religions born at the Parliament resolved to collaborate together on the critical issues. The primary one is of course the environmental crisis. This crisis has greatly concentrated minds, and focused our efforts. This commitment to resolve the ecological crisis by changing our relationship with the earth is enshrined in the declaration, *Towards a Global Ethic.* Many other critical issues are similarly addressed in the *Ethic,* but there is no detailed formulation of how to *live* the *Global Ethic,* nor how to change direction. It is hinted at in the final paragraph where there is an opening to the role of spirituality without mentioning it by name, but clearly it is the inner life that is to spark the change in consciousness that will permit us to advance.

Spirituality is the time-honored way to bring radical change in us. At the historic Parliament this spirituality was very present. More precisely, the spirituality of the third millennium was glimpsed. We saw its fruit in the thousands of exchanges between participants: in the openness, mutual respect, the quality of listening, the humor and affection that were universally operative during the Parliament.

In what follows, I want to discuss the nature, elements, and capacities of third millennial or global spirituality. This multifaith view of spirituality is thus a universal approach, a fresh understanding of its nature and role as a resource for transformation of persons and societies with the goal of assisting the birth of a new civilization, a civilization that has a compassionate, loving *heart.*

Global Spirituality

The terms "global," "universal" or "multifaith" spirituality do not signify or imply a notion of a superspirituality, an overarching new form that is a creation of syncretism, a forced, unreflective synthesis of all the types of spirituality present in the various religions and part of a larger, perennial tradition. Although this perennial tradition certainly exists in a metaphysical sense, there is no all-embracing spirituality that represents it and actualizes it in human life. To detail the nature and scope of a global spirituality is a much more modest enterprise. It aims at a consensus of experience on the common elements present in every viable form of spiritual life, regardless of the tradition. But here of course what is referred to as spirituality in this sense is *not* the lowest common denominator; it is rather the most mature form embodied in the lives of truly enlightened, fully aware, vitally conscious persons.

Universal spirituality is concerned with those common insights, intuitions, experiences, values, and practices that are essential in every solid form of spiritual life. A mature or viable kind of spirituality will greatly improve us as human beings, particularly on the psychological, moral, and mystical levels.

We must further clarify by making a distinction between theoretical and practical spirituality. I am not referring primarily to the former. That is the conceptual dimension of the enterprise, a highly complex matter fraught with numerous difficulties. The theoretical dimension would have to include and build on the perennial philosophy, the primordial universal tradition, adding many insights from more than a century of comparative studies, interfaith encounters and common approaches to understanding the feasibility of such a multifaith view of spiritual life.

Concerning the mystical nature or origin of all spirituality, it can be said to be a direct, immediate, experiential awareness of Ultimate Reality, however that is *known* and conceived. All mysticism is either personal or impersonal, or relational, intimate, and loving, or nonrelational, purely unitive, nonemotional and nonaffective. Some forms may have both the personal and the impersonal aspects, but they are very rare and constitute a more total type that possesses greater understanding.

All mysticism is also either, or both transcendent and immanent, *apophatic* and *katophatic*. A nonrelational mysticism, i.e., a Buddhist form, etc., is essentially transcendent, while the personalist mysticism of Christianity, Islam, and Judaism, etc., are both immanent because of God's nearness to the human, and transcendent—that is, beyond us, beyond our grasp. At the same time, the experience of Ultimate Reality is profoundly apophatic, that is, experienced in an ineffable way that transcends the capacities of reason, intellect, memory, imagination, and the senses. Where these are employed in our conceptions of Ultimate Reality, the katophatic approach is at play because it draws its terms from their operations and applies its concepts to the Ultimate by the method of analogy.

The concern here is with the *practical* dimension of spirituality: spirituality as a universal property of religious consciousness that expresses itself in many ways, i.e., through prayer, liturgy, chanting and other forms of music, meditation, yoga, diet, ascetical discipline, self-control, contemplation, art, and service, all of which engage one's inner being, *how* one is, and indeed, *what* one is because of the exercise of this *how*.

Spirituality, in its most basic sense, originates from an inner movement of the heart, with the assistance of the mind and affecting the total consciousness of the individual. The heart or will, the mind, intelligence or intellect, and the consciousness or awareness or understanding work together in the deep stirring of desire that is essentially seeking relationship with Ultimate Reality or with the Divine, regardless of how it or they are known or conceived. In this general sense, spirituality is

also the fundamental essence of all genuine religion, and so, is the animating core of human life and experience. Many passages from various
texts across the traditions could be adduced to characterize this impulse
of the soul, but St. Augustine gave it precise and eloquent expression in
his prayer at the beginning of his *Confessions,* the great autobiography
that articulates the inner nature of us all: "Our hearts, O Lord, are
restless until they rest in you, because, O God, they were made for
you."[1]

A further distinction should also be made before outlining the elements of all spirituality in the age to come, that is, in its universal or
multifaith sense, and that distinction recognizes both an individual and
a social dimension to all authentic spirituality. The social dimension
shows itself in a concern for others, especially for the larger community
of the earth itself. An *acosmic* or totally otherworldly spirituality lacks
this social aspect, which is becoming in our time a very urgent necessity,
particularly as we consider the demands of justice, the needs of the
poor, the issue of human rights, the preservation of endangered cultures,
the care and protection of the earth and other species. These are just a
few areas that vitally aware individuals will include in their vision of
compassion and love. These concerns will then guide their action.

The Elements of Global Spirituality

Every fully realized form of spirituality has seven elements in common
with every other type, although in varying degrees of emphasis. These
elements include: (1) a capacity to live morally, (2) deep nonviolence,
(3) solidarity with all life and the earth itself, (4) a spiritual practice
and a mature self-knowledge, (5) simplicity of life, (6) selfless service,
and (7) prophetic action. The first three are foundational dispositions,
compelling attitudes, and enduring commitments; four is the means of
spiritual living, while the last three are the fruits.

The capacity to live morally becomes a solid foundation for spirituality when this capacity is actualized in practice, in one's daily life. It is an
indispensable first and enduring condition. Each religion and spirituality
emphasizes this insight. We see it in the Ten Commandments, in Jesus'
two great commandments or conditions for salvation "to love God"
and one's "neighbor."[2] It is present in the yogic tradition of Hinduism

---

1. St. Augustine, *Confessions,* I.1.
2. For the Ten Commandments see Exodus 20:3–17, and for the two great laws of Christ,
see Matthew 22: 36–40, and for his ultimate commandment, turn to John 13: 34–35.

in the notion of *yama* (restraint) and *niyama* (discipline),[3] and the Eight-Fold Path of the Buddha. The Global Ethic draws on this foundational role of the moral part of human being, and appeals it. Spiritual life is not possible without moral character, but the moral dimension is only the beginning.

Secondly, genuine spirituality—one that also accounts for the new context we now find ourselves in—requires a commitment to *deep non-violence*. This sort of nonviolence is similar to the *ahimsa* of the Indian tradition as it is found in its Jain, Buddhist, and Hindu types. This kind of nonharming extends to all sentient beings and to the planet itself. It is not simply a focus on the human species. Deep nonviolence is clearly necessary to the successful growth and development of spirituality and to the evolution of a new culture because it adjusts our outer actions and inner attitudes to the consistency of compassion and the demands of love. As one grows in holiness, one also becomes more sensitive to the rights of others, including other species.

Thirdly, this commitment to such a profound nonviolence is based on a tangible sense of spiritual and moral solidarity, an interconnectedness with all members of the human family, but also, with all other species and the whole world as well. It is this realization of interdependence that gives rise to the insight of solidarity, and incarnates our attempts to live nonviolently, an urgent need for spiritual life and society.

The fourth element of every spirituality concerns spiritual practice. No spirituality is vitally authentic and effective without some sort of spiritual discipline that is the means of inner growth in the attitudes, dispositions, habits, and commitments of the life of meaning, depth, and human maturity that is glimpsed in the best of religious consciousness. This point goes to the heart of the matter since spiritual practice is the factor of human effort in the work of our transformation. It is the *living*, transformative power of the inner reality taking form in a disciplined habit of relating to the Divine or Ultimate Reality. Without a spiritual practice, spirituality is a hollow affair; it has no substance, and is reduced to the formalism of external religiosity.

Spiritual practice(s), notably contemplative forms of prayer, meditation, sacred reading, or what is called *lectio divina* in the Christian tradition, which literally means "divine reading"—a restful, awake presence at liturgy and ritual, an active participation in them, music, chanting, yoga, even walking, are all transformative, for they change us

---

3. *Yama* and *Niyama* essentially deal with the self-control that ethics imposes on us.

within, and make this change consistent with our actions in the world, in our daily lives.

Transformation happens slowly as we gain self-knowledge, and uncover the hidden motives that lie deep within us, perhaps even in the unconscious part of ourselves. This self-knowledge is salutary and profoundly useful to us in our process of inner growth. It is also seen as a gift of divine grace, and contains the wisdom to guide us in our contemplative development. In some traditions, for example, certain Hindu and Buddhist schools, this grace can be mediated through a guru or spiritual master, but it represents a significant factor in our growth to wholeness in most—if not all—traditions.

Self-knowledge, when it reaches maturity, when we go beyond denial and projection—denial of our limitations and faults, buried motives; projection, meaning judging others rather than working on overcoming the obstacles in us to spiritual/human wholeness, hence "projecting" onto others this need for inner work—becomes the basis for very deep changes within us. This quality of inner change is what I mean by the term "transformation." It is a radical alteration of our inner "form," our character, will, and all our old habits of thought and action.

This possibility of transformation is what gives evidence of authenticity and maturity in the spiritual journey itself; indeed, it is difficult to regard a spirituality, as it functions within a person's life, to be either authentic or mature unless it contains a self-knowledge that leads to actual changes within the person. Thus spirituality is meant to make us better by unlocking our potential for divinity, in a sense, to be *like* God in some participatory way, or as the Christian theologians of the Greek Orthodox Church called it in the early centuries of the Gospel, *theosis* or deification: becoming *like* God!!! Another way of saying this is that it awakens the Buddha nature in us. If spirituality does not offer access to actualizing our potential for this higher form of life, which is what we are made for to begin with, then what ultimate value can it possibly have?

The transformation to which spirituality summons us has four basic levels to it, and I say "basic" because it involves more of the faculties, like imagination, memory, intellect, and reason, the emotions and the senses, but for our purposes here, they can be identified primarily as consciousness, will, character, and action or behavior.

Consciousness affects our understanding of reality and life. Our awareness grows, expands, takes in more, and the more it expands, the greater becomes our capacity to understand, to change, to *realize* what we are potentially: images and likenesses of the Divine Reality. As our understanding increases, ignorance is dissipated, and we can then modify or alter our motives; we can outgrow the selfish ones. Our will knows an inner change, a purification, and this change affects a radical transmutation in our character and action or behavior.

The will becomes stable in desiring the Good, in transcending self-concern, so that we can respond to others in love and compassion. The will seeks less the goods that are mutable, but desires ones that do not change—e.g., wisdom, spiritual knowledge, the virtues, mystical awareness and unitive vision/life. This change gradually habituates the character to be informed by these values and spiritual treasures—to be formed *in* them—and to be transformed from self-preoccupation to love, from hypocrisy to sincerity, from sin to holiness, from human limitations to the power of grace. The character takes on the form and substance of virtue, slowly becoming deified. Finally, a living, mature, effective spiritual life transforms our action or behavior, making it conform to grace and the requirements of love. All these levels of transformation happen in tandem as we grow into our ultimate nature and identity.

Spiritual practice, which of course includes and demands self-knowledge, manifests a realized or transformed being, or nature in the latter three aspects of spirituality—that is, in simplicity of life, selfless service, and prophetic action. These are some of the fruits of transformation in the domain of action, and no genuine spirituality today would be without them.[4] They represent inner resources needed for changing the direction of the human family so that it can accept its *universal responsibility,* as the Dalai Lama puts it, for the earth, etc.[5]

One of these inner resources that advances this common responsibility, and could effect a decisive change in humankind's relationship to the environment and the issues of social justice, poverty, etc., is simplicity of life. Spirituality has always espoused this value and practice in every form it has assumed, particularly in the monastic traditions and other forms of religious life. Simplicity of life has a profound contemporary relevance, for it can have a major impact on altering how we relate to the earth, other species, and the poor. This point of global spirituality has a subtle necessity to it because—let us face the fact—*we have to*

---

4. We must keep in mind that this whole discussion is centered on a socially engaged global spirituality. There is a long tradition of an *acosmic,* ascetical spirituality in the Asian traditions, and in Christianity—and these are certainly valid—but the need of the planet in our time is for a general spirituality that is also capable of action.

5. Tenzin Gyatso the Fourteenth Dalai Lama, *The Global Community and the Need for Universal Responsibility* (Boston: Wisdom Publications, 1990).

simplify our lives if the Ecological Age[6] is really to take root. Simplicity of life reveals itself concretely in the great generosity of embracing a more simple lifestyle that doesn't require using up so many precious resources, a use that degrades the environment, threatens and oppresses other species, and deprives the poor. There is wonderful adage: "Live simply so others may simply live." This wise saying sums up the whole point, and demonstrates the practical efficacy of true spirituality. "To live simply so others may simply live" applies to the planet itself. It is the chief "other" for all of us, but it also applies to our relationship with other species as well as the poor. This dictum is a way to concentrate our minds, and our efforts, on changing how we live. It is not enough only to talk about the need to change. We *must* change! We have to embrace a more simple way of life, or we have no right to speak! It has to begin with each one of us, or else our words are meaningless. A spirituality that ignores simplicity is bogus! Furthermore, there is no "upper class," "middle class" and "lower class" spirituality. There is *only* the dimension of spirituality itself as part of human experience, and its requirements are universal.

Similarly, true spirituality is always open to service; it never evades service, especially as need arises, but the spiritual life summons us to a selfless kind of service, a form of action, that as the Bhagavadgita so powerfully emphasizes, does *not* seek a result, that is, is not attached to the possible fruits of any action, and so, is not performed with any result or purpose in mind other than to respond to the perceived need. This quality of selfless action does not come easy to us. It is something we must learn through education, other kinds of training or formation, and much practical experience.

The seventh aspect of Global Spirituality is prophetic action: the necessity to speak out when injustice, oppression, the abuse of human rights, the rights of other species and the Earth itself occur. This element is a very critical function of all spirituality, particularly through the collective voice of religious and spiritual leaders, and it is something desperately needed in our time—at the very dawn of the Interspiritual Age—because often most religious and spiritual leaders are curiously silent before these kinds of challenges. For example, although much has been said about Bosnia and Rwanda where the cost of speaking out prophetically is rather low, virtually nothing has been uttered by any religious or spiritual leader about the systematic violation of the human rights of Tibetans by the Chinese colonial government in Tibet! Person-

---

6. The term "Ecological Age" was coined by Thomas Berry. See his *The Dream of the Earth* (San Francisco: Sierra Club Books, 1988), pp. 36–49.

ally, I find this silence quite disturbing; it illustrates a lack of courage and moral strength that hides behind considerations of prudence and discretion, but appears as weakness, while placating a worldly power.

Tibet itself—if I may be indulged a digression—is, I believe, an important *test* case and an *opportunity* for the religions in their evolution into becoming more fully the Community of Religions. It offers them an opportunity to contribute to the emergence of a new culture that is founded on justice, compassion, and love. Such a new global culture— a civilization with a *heart*—will never be until the religions can speak out and act collectively when confronted with such a challenge as China's arrogant and shameful behavior in Tibet. Intense spiritual life grants the moral clarity and the courage to confront evil with the truth.

Genuine spirituality—and certainly this is true a fortiori of a multifaith approach to spiritual life, culture and action—is willing to engage in moral and political action when justice is at stake. If it cannot, it then vitiates the potentially effective and prophetically incisive contribution of religion in encouraging the establishment of a universal culture that is spiritually viable. An attitude of business as usual simply will not do, and such an attitude reveals a vacuousness to moral and spiritual authority that is following such a bankrupt policy in the face of grave moral evil, such as exists in the Tibetan situation.

Spiritual leadership, guided by a deeply *alive* spirituality, or mystical life, is always ready to take a stand when required by the demands of justice. I believe that the religions, all comtemplatively aware persons, and all decent people must stand unambiguously with Tibet in its consistently nonviolent, moral struggle with China. We should avail ourselves of the inherent lessons to be learned in endorsing the Tibetan People's approach and identifying with their higher moral position vis-à-vis the People's Republic of China. Supporting Tibet in this way would educate us in nonviolence, habituating us to this way of action, while allowing us to emerge slowly with an enhanced identity as the Community of Religions because we have learned and exercised the prophetic function together. To put the matter rather bluntly: can we carry the cross with Tibet? Do we have the moral depth and spiritual wisdom to do so? More basically still, are we worthy to do so? The point of prophetic action is that an effective and mature spirituality always produces the fortitude necessary to rise to the exercise of the prophetic voice in relation to the actions of governments, nations, cultures, religions, and persons. The Interspiritual Age will focus this prophetic function as a collective responsibility of the religions, and it will be uncompromised in its operations.

The Capacities of a Universal Spirituality

Mystical life, contemplative interiority, and mature spirituality awakens and develops a number of gifts. These can be called the capacities of contemplation or spirituality. The reason why they are capacities is simply that they facilitate our sensitive, loving, compassionate relationship to the other, whoever this *other* is: human beings, different species, the natural world, the earth as a whole, or the Divine. The capacities are very beneficial in the area of interreligious dialogue, cooperation, and so are quite useful in the task of building the global, multifaith civilization. They are really indispensable skills for the works of dialogue, collaboration, peacemaking, and prophetic action. These capacities are: *openness, presence, listening, being, seeing, spontaneity,* and *joy*.

Briefly, *openness* is a receptivity to everyone and everything. It is quite fundamentally an other-centeredness, a disposition of availability to others. Similarly, the inner life gives us the ability to be present to others in all senses. By being present we meet them in the eternal *Now* where everything is already and always happening. Through the gift of *presence* we fashion ourselves as a *home* for the Divine, for creation, for all others. The present moment is thus sacramental because it is filled with the reality of the Ultimate, with God, as Pierre de Caussade reminds us in his little masterpiece. *Abandonment to Divine Providence.*[7]

Deep spirituality also grants us the capacity to *listen,* but the quality of this listening is much more subtle and comprehensive than ordinary listening; it is a complete inner attention, a *listening with the heart*. Here again we are listening to the Divine, to nature, the earth, to persons, members of other species, and to ourselves.

People who are mystically awake, or spiritually enlightened, also have the ability to just *be,* and they are very conscious of the importance of this capacity for simply *being*. Our technological society stresses *doing,* and many of us are always rushing around *doing* many things. Contemplative spirituality is a call to *be:* to *be* just who we are in the deepest sense of our nature.

Closely associated with the ability to be is the capacity to *see:* to see reality as it is; to see ourselves as we are. This *seeing* arises from the depths of contemplative interiority, from spiritual discipline; it is a seeing with the heart. Contemplative, mystical seeing, which also re-

---

7. Jean-Pierre de Caussade, *Abandonment to Divine Providence* (Garden City, NY: Doubleday, 1975), cf. ch. 2.

quires and *is* self-knowledge, is actually the gift of *perspective,* of seeing everything in its proper place.

Spiritual life, as it advances into its fullness, also awakens in us the capacity for real *spontaneity* in our actions and responses to others. This spontaneity leads us into appropriate actions in all the situations of life. It inspires us to spontaneous acts of compassion, kindness, mercy, charity, love, patience, and gentleness, and is ultimately a very well developed and subtle sensitivity to all beings, including the earth and the cosmos.

The crown of all these capacities is unitive *joy.* Joy is an unmistakable sign of the deeper life in a person. In the mystical process, it comes to be an abiding gift when the individual has reached, in the ultimate state of mystical consciousness in the unitive experience, union with God, or with Ultimate Reality. Joy *is* the presence of the Divine in us, or the completion of our goal in the earthly pilgrimage. Joy is the plenitude of spirituality. A sense of humor is a real indication of this spiritual fullness or maturity. This joy, and all these other capacities, culminate in a mystical kind of peace that is very deep and abiding; it is a supernatural peace, that peace that is the possession of the Ultimate, the Divine, or God. Ultimately that peace is *rest* in the Absolute.

We must allow all our efforts at building a new civilization to breathe with the inner life, and that is spirituality, the interior awareness of contemplative mysticism. Spirituality can clear a path for the return of the Sacred to the realm of culture after it had been banished by the Enlightenment. This does not mean or imply that the good points of the Enlightenment should be reversed, nor is it the beginning of the dominance of the Sacred over culture, but simply its readmission as a positive, greatly needed influence on world society. We have a unique opportunity for a genuine renaissance of the Sacred with the promise of creating a universal civilization with a compassionate, loving *heart.*

26

Toward the Dialogue of Love

ROBERT L. FASTIGGI

The story is told of a young Capuchin friar who had consulted the great French Islamicist Louis Massignon about how to overcome his negative feelings towards Islam. The scholar provided the friar with two thoughts to ponder. The first was from Augustine, *"Amor dat novos oculos"* (Love gives new eyes); the second was from John of the Cross: "Where there is no love put love, and you will find love Himself." These two thoughts helped to transform the young friar into an Islamic scholar capable of finding in a religion he once feared "the reflection of the infinite goodness of God" (See Giulio Basetti-Sani, *The Koran in the Light of Christ,* p. 18).

This story serves as an example of the central role of love in authentic interreligious dialogue. The new eyes given by love enable us to see people of other religious as brothers and sisters engaged in a common search for wisdom and truth. Without love there is the danger of demonizing those of other faiths—of seeing them as competitors and enemies rather than as fellow human beings who share a common humanity and common human questions. In reflecting on the meaning of the 1993 Parliament of the World's Religions, one question continuously comes to my mind: "Is it possible for people of many religions, of many races, and of many languages to truly love one another? It is a question that is deceptively simple—for in the answer lies the destiny of our planet.

The amazing truth is that love *is* possible in spite of the differences of belief and practice that exist among the religions. These differences are real and will not go away. We should not attempt to ignore these differences and pretend that all religions are homogeneous for they are not. However, the people who practice these religions share a common language of love and compassion. For in every continent people have learned the language of love—whether from the arms of a mother or the gentle wisdom of a grandfather or the companionship of a friend. It should come as no surprise to learn of the beautiful words for love and compassion that emerge from the different traditions. From the *karunā* of the Bodhisattva to the *hesed* of YHWH; from the *agape* taught by Jesus to Allah *Ar-Rahmān, Ar-Rahīm*—there is a common recognition that compassion, mercy and loving kindness are the qualities we most wish to imitate as humans reaching towards transcendence.

As we near the end of this century, we must look for ways of growing in love. One way is that of collaborative work. When people of different religions work on common projects for better health care and family life, for cleaner air and safer cities, for more just laws and structures for peace then the common humanity of fellow workers is perceived and loved. Another way is through the study of different religions—not a study that simply looks for patterns and archetypes—but a study that seeks to penetrate the heart of each tradition with empathy and a true desire to understand (insofar as possible) how the world is seen from within the vision of that tradition. And finally, we learn to love, as John of the Cross tells us, by putting love where there is no love, by being loving even when others are not loving, by seeking to understand even when others do not understand.

The dialogue of love is the first step needed for what has been envisioned as "the civilization of love." The shadows of war and fratricidal killing still hang like gloomy clouds over the sky of a world, which is taking its first steps in learning to love. However, if love is the starting point for the survival of our planet then all will be in vain if the various religions that preach love, compassion, and mercy fail in the exercise of these virtues. If religious people cannot learn to love each other, what are we to expect from nonreligious people? *"Amor dat novos oculos"* (Love gives new eyes). Let us love so we may have new eyes—eyes that see into the hearts of our brothers and sisters with love and eyes that can see in the future a civilization of love and not hate.

27

Music as a Way of Intuitive Wisdom and Self-Knowledge

RUSSILL PAUL D'SILVA

We all seek the ultimate mystery of the Divine in our own way. The Parliament of the World's Religions was and is a celebration of this essential truth. Prayer, liturgy, chanting, and meditation are the usual ways. Communion with nature, art, and beauty are other ways. Complementary to the need to seek and remain in the experience of the presence of the Divine is the need to find ways of expressing it. For me it is music and poetry that answer this need, while for others it could be dance, painting, or some other art form.

At first I used the harmonic music of the Western tradition for this purpose. I grew up studying and playing Western music since the age of four, and it came as a natural gift with which I seem to have been born. This music has its value, but it is not sufficient to express and experience the whole of divine nature. It is only one half of the musical revelation that is God's gift to the world for this purpose. I term Western music as horizontal music, as it helps me to relate to nature, society, and my personal life and relationships. Although I composed lyrical as well as instrumental songs to express certain particular experiences, a free-style jazz playing has been my way of using music as a meditation technique.

Allowing a free expression of the unconscious through my instruments—the guitar, harmonica, keyboard or the unique handmade synthesis I call a unitar—I can understand and be aware of what is happening deep down by listening to the music I am playing and by being aware of my inner attitudes, feelings, and thoughts as I play. Frustration, anger, love, joy, hatred . . . all have their own tone and resonance. A constant watchfulness while playing has helped me discern these various moods and experience them in my being, both subjectively as well as objectively. I try to sustain this practice in all other activities as well. The Buddhists term it "mindfulness," and did not Jesus tell us to "watch and pray"?

Now it is also possible to transform these moods by deliberately using patterns of their opposites to express the complementary balancing engines. This has to be done slowly and gently, but firmly and consciously. It is not so simple as it sounds, for there are many factors involved. For this technique I use guitars, the unitar, and vocal improvization by way of ragas (scales) accompanied by a shruti box or tanpura, the former being a reed drone and the latter a string drone instrument, both of which are used in traditional Indian music. There are morning ragas and evening ragas, and one has to be careful with these things for they are very powerful and can activate strong energy systems within the physical and psychic bodies.

I was a monk for some years with Dom Bede Griffiths in Tamil Nadu, South India, and during my years of monastic training, I spent much time studying South Indian classical music of the ancient Carnatic tradition. I term this music vertical music, for through it I can enter deep into myself. I find it to be nondualistic and unitive in its consciousness. I discovered this musical form to be a very fulfilling expression of my experience of God and also a way of yoga, bringing about a profound integrity in my being. Devotional music in this tradition involves singing about the various attributes of God that are personified in the Hindu tradition. Even though I am most comfortable with the use of the words Christ and Jesus in prayer, I have always felt quite free to use any name to relate to the Holy Mystery, that is, provided it resonates with my own experience at the moment. This does nothing to impede my being Christian in any way. Rather, it deepens and enriches my faith in Christ.

I am surprised that most Christians seem overconcerned and often reluctant to use a name for God that comes from another tradition. Most often, these names refer to an attribute of God or a term that symbolizes the totality of the Godhead. Why is it that, when we can feel comfortable about using words such as water, earth, or love in another language when we travel to a foreign country, we can feel so uncomfortable about using terms about God in their language, when we freely admit that God is that great mystery of being that pervades all existence and is the ground of all being? The words and sounds for God in other languages contain the seed energies of their own experience of the Divine and by using them we can acquaint ourselves with this experience and expand our own consciousness of the nature of Christ in us. If not, don't we limit ourselves to a very narrow experience of God in Christ and of course greatly limit the nature of Christ for ourselves as well? This is probably one of the chief reasons for our lack of tolerance towards other traditions and that ridiculous sense of superiority Christians generally cultivate. As Gandhi once remarked, "Christians should preach the gospel by giving out a fragrance like the rose, and people will be drawn to them through their state of being." Spirituality must primarily be lived, for the deepest conversions in others take place in the transformational effect of a holy life well lived. In musical terms this will be by giving out the right vibrations, harmonious sounds, and tonal patterns.

Music is very important to me, and I suppose it is to everyone, for music communicates consciousness. Through sound and music, we can enter deeply into the experience of a person or culture, so it is important that we pay close attention to the music we choose to listen to. Music for me is very sacred and very personal, and is essentially a way of self-knowledge. I rarely use it for entertaining others or as a way of personal amusement. It is not a one-sided affair anymore. I mean it isn't just me exhibiting my talent or presenting a piece in a matter-of-fact way, for I am a musician by profession. It is a *language* that I use to understand myself and to express that dynamic interplay between the two poles of my own psyche in harmonious patterns, giving the energies form and beauty. Hence, the attitude and disposition of the people I play for are very important since the music that comes through is a combined expression of the whole.

Music is very important to our spiritual life, as it is basically a way of intuitive wisdom. It develops the feminine within us and is a powerful expression both with and without words. Hence, it can communicate our experiences and our insights directly and clearly, beyond any barriers of sex, caste, or religion. It can and should "open the door of the mystic female" within us, as Bede Griffiths puts it so well in his book *The Marriage of East and West*. Music also has a horizontal effect between and among people of different religious traditions. Sacred music, especially contemplative music, has the capacity, like meditation itself, of providing a medium of profound communication that unites hearts in the mystery of the Divine and that yearning for the Sacred present in all of us consciously or unconsciously. Music is able to express the depths of our being; it can give voice to that ultimate mystery beyond all words, images, thoughts, and emotions, that mystery that dwells in the Silence.

28

Possibilities for an Ongoing Program

PAULOS MAR GREGORIOS

The Renewal of Religions

Someone characterized the present-day religious leadership of the world as "generally mediocre, incredibly naive, and lamentably underinformed." That may not be a fair characterization of all religious leaders. We know of a few exceptions. But the judgment generally holds true for a vast number of religious leaders we see in our interreligious gatherings.

Whenever religious renewal movements have been vitally effective in history, there were outstanding religious leaders who were unusually wise, spiritually mature, and full of a compassionate love that extends to all humanity. They had a deep and clear understanding of what humanity needed at that particular time in that specific cultural situation. That understanding and wisdom were based on a comprehensive knowledge of the science and philosophy of that time, integrated into a compassionate vision of the plight of humanity, and on a rare insight into the kind of healing needed.

That is not our current state of affairs. Despite a monumentally powerful wave of religious awakening among the masses, we have a great scarcity of mature and wise leaders among those who are called to be heads of religious movements. From my limited perspective, nearly every religion I know stands desperately in need of renewal among its own leadership. Without a spiritual renewal among the religious leaders of the world, capable of equipping them with deep spiritual power and with a wide range of learning so necessary for an informed dialogue with the culture, science, and philosophy of our time, religions will not be able to bring to humanity the healing it needs. I therefore regard the renewal of all religions and their leadership as a first priority in any agenda for interreligious cooperation. The orientation of that renewal will be towards wider learning and deeper spiritual power, as well as along the following two points:

Unity of Humanity as Growing Community in the Good

A primary goal of the interreligious movement is the unity of humanity. The most negative aspect of religion today is its role in dividing humanity into rival blocs and groups. So much of the conflict among human beings today has an ethnic or a religious label. And yet the power of true religion is always to transcend, in an all-comprehending love of the whole of humanity, all sectarian, nationalistic, religious, and racial differences. However, instead of transcending, religions today tend to reinforce the barriers that divide and separate.

It is clear that the unity we seek is unity in the good, not the unity of the criminal gang or of the robbers' den. Religions should now engage in thoroughgoing self-criticism, in dialogue with the secular world and its science/technology, and in a spirit of humility, in order to identify the evil now regnant in each religion and to eradicate that evil. Think of all the cheap power struggles going on in each religion as well as in most interreligious organizations; of the misuse of the wealth of religious institutions and endowments; of the support now being given by the religious establishments to many forms of dishonesty, corruption, and injustice in public life; of how religions use their political and economic clout for selfish and sectarian ends rather than for the good of all; the personal immorality of many religious leaders; the way religions build up and project false images of their leaders, and so on. Until religions are purged of some of the evil now manifest in them, how can they really work together for the harmony and unity of all humanity? When the religious leaders themselves are so prone to corruption and deceit, quarrel and division, what credibility will their efforts to unite have in the eyes of the public?

You will see the reason why I am not at all moved by the claims of religions and the interreligious movement to solve all the problems of humanity and quite naively to propose an unrealistic global ethic for all humanity and to arrogate for itself the formidably great and noble task of uniting that humanity. Religions in their present condition are hardly fit to undertake the task of promoting harmony and unity in the world. Even the attempts of religious groups to resolve conflicts such as those in Bosnia or the Middle East often tend to be motivated more by the desire for the limelight than for the welfare of humanity. Religions will have to regain their authenticity and integrity as a prerequisite preparation for their work for global unity.

Unity does not mean uniformity or conformity; nor does it mean the elimination of differences. Some differences are valuable and have to be celebrated; others have to be eradicated or resolved. Unity in diversity—that is a popular slogan. But not all diversity needs to be sanctified or absolutized. When the differences are brought into the dialogical dynamics of interreligious communities, mutual openness will lead to self-correction and grateful emulation of the good points of other religions. Each religion must be humble enough to recognize the good aspects of other religions and to foster these in their own communities. The good that unites is a growing and dynamic good. Pluralism does not mean permissiveness; the idea that everything can coexist does not work; there cannot be genuine pluralism without two conditions: a uniting core of agreement that is constantly expanding and a continuous process of mutual dialogue to reduce the differences that do not really matter without insisting on or imposing any form of conformity.

No one can ever permanently define the good. But we can always envisage some forms of the good, for our time. My present perception sees eight aspects of the good that we need to struggle to embody now:

(1) The unity of humanity and the just, nonviolent resolution of conflicts;

(2) Societies that foster human dignity, creativity, and freedom for all men and women;

(3) A culture that does not exalt science/technology above everything else like art, culture, and religion; a world in which science/technology is liberated from its present enslavement by war and profit and is made available for meeting the needs of humanity; a civilization that does not foster greed and covetousness; an industrial system that does not misuse or waste the resources of the planet or pollute it by excessive consumption of fossil fuels;

(4) Local, national, regional as well as global economic and political structures that are just; that care especially for the downtrodden, the oppressed, the marginalized, and the exploited; and that strive continuously and vigilantly to eliminate all forms of oppression, exploitation, and discrimination;

(5) The elimination and banning of war, of weapons of mass destruction, and of militarism in general and the healing of the culture itself, with its endemic social and personal violence;

(6) The repairing and maintaining of our life environment;

(7) A great exuberance of human compassion and love reaching out to the needy, the marginalized, the abandoned, the despairing; the victimized; and

(8) Models of spiritual discipline and pilgrimage that lead to finding meaning and fulfillment by human persons, families, and communities.

These are the forms of the good that each religion should, separately, on its own as well as in concordant concert with other religions, embody and manifest today. That is what I mean by the renewal of religions.

What humanity hungers for today are visible manifestations, iconic communities, of unity in the good. Communities need to embody the good that we seek, not simply preach it or profess it. People are looking for living icons that inspire, communities that practice what everybody preaches, not empty words about a global ethic printed on a piece of paper. We need icons of personal spirituality—more Dalai Lamas and Mother Teresas, more Mahatma Gandhis and Martin Luther Kings. But we need also visible interreligious, international, interracial communities that embody the Spirit of God in the very way people of different races and religions live together and pray together and serve together.

The Civilization of Tomorrow

We live today in a dominant global civilization that has its roots mainly in European or White Western history. It embodies both the positive values of a so-called Judeo-Christian religious heritage and the centuries-old aggressive-acquisitive tempo of White Western culture. Both its basic forms, the Western liberal and the Western Marxist, stand discredited today. The Urban-Industrial, Scientific-Technological model of development does not work. It is that model that unleashed war and violence, promoted exploitation and oppression, ruptured the life environment, and has made life miserable for millions; this is not to deny its positive contributions, for example, globalization, elimination of disease and premature death, large-scale production of commodities to sustain the growing population of our planet, wiping out much superstition and ignorance, and so on.

But one cannot overlook the fact that the secular civilization is at bottom a godless one that has consciously sought to cut its roots in the transcendent. Insofar as it succeeds, it withers and wilts. It has not merely banished religion from the public realm, privatizing it and marginalizing it in the process. It has imposed in its place the godless, soulless, scientistic religious ideology of secularism, which dominates our educational system, our healing system, our communication media, and our political economic institutions. Liberation from this dominant godless ideology in its many forms seems to me the most pressing need of our time.

Religion, including the secular ideology, is always the religion of a community, a very public affair, not a private affair created or purchased by the private individual. Neither is religion a department of one's life. Religion is not only an all-or-nothing commitment; for the members of the religious community, religion, including secularism, is the pervasive framework within which a community perceives reality and orients its life. It is not a hobby or an avocation; it is the foundation of human living and aspiring and acting.

The most daunting challenge facing the interreligious movement today is to bring back a pluralistic and free religious outlook into the center of public life without thereby handing over political power to the religious leaders. That is why it cannot be a universal religion or spirituality imposed on people. No one religion should dominate any society. All religious communities should have the same freedom to practice and propagate their religion. This freedom extends also to secularism, which, judging by its features, shows itself to be a religion based on belief in unscientific assumptions like: the world open to our senses is the only world that exists; humanity is free to know it by modern science and to exploit it by modern technology in any manner it wishes.

Secularism must be recognized for what it is: the religion of scientism born in the eighteenth and nineteenth centuries. It should not be allowed to dominate public life; it cannot decide what can be taught in the schools and universities; it cannot dictate what kind of a medical system should monopolize the healing ministry; it should not be allowed to dictate the political system and its institutions; secularism should not legislate that the Transcendent be kept out of the school, the healing system, the political economic institutions and their theoretical underpinnings.

It was once thought that Modern Science would replace all religion with a new so-called scientific outlook and worldview. It is now clear that science has a much more limited function within culture; it can help us to know how things work; technology can then give us the means to manipulate the world around us to suit some of our needs and purposes, based on the knowledge produced by science. We need science/technology to sustain human life; but it cannot tell us what is ultimately true; it has access only to operational truth, not to the transcendent source of all existence, of all meaning and fulfillment. Science cannot tell us what the purpose of human existence is; it cannot lead human beings to meaning and fulfillment. It cannot generate that spiritual energy that alone truly liberates and fulfills the human community.

And what we need most of all as a basis for a more human and more humane civilization is the large-scale generation of that spiritual energy. How can we expect Science/Technology to be the instrument through which that energy can be generated? Here is the big challenge before the interreligious movement, in dialogue with the world of science/technology—to help in the process of the fundamental transformation of our civilization, by bringing into public life the redeeming aspects of religion and providing a multireligious, pluralistic setting in which human beings can find meaning and fulfillment. This is why the renewal of religions is an inescapable prerequisite for healing humanity and for creating new civilizations in the twenty-first century. Can religions face up to this daunting challenge, trusting in the grace of the Transcendent?

The program of the follow-up of the Second Parliament of World Religions depends very much on the answer we give to these questions. Yes, we need to network; we need to promote dialogue; we need a mechanism for conflict resolution; but above all and before all, we need the renewal of religions, facing up to the challenge of the Western Enlightenment; we need iconic communities of human living together and working together to serve others; we need the upsurge of spiritual energy generated by prayer and spiritual disciplines; we need to lay the foundations for less godless, less soul-destroying civilizations. It is the Transcendent who calls us to this noble mission. Let us shed our lethargy and pettiness and begin our pilgrimage in that direction where the Transcendent beckons us. It is the Transcendent who will ultimately lead us to fulfillment.

Epilogue: Continuing the Dance

JEAN HOUSTON, WAYNE TEASDALE,

AND GEORGE CAIRNS

JEAN: The Parliament was an historic meeting that brought together a broad spectrum of ecumenism. Hindus, Buddhists, Muslims, Christians, Australian Aboriginal and goddess adherents were all in attendance as well as every type of feminist. This was like the world's spirit taking a walk with itself. The *anima mundi* came together for this event, while the evangelicals were outside picketing!

I spoke to a group of 1500 on the future of spirituality and then later attended a meeting of Buddhist and Christian monks and nuns.[1] The Dalai Llama attended this meeting, and all felt the singularity of his presence with us. He, as revered representative of Tibetan Buddhism, seemed representative of the group itself; his presence seemed to go broad and deep in the group, and I was profoundly moved by this occasion and by the lives of the monks. They seem to live by the *via negativa* whereas I live by the *via positiva*—mysticism more in touch with reality, which I feel is more a *plurosis* than a *kenosis*.

I wondered what I could bring to this meeting, and then I felt that nature was missing. I suggested that the tree was representative of the critical consciousness of the west. I felt that the tree was a symbol of importance both to Buddhists and Christians since Christ was crucified on a tree and Buddha was enlightened under a Bo tree. The tree represents both body and brain. A human scaffold is within us like a tree, like a garden of the inner state, so it could be a symbol.

WAYNE: I thank you for these fascinating thoughts. I like especially your image of the *anima mundi* and the tree. Another important theme

---

This epilogue is an edited version of a conversation that took place October 24, 1995.
1. The Buddhist-Christian Monastic Dialogue, September 4, 1993.

at the Parliament was the dance: the sacred Hoop Dance of the Native Americans, Brother David's Great Circle Dance of the Religions, Keith Cunningham's Dancing Honeybees, and the polyform dance at the closing Plenary of the Parliament. All these expressed something at a deeper level.

GEORGE: Jean, I am delighted to hear you reflections about the significance of the Parliament to the religious community. It reminds me of the work earlier in this century by William Ernest Hocking, who described the way that contemplatives were helping to bring people together—the idea of the religions of the world being joined at the top by the contemplatives—a mapping of consciousness. We are experiencing a converging method of praxis that includes contemplation, compassion, and social action creating a new *via positiva*. We are developing a common set of metatheories.

JEAN: I think the world soul brings in other dimensions of human consciousness, a harvest of human capacities. In the idea of harvest I can see a depth of human psyches coming to participate. The dimension of the psyche, the idea of many parts of the human journey, was neglected in the west so the harvest of the psyche and practice amounted to a completeness and a fullness. Access to other levels of consciousness combined with depth led to a celebration of praxis that transcended and to an organic coming together of the gnosis of the world.

WAYNE: I found it interesting that Jean mentioned the "*anima mundi* taking a walk with itself at the Parliament." That idea has stayed with me and reminded me of Teilhard's *noosphere*. Even before Jean said it, I realized something essential was being born. All the old categories were dissolving. All the old feuds seemed to melt. I sensed harmonization, a leap to planetary consciousness. The *noosphere* coming through. The Parliament was like a revolutionary experience; the veil was pulled back, and I began to see the skills needed if we are going to make a leap in awareness. I saw a vision of expanded consciousness and the fact that it worked.

JEAN: I feel that the spirit of the *anima mundi* was seen at the end as dancers joined in a world dance. Everyone danced. I danced, African men and Muslim women danced; there were hundreds of people spiraling and dancing a living dance. I lost my shoes—no matter—the dance went on.

WAYNE: The polyform dance as an image preserves the uniqueness of gift of each cultural expression. The matrix is harmony, which is better than unity. When we say "unity" isn't it this harmony that we mean?

JEAN: Ecstatic participation is better than harmony, or more accurate. The life form itself seemed to be present; it was like a green fuse driving them. At the end, when the crowds left, the mood of joy continued. Several representatives of the fundamentalists handed out comic books of Jesus Christ and said we were doomed to hell. I noticed an African man, wearing a white robe. One of the fundamentalists asked him if he knew Jesus, and he answered, "No, my brother, but the God in me sees and honors the God in you." The fundamentalist turned away saying, "Blasphemy!"

GEORGE: The fundamentalists were like wallflowers at the dance! They stood on the sidelines and only really spoke or listened to one another. There was a full-bodied, organic process at the Parliament. It was such a powerful movement for conscious integration—it helped dissolve boundaries and move across domains of body, mind, and spirit. There were ways of being within ourselves and simultaneously in all the communities. This was a powerful movement, but how can we reach out now to continue it?

JEAN: I remember Ma Jaya. It was a funny scene. Here was this Jewish Hindu dressed in her colorful sari, a life force incarnate, and a fundamentalist in a seersucker suit came up and asked if she knew Jesus. "Know him?" she said, "I'm his Mother!"

WAYNE: What was the reaction to that?

JEAN: "Utter falling back."

WAYNE: Dante used the image of dance to convey the sense of community in heaven.

JEAN: In Africa, there is a saying, "He who does not dance does not know what's happening."

WAYNE: I am reminded of Guido the Carthusian in terms of the flow of reality and consciousness. He says that God is singing a great song; our purpose is to flow along with it, but some people hear only one note and never grow. They are like the fundamentalists; they won't move beyond.

JEAN: I feel we are in the midst of systematic transition all around us, and we are unprepared for what is coming. Muchness makes me shiver. We are not ready for this immense transition. Women are rising, interconnected, extending the training and speaking, a revelation of whole humanness that can be. At the same time we are aware of the disenfranchised. There is radical downsizing at the same time a global economy is growing. Fearful people such as the fundamentalists look for a retreat in a haven of safe answers.

The Parliament represented the rising of a new story, and it apparently really scared the day and night lights out of the fundamentalists.

We saw the sun set on the current age and the darkness emerge as a gestation of a new story.

WAYNE: I agree that a new consciousness is dawning as the old story moves into an inner way.

JEAN: Once it is seen as *overt,* it is new.

WAYNE: George and I had been talking about the dialectic between religion and mysticism through history. What we saw was an explicit manifestation of mystical life. This was a dominant emphasis on experiential mysticism or experiential spirituality.

JEAN: I make a distinction between large against small, spirit and body, and I try to bridge the gap. This amounts to mapping three realities: "I am," "we are," "this is me." We are nested in several realities, and once we transcend them, we see we are citizens of several realms.

Sacred psychology equals psychology of praise of human nature and life. We exist in psyche, in history and in sexuality, in myth and in signs. Then I realize I am. Each realm has its own reality and exists in us as well. We can't escape from any part of reality. We are all woven together. If we negate any one realm we feel we are losing life. Many live only half a life. Full awareness would be to be conscious cocreators in all three realms.

Sexual existence represents our physical/fundamental awareness of our embodiedness: "this is me." This becomes a locked-in awareness and leads to frustration and resentment. "My soul could soar if not flesh." These ideas have led to mystical practices that want to escape the body. We can gain from the shamanic approach: the soul is not entrapped, it is on a continuum. There is resentment in the West. "This is me" became dead in the world in the West. I tap into dreams. Death and resurrection in every world is an archetypal symbol of the transhistorical world. The human psyche is inherently pantheistic. There is a place where the self is joined to the larger person. All forces are crystallized in human consciousness and then beyond psyche. Every culture has tapped into this realm. The people at the Parliament represented everyone. What we call gods that came down to us are really human borderline personalities. They are vehicles to greater understanding.

Patterns give us the larger story; myth also provides the larger story, a copartnership. The Parliament represented the gods rising, the personification of sources of spirit trying to get together to form a new story.

In certain states of consciousness, the mind rises. We meet new forms of consciousness in the archetypal state, and so we can merge or unite with the Divine. Mother Theresa can do her work because she considers herself married to Jesus, in love with Jesus, and she can see the face of

Jesus in all faces. For her the belief archetype is Christ. At the Parliament we saw an ecumenism of the psyche. The shadow also arises because the sun is so bright, and this is a real danger.

WAYNE: The Gods are numinous "borderline personalities" . . . another dimension to cosmic mystery, and are in the real of pure mysticism, whether theistic or nontheistic, Western religious or Buddhist, advaitic as in the East. Beyond archetypes, there is the realm of the Divine itself. It imposes itself on human experience. It imposes itself on history. The Divine is utterly real, and we can know this from direct and immediate experience.

For you may be sitting alone in a room, and all of a sudden you experience a cosmic wind, though the windows aren't open. You surrender to the presence of the Divine, and you are absorbed into its consciousness. Then you experience reality in and through divine consciousness. This is not under human control.

GEORGE: I would like to talk about decenteredness as experienced by Native Americans. I was on our farm once. I offered a prayer, and I offered tobacco. A large hawk appeared. The winged ones sometimes break through when we decenter ourselves. The hawk flew directly at me; I could literally feel the wing beats on my shoulders as the hawk circled me and then flew off crying. I had a sense of falling into something much larger, being in a wholly different way, being present to the possibility that the sacred offers us "This is me." "We are." "This is beyond." God offers us an infinite number of unfoldings if we allow ourselves to be open to the experience.

JEAN: The local self has to release its grasp on reality and allow it to happen. My father was a comic writer. When I was attending Catholic school, he coached me with embarrassing questions and got me into so much trouble! He took me to see *The Song of Bernadette,* with Linda Darnell as the leading lady, which sent my father into hilarious laughter. Later, I begged the Virgin to show up, and a door opened up. The world has never been the same since. The Virgin Mary became part of everything; all worked together and was very good. I had awakened to a consciousness that spanned centuries. My mind was the universe. I knew and was *everything*. It was a state of resonance with everything. I was *in* a universe of love. Friendship filled everything. It was a dance of life that went on forever in only two seconds.

Many people feel this, especially children. It is not to be kept locked within. Maybe that led me to do my work, continual creative experience. I accept it as given. Native people *assume* it is there. The ceremony is only a reminder. In Western ceremony the words are there, but no assumption of a natural bridge exists.

WAYNE: "Native Americans *know* it while our culture doesn't. Father Theophane Boyd conducted a eucharistic celebration within a Zen framework at the East-West Monastic Conference in Petersham, MA, in June 1977. He spoke only eight sentences during the whole Mass. What I saw happen was Theophane transformed into the presence of Christ.

JEAN: He looks like Christ.

WAYNE: He created the archetype; silence allowed it. Most priests have absolutely no idea when they celebrate the mass what they are doing.

JEAN: Theophane became the living presence.

WAYNE: Without trying.

JEAN: He did his human homework.

GEORGE: I wonder if the Parliament wasn't a multicoevoked birthday party for being different, for going beyond ourselves.

WAYNE: It was a birthday for numinous borderline personalities! Where are we going? What does the future hold?

JEAN: Do you mean the future of spirituality or the future of the world.

WAYNE: If the Parliament was historical corporate mystical experience, a historical altered state, we might see the breakdown of religions and the coming out of mysticism. What is the future of the planet?

JEAN: Seeing and experiencing, I hope, taking up of daily life as a spiritual experience and allowing this to flood into daily life. We can look back to the Parliament to provoke a process of spirituality, a process that transcends. The Human heart *must* go to the heart. It would be a good idea to reinvoke a series of Parliaments every few years. There is a marvelous film on the Parliament, *Peace Like a River,* which evokes this feeling. Maybe it can become part of the Zeitgeist. It works. The Parliament was part of time. It was a world historical event that radically became a vehicle through which little and later Parliaments can continue to allow empowerment at the local level. We need institutions that allow for the spiritual basis, that involve spiritual artists, that are spiritually wise. The notion of a Parliament has to be kept available. It was so potent. The resonance continues.

GEORGE: I agree. For me, the Parliament was an event that was a catalyst, a coming together of many networks and resonating networks in ways never experienced before. It was an event of global singularity, the coming together in one place at one time of these networks and simultaneously pluriform, reconnecting concurrent processes. We can continue to work within these networks and develop them. Perhaps both the metatheory and the reality of the internet offers us a metaphor for this process—to network broadly and deeply and then to recoalesce in order to supercharge the process—to hear the full range of multiplicity of voices and to tap the riches of all of creation.

WAYNE: I knew, I intuited that this was a major historical event. I was certain that it was the most important thing in the twentieth century, perhaps even in the last thousand years. I observed three omens, one on the day before and two on the day the Parliament opened. On the 27th of August, the *Times* headline said, "Spiritual Leaders from around the World Flock Together . . . Global Talks Begin Tomorrow." On the 28th, a breakthrough occurred in the Middle East with the opening of peace talks between Israel and the PLO. This breakthrough was an incredibly important harbinger that pointed to the significance of the events unfolding in Chicago! One thousand years from now the Parliament of 1993 will be seen as one of the greatest world historical events because it constituted a turning point in consciousness. The third omen was of a more personal nature. I was having breakfast on the morning of the Parliament's opening with as Franciscan brother and with Sampdong Rinpoche, the head of the Tibetan delegation. I fetched him a cup of coffee. Now I don't know how it happened, but the entire cup with the coffee ended up in his lap! He never showed the slightest irritation. He looked up and said with a smile "This a most auspicious sign." I intuitively knew that his comment referred to the meaning of the Parliament itself.

JEAN: Other ways of knowing became prominent.

WAYNE: A basic shift occurred at the Parliament. Community was born among the religions. A shift from competition to community occurred in how the members of different faiths relate to one another. The old exclusivism was ending. This amounts to the coming out of the world soul. On a personal level, more and more awakened beings will be speaking out.

JEAN: This is a very powerful thought! A metanet, a morphogenetic field, more than one or two or ten or twenty people have to hold it!!!

Appendix A
Towards a Global Ethic
(An Initial Declaration)

The world is in agony. The agony is so pervasive and urgent that we are compelled to name its manifestations so that the depth of this pain may be made clear.

Peace eludes us . . . the planet is being destroyed . . . neighbors live in fear . . . women and men are estranged from each other . . . children die!

This is Abhorrent!

We condemn the abuses of Earth's ecosystems.

We condemn the poverty that stifles life's potential; the hunger that weakens the human body; the economic disparities that threaten so many families with ruin.

We condemn the social disarray of the nations; the disregard for justice that pushes citizens to the margin; the anarchy overtaking our communities; and the insane death of children from violence. In particular we condemn aggression and hatred in the name of religion.

But this agony need not be.

It need not be because the basis for an ethic already exists. This ethic offers the possibility of a better individual and global order, and leads individuals away from despair and societies away from chaos.

The Declaration "Towards a Global Ethic," also includes "The Principles of a Global Ethic," which we have not included here. The Declaration itself was written by two members of the Council for a Parliament of the World's Religions, Dr. Daniel Gómez-Ibáñez and Rev. Thomas A. Baima, while the Principles were formulated by Hans Küng. See *A Global Ethic: The Declaration of the Parliament of the World's Religions,* commentaries by Hans Küng and Karl-Josef Kushel (New York: Continuum, 1994). Also see *A SourceBook for Earth's Community of Religions,* ed. Joel Beversluis (Grand Rapids: CoNexus Press, 1995), pp. 124–38. The latter

We are women and men who have embraced the precepts and practices of the world's religions:

We affirm that a common set of core values is found in the teachings of the religions, and that these form the basis of a global ethic.

We affirm that this truth is already known, but yet to be lived in heart and action.

We affirm that there is an irrevocable, unconditional norm for all areas of life, for families and communities, for races, nations, and religions. There already exist ancient guidelines for human behavior that are found in the teachings of the religions of the world and that are the condition for a sustainable world order.

We Declare:

We are interdependent. Each of us depends on the well-being of the whole, and so we have respect for the community of living beings, for people, animals, and plants, and for the preservation of Earth, the air, water and soil.

We take individual responsibility for all we do. All our decisions, actions, and failures to act have consequences.

We must treat others as we wish others to treat us. We make a commitment to respect life and dignity, individuality and diversity, so that every person is treated humanely, without exception. We must have patience and acceptance. We must be able to forgive, learning from the past but never allowing ourselves to be enslaved by memories of hate. Opening our hearts to one another, we must sink our narrow differences for the cause of the world community, practicing a culture of solidarity and relatedness.

We consider humankind our family. We must strive to be kind and generous. We must not live for ourselves alone, but should also serve others, never forgetting the children, the aged, the poor, the suffering, the disabled, the refugees, and the lonely. No person should ever be considered or treated as a second-class citizen, or be exploited in any way whatsoever. There should be equal partnership between men and women. We must not commit any kind of sexual immorality. We must put behind us all forms of domination or abuse.

We commit ourselves to a culture of nonviolence, respect, justice, and peace. We shall not oppress, injure, torture, or kill other human beings, forsaking violence as a means of settling differences.

includes two articles on the document, the Declaration and the Principles, with the original signatories.

We must strive for a just social and economic order, in which everyone has an equal chance to reach full potential as a human being. We must speak and act truthfully and with compassion, dealing fairly with all, and avoiding prejudice and hatred. We must not steal. We must move beyond the dominance of greed for power, prestige, money, and consumption to make a just and peaceful world.

Earth cannot be changed for the better unless the consciousness of individuals is changed first. We pledge to increase our awareness by disciplining our minds, by meditation, by prayer, or by positive thinking. Without risk and a readiness to sacrifice there can be no fundamental change in our situation. Therefore we commit ourselves to this global ethic, to understanding one another, and to socially beneficial, peace-fostering, and nature-friendly ways of life.

We invite all people whether religious
or not, to do the same.

Appendix B
Resources for Study
and Networking

JOEL BEVERSLUIS

Although the 1993 Parliament in Chicago was a highly visible commemoration of the 1893 World's Parliament of Religions, the worldwide interfaith movement has been increasingly active in many other ways during the past few decades. A few examples follow: the World Conference on Religion and Peace (WCRP), which was founded in the late 1960s in response to the expanding war in Vietnam and the cold war, has held many regional and international conferences and worked behind the scenes at the United Nations. The predecessor of what is now the Inter-Religious Federation for World Peace held the first of many interfaith conferences in 1985. Shortly thereafter, a coalition of international interfaith organizations, including WCRP, the Temple of Understanding, the International Association for Religious Freedom, and the World Congress of Faiths named 1993 the Year of Inter-Religious Understanding and Cooperation and began planning programs linked by that agenda. About the same time, monks of the Chicago Vedanta Society began promoting the concept of an interfaith commemoration of the 1893 Parliament to be held in Chicago in 1993. Working mostly independently, these organizations and others planned substantial conferences and celebratory meetings that would be held throughout the year in places ranging from Chicago to the United Kingdom, Japan, and India.

Concurrent with these activities, a groundswell of both grassroots and high-level interactions among members of religious and spiritual traditions, combined with the extraordinary challenges and opportunities of our time, have given new direction and impetus to many local and international interfaith movements. Within religious traditions themselves, ranging from Won Buddhism in Korea and Risho Kosei-kai in Japan, to the World Council of Churches and the worldwide Catholic Church, a wide variety of motivations, programs, and concerns have given this movement an exciting and sometimes challenging diversity. Nevertheless, this groundswell demonstrates that there is now a considerable amount of common concern across traditions, a very inspiring idealism, and a refreshing commitment to the religious, spiritual, and ethical components in all aspects of life.

The annotated listings that follow identify a selection of organizations and resource materials that address or further the visions of interreligious understanding, cooperation, and ethical response. It is by no means an exhaustive listing. (Much of the data that follows has been extracted from the more comprehensive *A SourceBook for Earth's Community of Religions,* Revised Edition, edited by Joel Beversluis). Many of the entries listed here relate to the legacies of the two Chicago Parliaments and the Year of Interreligious Understanding and Cooperation (1993), but information about other interfaith organizations and resources is also included to provide a more complete picture of the larger context of interreligious activity.

Within that context, the events of 1993 may be seen as stepping stones toward the formation of a global ethic and an emerging sense of interreligious community. Some visionaries would like that community to be a formally structured United Religions organization similar to the United Nations. Others see the concept of a community of religions as a more informal phenomenon, an interpersonal and interspiritual movement linked by a global ethic and cooperative service rather than by bureaucratic ties and competing agendas. Whatever the future holds, we can observe that, since 1993, interfaith events surrounding the commemoration of the fiftieth anniversary of the United Nations and other assemblies and conferences continue to move the process along. We perceive that this is a historic path, one that has intersected and is beginning to bridge the swelling current of our personal, spiritual, and global crises.

Readers are therefore encouraged to learn more about these events and many other related organizations and resources. This Appendix provides a starting point toward a fuller understanding of the historic changes that are now taking place in the relationships of the world's religions and spiritual traditions to each other and to the world in which we coexist.

A. Archives

The official archives of the 1993 Parliament of the World's Religions are gathered and indexed at the DePaul University Library Archives, 2350 North Kenmore Avenue, Chicago, IL 60614. These include documents, correspondence, minutes, media releases, several thousand news clippings, audio and video tapes, and other items from the board and staff, cosponsors, committees, participants, the media, and other commentators.

B. Books and Booklets
(1) Resources for Personal and Group Study

Cosmic Beginnings and Human Ends:
Where Science and Religion Meet
Edited by CLIFFORD MATTHEWS and ROY ABRAHAM VARGHESE
Initially presented at the Symposium on Science and Religion held in conjunction with the Parliament, these essays by leading scientists, philosophers, and educators from diverse religious orientations are thematically linked around the proposal that the story of the universe is the primary place where the religions of the world can meet each other with a common point of reference. Other essays explore mysteries of the origin of the cosmos and their implications for human striving—where the religions and sciences can meet. Published 1994 by Open Court Press. pb. $17.95; cl. $41.95.

The Earth Charter: A Religious Perspective
A distillation of several charters written by many international and interfaith organizations since the early 1990s, the Earth Charter is used in personal and group study as the foundation for a new society with new kinds of agreements and structures between peoples and between people and the earth. Uses include endorsement by some of the United Nations Associations as the focus for the proclamation of a charter in 1995, the fiftieth anniversary of the U.N. Available from the International Coordinating Committee on Religion and the Earth, P.O. Box 194, Cross River, NY 10518. See also *A SourceBook* for this and other public documents and declarations.

Earth in a Global Age: The Interfaith Movement's
Offer of Hope to a World in Agony
MARCUS BRAYBROOKE, Foreword by JOHN HICK
This extensive booklet published by Marcus Braybrooke, the leading historian of the international interfaith movement, offers his personal

perspective on the events, networks, theological frameworks, declarations, and understandings of global spirituality that have emerged during his many years of service to and observation of the interfaith movement. Reverend Braybrooke also looks ahead to the tasks that now confront the interfaith movement as we all learn to live in a global society. Available from Braybrooke Press, The Rectory, Marsh Baldon, Oxford OX44 9LS United Kingdom. 120 pp. U.S. $7.99 or British £4.99.

A Global Ethic: The Declaration of the
Parliament of the World's Religions
Commentaries HANS KÜNG and KARL-JOSEF KUSHEL
This paperback presents the complete text of the declaration as it was signed (provisionally), and describes the process of consultations with numerous religious scholars, the drafting process, and the nature of this minimum ethic based on a "common set of core values" derived from the ancient wisdom and teachings of the world's religions. Available at stores and libraries; published by Continuum in the U.S. and SCM in the U.K. pb. $9.95.

Global Responsibility: In Search of a New World Ethic
HANS KÜNG
Presents a compelling argument that this world needs at least a minimum of shared ethical principles on which we can all agree if we are to survive in this time of new opportunities and dangers. "Our society does not need a uniform religion or a uniform ideology, but it does need some binding norms, values, ideals, and goals." Küng addresses the world faiths in particular but also nonbelievers in this preliminary study to his work of drafting the Global Ethic for the Parliament. Published 1991 by Continuum Publishing Co., 370 Lexington Avenue, New York, NY 10017. pb. $14.95.

Global 2000 Revisited: What Shall We Do?
DR. GERALD O. BARNEY, JANE BLEWETT and KRISTEN R. BARNEY of The Millenium Institute (see listing below)
Prepared and published by the Institute for the Parliament of the World's Religions, this report is an update, specifically addressed to the religions, of the *Global 2000* report that Dr. Barney directed for Jimmy Carter's administration. In its own words, the book "is an invitation to reflect deeply on the critical issues we face today: threats to the global environment; divisions within the human community, such as racism, interreligious hatred, sexual discrimination, and xenophobic national-

ism; extremes of affluence and poverty; and the prevalence of violence, oppression, and exploitation of all kinds." Paperback $20. Available from Public Interest Publications, PO Box 229, Arlington, VA 22210 USA. TEL: (800) 537-9359 in the US, Canada and Mexico, or (703) 243-2252 elsewhere. The official *Summary of Global 2000 Revisited* is also available for $8.

Multifaith Information Manual
Substantially revised and published in a paperback edition in 1995, this excellent resource was first produced especially for use by caregivers and chaplains who must provide spiritual and religious care to persons from many traditions. Its value goes beyond those users, however, in that the *Manual* provides essential information on history, beliefs, scriptures, cultural elements, dietary needs, laws, rituals, symbols, calendar, responses to illness and death, worship and festivals. Large format paperback, 230 pages, CN$33.95 (plus 15% tax). Published by and available from Ontario Multifaith Council on Spiritual and Religious Care, 35 McCaul St., Suite 200, Toronto, ON M5T 1V7, CANADA Tel. 416 326-6858 Also available in the U.S. from Multifaith Resources (listed below) for U.S. $23.95 including postage and handling.

A Parliament of Souls:
In Search of Global Spirituality
Edited by MICHAEL TOBIAS, JANE MORRISON, and BETTINA GRAY
This book has been derived from video interviews held during the Parliament of the World's Religions with twenty-eight spiritual leaders from fourteen religious traditions and numerous countries. In addition to printing edited transcripts of the interviews, the book offers photographs and sidebars with pertinent excerpts from quotations, declarations, and statistical documents. Leaders such as His Holiness the Dalai Lama, Charles Colson, Dr. Hans Küng, Dr. Azizah al Hibri, Robert Muller, and Swami Chidananda reflect on universal dilemmas such as: Is there a universal code of ethics? Can religion combat racial and ethnic bigotry? How does spirituality inform daily life? and What kind of environment will we bequeath to our children? Pb. 292 pp., $18.95. Published by KQED Books, available at bookstores and from Multifaith Resources (listed below).

A SourceBook for Earth's Community
of Religions (Revised Edition)
JOEL BEVERSLUIS, Project Editor
Packed with essays, sidebars, scriptures, prayers, spiritual wisdom, declarations, and organizational and resource listings. *SourceBook* chal-

lenges the world's religious and spiritual traditions to respond to critical global issues—the environment, sustainable development, interfaith conflict, poverty, hunger and the next generations. Portraits of many religions of the world (from African indigenous to Zoroastrian) survey their beliefs, wisdom teachings, and interfaith relations, and propose new possibilities for cooperative action and personal transformation. Voices from diverse religious, scientific, and philosophic traditions express the vision of the 1993 Parliament that humanity can address our common problems if we are guided by both spiritual wisdom and by the enlightened application of modern knowledge. Available in stores and libraries or from CoNexus Press—SourceBook Project, PO Box 6902, Grand Rapids, MI 49516. 376 pp., large pb ($18.95 plus $3.00 S&H).

"Towards a Global Ethic: An Initial Declaration"
Council for a Parliament of the World's Religions
This is the document prepared for the 1993 Parliament and then discussed and signed, provisionally, by most participants in the Assembly of Religious and Spiritual Leaders. It is printed and discussed elsewhere in this book and in *A SourceBook for Earth's Community of Religions* (Revised). The document is also available from the Council for a Parliament of the World's Religions and in Hans Küng's *A Global Ethic*. Since it was signed provisionally at the Parliament with the understanding that the document would be discussed, refined, and perhaps redrafted, a new version may some day be prepared. Meanwhile, the document as it stands provides an excellent forum for teaching about the ethical norms of the world's religions and for discussing its observation that a minimum ethic already exists that can help guide us to a more peaceful, just, and sustainable world.

(2) The 1893 Parliament and History of the Interfaith Movement

The Dawn of Religious Pluralism: Voices from the World's Parliament of Religions, 1893
Edited and Introduced by RICHARD HUGHES SEAGER, with RONALD R. KIDD, and with a Foreword by DIANA L. ECK
This volume contains a selection of sixty representative addresses given to the Parliament of 1893. Contributions include speeches by Protestant mainstream ministers, African-Americans, Roman Catholics, Orthodox Christians, Jews, Muslims, Buddhists, Hindus, and representatives of other Asian religions. Also included are various "points of contact and

contention," in which religious leaders attempt to analyze or reach out to their counterparts in other traditions. Published 1993 in Association with The Council for a Parliament of the World's Religions by Open Court Publ. Co., LaSalle, IL 61301. pb. $28.95; cl. $59.95

A Museum of Faiths: Histories and Legacies
of the 1893 World's Parliament of Religions
Edited by ERIC J. ZIOLKOWSKI
Reassesses the meaning and significance of the 1893 Parliament and its impact on the development of the academic study of religion. Contents include an extensive introduction, six papers on comparative religion from the Parliament's original proceedings, two articles expressing an early appraisal of the event's significance for world religious history and the comparative study of religion, and eight essays written during the last ten years reassessing the Parliament and its impact on interfaith dialogue and comparative religion. Published 1993 by Scholars Press of the American Academy of Religion, Atlanta, Georgia. pb. $29.95; cl. $44.95.

Pilgrimage of Hope: 100 Years of the Interfaith Movement
REV. MARCUS BRAYBROOKE
Details the history of interfaith organizations, events, and trends, as well as the people and historical contexts that helped shape the movement since the 1893 Parliament. This volume was published in anticipation of 1993, the Year of International, Interreligious Cooperation and Understanding. Written by an Anglican clergyman with wide interfaith experience and respect worldwide for his leadership in organizations and activities, this volume widens the focus of study well beyond North American experience to the global arena. Braybrooke is also editor of *Stepping Stones to a Global Ethic,* which introduces and reprints significant declarations and documents that helped shape the movement toward a global ethic. Both volumes are published in the U.S. by Crossroad and by SCM in the U.K.

WCRP: A History of the World Conference
on Religion and Peace
HOMER A. JACK, with Forewords by DANA MCLEAN GREELEY and NIKKYO NIWANO
Afterword by Archbishop Angelo Fernandes. (Illustrations)
Founded in 1969 at Istanbul, Turkey, after many years of discussions and negotiations, WCRP has been a unique and fully representative interreligious body, dedicated to the cause of world peace. In addition

to its detailed description of the formation, assemblies, initiatives, and relationships of WCRP, the book presents the vision of Homer A. Jack, a veteran activist who was prominent in directing the focus of the interfaith movement toward issues of peace and justice. Published 1993 by the World Conference on Religion and Peace, 777 United Nations Plaza, New York, NY 10017.

C. Audio and Video Tapes
from the Parliament

These can be used as great discussion starters for study groups and gatherings of friends. Instead of spending dollars on movie tickets, consider buying a video for your group and listen to or watch these moving portraits of the Parliament as a prelude to your own interfaith dialogue.

Audio Tapes of several hundred major speeches, presentations, and workshops from the Parliament, by a wide range of scholars, clerics, and other leaders from the world's religions, on numerous topics. Brochure and tapes are available from *Teach em,* 160 East Illinois St., Chicago, IL 60611 (312) 467-0424.

A Parliament of Souls

This is fine series of video interviews of visionaries, religious leaders from many traditions, and Nobel and Templeton prize winners who were participating at the Parliament of the World's Religions. The interviews were hosted by Bettina Gray and produced by Michael Tobias for cable stations VISION (Canada) and the Faith and Values Channel (VISN/ACTS), with the support of the Presbyterian Church (USA) and the North American Interfaith Network. A collection of sixteen of the interviews is now available for $29.95 by calling 1-800-647-3600.

How to Find God: Mystics Explore the Path to God

Produced by DR. KIRK LAMAN with Majestic Film & Video

This video addresses questions about the mystical and religious encounters that some people have with God. The footage includes interviews that Dr. Laman held at the Parliament with Brother Wayne Teasdale, a Roman Catholic monk; Sister Jayanti, a nun from the Brahma Kumari World Spiritual University; Reverend Robert Thompson, a Baptist minister, Brother Anandamoy from the Self-Realization Fellowship, and Ma Bhagavati, a former Jewish housewife who had a personal experience with Christ and now works with AIDS patients. 55 minutes; $19.95 from Mosaic, Inc. 2801 N. Woodward, Suite LL120, Royal Oak, MI 48073.

The Interfaith Message of the Parliament
of the World's Religions
Directed and produced by ANDRE PORTO
This video portrays a fine montage of the speakers and topics, the music and dance, and the diverse participants, as well as a dramatic reading of part of the declaration, Towards a Global Ethic, "all ways to find the common spiritual heart." $25. Available from InnerSong, 4095 Jackdraw St., San Diego, CA 92103.

Live, the Dalai Lama in Chicago.
Features the keynote speech to an audience of 30,000 in Grant Park, at the dramatic, public conclusion to the Parliament of the World's Religions. Includes montages of the diverse and enthusiastic audience and chants by Tibetan monks. Available (for $20 plus $4.95 S/H) from Lioness Films, 1535 W. Estes Ave, 3rd Fl., Chicago, IL 60626.

Peace Like a River: The 1993 Parliament
of the World's Religions
Shown nationwide on PBS, this remarkable film captures the Parliament's focus on the critical issues. Using excerpts from speeches and interviews, combined with video clips highlighting contemporary political, ecological, and social issues, this fifty-five minute video is an excellent introduction to the interaction of religions with global issues. The video cassette was created by and is available (for $25 plus $5 S/H) from the Chicago Sunday Evening Club, 332 S. Michigan Avenue, Suite 820, Chicago, IL 60604.

Voices from the 1993 Parliament
Two thirty minute video tapes feature an introductory montage of music and performances interspersed among interviews. Available from Greater Chicago Broadcast Ministries, 112 East Chestnut St., Chicago, IL 60611. Cost: Parts 1 and 2 can be bought separately for $20 each, or together for $35.00.

D. Interfaith, Educational and Networking Organizations

Council for a Parliament of the World's Religions
PO Box 1630
Chicago, IL 60690-1630 USA
Ph. (312) 629-2990; FAX: (312) 629-2991

As the body that organized the 1993 Parliament, the Council's Trustees and its office continue to handle day-to-day business, including coordination of the Metropolitan Council, the newly formed Chicago-area interfaith council, and other national and international initiatives. A second Assembly of Religious and Spiritual Leaders is being planned, as is another Parliament, which may be held in 1999 in South Africa. An "Executive Summary" of the Parliament, comments on recent developments within the CPWR, and reflections on the long-term legacies of the Parliament by this author are available in *A SourceBook*. (Also see other references to CPWR elsewhere in this book.)

Environmental Sabbath/Earth Rest Day
United Nations Environment Programme,
DC1-803, United Nations,
New York, NY 10017

Established in 1987 by the United Nations Environment Programme (UNEP) and its advisory committees, the Earth Rest day provides a way to meld spiritual values with environmental science. Many churches, temples, synagogues, mosques, and other religious bodies have adopted the first weekend in June as a time for special commemoration, education, and personal commitment, often utilizing resources provided or recommended by the UNEP, including the materials provided in its annual Environmental Sabbath/Earth Rest Day publications. UNEP is the international organization given authority to monitor and control the global environment, which ensures that environmental work done by other agencies of the United Nations incorporates an ecological perspective.

The Faith and Values Channel
This twenty-four hour-a-day cable television channel serves 8000 communities in the U.S. and over 20 million homes. The channel is programmed by two networks—the Vision Interfaith Satellite Network (VISN), which provides two-thirds of the daily programming, and the American Christian Television System (ACTS)—working together. The channel brings together over sixty national Catholic, Protestant, Jewish, Evangelical and Eastern Orthodox faith groups, but allows no maligning of any faith group, no on-air fund-raising, and no proselytizing. Diversity of programming brings documentaries, dramas, worship, call-in talk shows, music, and children's fare. *A VISN Special Report: The Parliament of the World's Religions* offered numerous interviews with participants and excerpts from speeches; this thirty-minute broadcast surveys the Parliament's context, goals, and issues, including divergent perspectives from Christians on how to relate to persons of other faiths.

Cable system managers will respond to customer input and to the requests of potential subscribers. (For more information, call 1-800-841-8476 x106.)

International Association for Religious Freedom
3 Carlton Road
Oxford OX2 7RZ, United Kingdom

or, in the United States, addressed to:
IARF, 777 United Nations Plaza, New York, NY 10017

IARF is a world community of religious organizations—interreligious, intercultural, and interracial in composition and vision. It encompasses fifty-five member groups in twenty-one countries that seek to expand its spiritual horizon, giving IARF a worldwide identity and moral involvement in response to the global issues of our time. The IARF world community is based on personal sharing to foster openness, understanding, compassion, service, and solidarity. Congresses were most recently held in India (1993), Germany (1990), United States (1987) and Japan (1984). In cooperation with local IARF groups, the Social Service Network has some fifty projects such as emergency relief, cooperative development projects and neighborhood women's centers. IARF also publishes a magazine, *IARF WORLD.*

International Council of Christians and Jews
Werlestrasse 2
Heppenheim, 6148 Germany

The ICCJ is the umbrella organization of twenty-three national Jewish-Christian dialogue organizations worldwide. Envisaged to deal with relations between Christians and Jews, its activities also serve as a model for wider interfaith relations. The ICCJ also creates a wide local outreach with international flavor. *See* National Conference, below.

International Interfaith Centre
2 Market St.
Oxford, OX1 3EF United Kingdom

This center is a joint project of International Association for Religious Freedom and World Congress of Faiths in cooperation with other organizations and with colleges in the Oxford area. The idea for the center emerged out of the cooperation among interfaith groups for the year of Interreligious Understanding and Cooperation (1993). The Centre's goals include providing a place for study and research, the development of educational materials, consultations, hospitality, and encouragement.

Inter-Religious Federation for World Peace
4 West 43rd St.,
New York, NY 10036

This global organization brings together believers and scholars from the many religious traditions of the world to work for world peace. IRFWP's program of congresses, conferences, consultations, research, service projects, and publications work to promote peace personally, socially, regionally, and globally. Peace among the religious traditions of humankind as well as the utilization of religious wisdom and ethics are seen as essential to the development of both interpersonal and universal peace. Founded and mostly funded by the Reverend Sun Myung Moon and the Unification Church, IRFWP now has an interreligious and prestigious board of Presidents and Presiding Council members. Individual and institutional memberships are also welcome.

Monastic Interreligious Dialogue
104 Chapel Lane
St. Joseph, MN 56374-0277

Originally called the North American Board for East-West Dialogue, MID was established in 1978 by the Benedictine Confederation to assume a leading role in dialogue between Christianity and the great religions of the East. It aims to foster the contribution of Christian monastics and other religious persons engaged in the dialogue between contemplative traditions. MID publishes a bulletin, assists in networking, participates in conferences, and promotes dialogical sessions.

Multifaith Resources
PO Box 128
Wofford Heights, CA 93285
Tel & Fax: (619) 376-4691

Multifaith Resources provides helpful aids to persons of many traditions who are working to respond to a variety of human needs while promoting and enhancing interfaith understanding and cooperation. While based in the Christian principles of its founder, the Reverend Dr. Charles White, this educational ministry encourages and supports the expression of thoughts and actions that are consistent with the highest values found in each of the world's religions. Resources include bibliographies, calendars, videotapes, books about the world's religions and religious education, study guides, workshops, consultations, and a full-color catalog describing all of the resources ($3.00).

The National Conference

Although its name was recently abbreviated from The National Conference of Christians and Jews, this human relations organization has been working since early in the twentieth century to fight bias, bigotry, and racism in America. Having expanded its work beyond the Christian and Jewish religions, the National Conference promotes understanding and respect among all races, religions, and cultures through advocacy, conflict resolution, and education. The national office in the United States, at 71 Fifth Avenue, Suite 1100, New York, NY 10003, helps to coordinate numerous local and regional chapters. Addresses outside the U.S. can be gotten from the International Council office, listed above.

The National Religious Partnership for the Environment
1047 Amsterdam Avenue
New York, NY 10025
Phone: 212-316-7441

In July 1993, four major faith groups and denominations—The U.S. Catholic Conference, the National Council of Churches of Christ, the Consultation of the Environment and Jewish Life, and the Evangelical Environment Network—initiated a three-year, $5 million mobilization representing on behalf of environmental integrity and justice. Now representing more than 100 million people, the Partnership began at a Summit on the Environment in 1992, sponsored by the Joint Appeal in Religion and Science; its origins, however, date back to the Open Letter to the Religious Community issued in January 1990 by thirty-four internationally prominent scientists. Each of the four traditions has published its own Resource Kit for congregational uses; these may be gotten directly from the affiliated partners (by contacting the NRPE). In addition, the somewhat obsolete *Directory of Environmental Activities and Resources in the North American Religious Community* (published in 1992) provides resources, ideas and networking information.

North American Interfaith Network (NAIN)
PO Box 1770
Dallas, TX 75221

NAIN is a nonprofit association for communication between and mutual strengthening of interfaith organizations, agencies, and programs along with offices of religious or denominational institutions pertaining to interfaith relations in the United States and Canada. The Network seeks to affirm humanity's diverse and historic spiritual resources and bring these to bear on contemporary global, national, regional, and local issues. The Network also sees its role as facilitating the networking possibilities of these organizations. It seeks to provide a coalition model for cooperative interaction based on serving the needs and promoting the aspirations of all member organizations. Membership includes a newsletter and links to other affiliates.

The North American Coalition on Religion and Ecology
5 Thomas Circle, NW
Washington, DC 20005

NACRE is designed to help the North American religious community enter into the environmental movement with a more informed understanding of the environmental crisis and a dynamic sense of ecological mission. The Coalition also assists the wider society in understanding the essential ethical and value dimension of the environmental movement. "Caring for Creation" is the motto and vision that NACRE communicates through the development of resource materials and collaborative programs with religious, scientific, and environmental leaders, in the United States and internationally through its Consortium on Religion and Ecology—International.

Religious Education Association of the U.S. and Canada
409 Prospect St.
New Haven, CT 06511-2177

The REA brings together people involved in all aspects of religious education for dialogue across denominations and faith traditions. Founded in 1903, the REA has a long history of concern and activity regarding the theory and practice of religious education, religion, and public education, adult faith development, and interreligious dialogue. Membership benefits include a professional journal titled *Religious Education,* a newsletter, conferences, and interfaith networks.

The Temple of Understanding
1047 Amsterdam Avenue
New York, NY 10025

The purpose of this global interfaith organization is the promotion of interfaith dialogue and education to achieve understanding and harmony among the people of the world's religions and beyond. The Temple of Understanding maintains a strong commitment to the integrity of each religion or faith tradition and believes that each can better remain true to itself by honoring the truths inherent in all traditions. Among its publications is the *1993 Global Interfaith Directory,* which lists and describes the international and national organizations as well as numerous regional and local chapters and organizations. The Directory is becoming obsolete but can serve as a starting point. pb. $15.

The World Conference on Religion and Peace
777 United Nations Plaza
New York, NY 10017
Tel: (212) 687-2163; Fax: (212) 983-0566

WCRP was formed in 1970 as a consolidation of separate movements in Japan, the United States, and India to promote interreligious encounter and cooperation throughout the world. Members have formed three regional committees in Asia, Africa, and Europe, and twenty-three national committees. On the local, national, regional, and global levels, WCRP convenes periodic meetings and assemblies, gathering religious leaders and representatives for the purpose of exploring urgent issues, sharing experiences in working for peace with justice, and making interreligious commitments for common actions to promote peace and harmony among religious bodies, nations, and ethnic groups, as well as between human beings and the natural environment. Foci include: conflict resolution, peace education, human rights, investment in children and youth, assistance to refugees, economic and social development, and environmental protection.

World Congress of Faiths
2 Market St.
Oxford, OX1 3EF United Kingdom

WCF aims to bring people of different faith commitments together in mutual respect and trust in order to promote better understanding between religious communities and to further dialogue between people of different convictions about religious truth and practice. It arranged conferences and cooperated with other interfaith organizations in the commemoration of 1993 as the Year of Interreligious Understanding. Its journal, *World Faiths Encounter,* is a major resource for dealing with new questions and issues that arise from living in a multifaith society. The internationally available journal bridges the interests of laity, clergy, community workers, students, and scholars from many faith communities. In the U.S.A, order from Multifaith Resources (listed above).

Contributors

Rev. Thomas A. Baima is the director of the Archdiocese of Chicago's Office of Ecumenical and Interreligious Affairs. He worked on the Global Ethic document.

Dr. Gerald O. Barney is the founder and director of the Millennium Institute in Arlington, Virginia. He was commissioned by Jimmy Carter to do the *Global 2000 Report* during the Carter Administration, and he has co-authored its updated version, *Global 2000 Revisited.*

Kristen R. Barney is a research associate at the Millennium Institute and is co-author of *Global 2000 Revisited.*

Barbara Fields Bernstein is the coordinator of the United Communities of Spirit, a grassroots interfaith network inspired by the Parliament, and the assistant director of the Dearborn Institute near Chicago.

Rev. Thomas Berry, C.P., is a celebrated and eloquent geologian. For many years he was a professor of the history of religions at Fordham University. He is the author of *The Dream of the Earth* and, with Brian Swimme, *The Universe Story.*

Joel Beversluis is the founder and publisher of CoNexus Press in Grand Rapids. He is the editor of *A SourceBook for Earth's Community of Religions* and is a significant commentator on the interfaith movement.

Ma Jaya Sati Bhagavati is a spiritual teacher and founder of the Kashi Ranch in Sebastian, Florida. She is well-known for her tireless work with AIDS patients.

Jane Blewett is the founder and director of the EarthCommunity Center and is co-author of *Global 2000 Revisited.*

Dr. Beatrice Bruteau is a writer, spiritual director, and founder of a monastic community in the Winston-Salem region of North Carolina.

She edits *The Roll* with her husband, James Somerville. She compiled *The Other Half of My Soul: Bede Griffiths and the Hindu-Christian Dialogue.*

Dr. George Cairns is a professor at the Chicago Theological Seminary. He edited *Healing and the Healer* with Nancy Cairns, his wife, and Lawrence Pottenger.

Dr. Ewert Cousins is an internationally known scholar who teaches theology and spirituality at Fordham University. His most recent book is entitled *The Christ of the Twenty-First Century.*

Keith Cunningham, a filmmaker and lecturer, was a close friend and associate of Joseph Campbell, and is active in the Joseph Campbell Society.

The Dalai Lama, XIV, is the exiled spiritual and temporal leader of Tibet. In 1989 he was awarded the Nobel Peace Prize for his untiring commitment to world peace through nonviolence.

Russill Paul D'Silva is on the faculty of the Institute of Culture and Creation Spirituality in Oakland, California. He is a musician, composer and writer.

Dr. Robert L. Fastiggi teaches religious studies at St. Edward's University in Austin, Texas. He is the author of *The Natural Theology of Yves de Paris.*

Rev. Dirk Ficca is director of the Parliament's Metropolitan Taskforce (Chicago) and has done much to organize interfaith encounters in the metropolitan area.

Samdech Preah Maha Ghosananda is a patriarch of Cambodian Buddhism and an eminent leader of the peace movement in Cambodia.

Archbishop Francesco Gioia, OFM Cap., serves in the Vatican's Pontifical Council for Interreligious Dialogue.

Magdalena Gómez is a poet, writer, dramatist, and teacher.

Dr. Daniel Gómez-Ibáñez is the founder and executive director of the Peace Council. He worked on the Global Ethic Document.

Archbishop Paulos Mar Gregorios is the retired Orthodox Metropolitan of Delhi. He is the doyen of the interfaith movement and is a past president of the World Council of Churches.

Dr. Jean Houston is a well-known writer and lecturer. Her most recent work is called *Lifeforce.*

Jim Kenney is the founder of Common Ground in Chicago and is the director of the Parliament's International Interreligious Taskforce.

Irfan Khan is a philosopher and celebrated scholar of the Qu'ran. He teaches at the American Islamic College in Chicago.

Dr. Paul Knitter teaches theology at Xavier University in Cincinnati. He has made numerous contributions in the area of missiology. His latest book is entitled *Mission as Dialogue.*

Burton Pretty on Top is a Crow spiritual leader and Pipe Carrier.

Jackie Rivet-River is a writer and a film documentarian.

Richard Hughes Seager, distinguished historian of the first Parliament (1893), is a professor of Religious Studies at Hamilton College in Clinton, New York.

Rabbi Byron L. Sherwin is a professor and Vice President of the Spertus Institute of Jewish Studies in Chicago.

Brother David Steindl-Rast, O.S.B., is hermit-in-residence at the Esalen Institute and, with Fritjof Capra and Thomas Matus, is the author of *Belonging to the Universe.*

Brother Wayne Teasdale is a Christian *sannyasi* (monk) in the Indian tradition and is an adjunct professor at DePaul University. He is a writer, spiritual director, lecturer, and retreat master. He is the author of *Toward Christian Vedanta.*

Sister Georgene Wilson is a Wheaton Franciscan, an anchoress, spiritual director, teacher, and writer.

Of related interest from Continuum

A GLOBAL ETHIC
The Declaration of the Parliament of the World's Religions
With commentaries by Hans Küng and Karl-Josef Kuschel

In September 1993 the Parliament of the World's Religions held in Chicago approved a "Declaration Toward a Global Ethic." This book presents the text of the Declaration with two commentaries. Hans Küng describes how the Declaration came into being and what it sets out to do. Karl-Josef Kuschel describes the historical background of the Parliament and gives an account of its proceedings.

YES TO A GLOBAL ETHIC
Edited by Hans Küng

Leading world figures in the worlds of politics, culture, and religion offer witness to a new global awareness and a new ethical consensus. From the worlds of politics and culture come Ireland's president Mary Robinson, former chancellor Helmut Schmidt, Jerusalem's former mayor Teddy Kollek, and Nobel Prize recipients Desmond Tutu, Rigoberta Menchú, and Aung San Suu Kyi. From the world's religions come representative from Buddhism, Hinduism, Islam, Judaism, and Christianity, including Elie Wiesel, Crown Prince Hassan of Jordan, the Archbishop of Canterbury, the General Secretary of the World Council of Churches, and Cardinals Franz König, Joseph Bernardin, and Paolo Evaristo Arns.

Hans Küng
CHRISTIANITY
Essence, History, and Future

"A mammoth and important rendering of the Christian faith by one of the most important Roman Catholic theologians. Küng surveys Christianity from its origins to the present in a highly readable account that illuminates without being didactic. . . . Küng does not skirt thorny issues, including papal infallibility, the changing role of women, and the encounter with other faiths."

—Kirkus Reviews

"This is a big book on a big subject by the biggest name in contemporary theology, and it does not deserve a small welcome. . . . [A]ny reader who is capable of tackling such a work and is deeply interested in Christianity would find Hans Küng's latest masterpiece a permanent enrichment of the mind."

—Church Times

Hans Küng
JUDAISM
Between Yesterday and Tomorrow

"A stunning achievement. What erudition this man has! The section on the Bible alone would be worthy of an Old Testament specialist."
—The Expository Times

"Küng's work contains a mine of information about Judaism, and its discussions of issues facing Judaism and the Jewish people today are clear, sympathetic, and insightful."
—The Journal of Religion

"This is . . . without doubt one of the most serious and learned encounters with Judaism by a non-Jewish scholar and thinker in our time."
—Shofar